To the incomparable
Ame. Lia, the
true guru of HIA
in the United States

Health Impact Assessment in the United States

Catherine L. Ross • Marla Orenstein
Nisha Botchwey

Health Impact Assessment in the United States

 Springer

Catherine L. Ross
Center for Quality Growth and Regional
    Development
Georgia Institute of Technology
Atlanta
Georgia
USA

Nisha Botchwey
School of City and Regional Planning
    College of Architecture
Georgia Institute of Technology
Atlanta
Georgia
USA

Marla Orenstein
Habitat Health Impact Consulting Corp.
Calgary
Alberta
Canada

ISBN 978-1-4614-7302-2   ISBN 978-1-4614-7303-9 (eBook)
DOI 10.1007/978-1-4614-7303-9
Springer New York Heidelberg Dordrecht London

Library of Congress Control Number: 2014931691

Printed on acid-free paper

Springer is part of Springer Science+Business Media (www.springer.com)

Health Impact Assessment in the United States *is an important resource... helping to uncover hidden causes of health inequities in proposals and identifying potential solutions before the proposals are implemented.*

Angela Glover Blackwell, Founder and CEO, PolicyLink

Preface

This book is intended to give the reader a comprehensive view of health impact assessment (HIA) as it is practiced in the USA today, as well as some practical tools that are useful in conducting, commissioning or evaluating HIAs. It reinforces the what, why, and how of HIA through reference to US and international case studies of completed HIAs. The book is structured in four parts:

Part I discusses HIA and its integration into public health, planning, and policy development. Part II introduces the core concepts of HIA and provides case studies from both the US and other countries. Part III discusses each of the six steps of HIA in detail, describing the purpose, the methodology and the outputs of each step. Part IV discusses how HIA has developed in the USA.

This book is written so that the reader develops an in-depth understanding of the concepts and methods that are the foundation of HIA. It is our hope that the book is also a step-by-step guide to conducting HIA and an introduction to other impact assessment methodologies that may be used in conjunction with HIA. As well as the need to discuss and make clear the health implications of policies, programs, and projects, there is a need for the development of methodologies and strategies to make these implications explicit. We hope this book makes a small contribution to that effort.

Acknowledgments

There are numerous people we would like to thank for their support and contributions to the development of this book. First and foremost are the many colleagues, friends, and the dedicated cadre of individuals who work tirelessly to integrate health into the decision-making framework of policies, programs, and projects in the USA and abroad. These people serve as an inspiration and have played a critical role in shaping many of the ideas put forth in this book. We have drawn heavily on their work as they exemplify the best thinking about health impact assessment (HIA) and current practice.

Of course, there are institutions and people that provide resources and leadership in any new and emerging field and that provide the basis for it to flourish. The Pew Charitable Trusts and its Health Impact Project have been a primary source for funding many of the HIAs completed to date in the USA. Many of the HIAs funded by Pew have contributed significantly to the increasing recognition of health assessment as an important consideration in today's decisions. Other institutions, too many to be identified singly, have promulgated HIA as a part of their ongoing mandate to share information and resources aimed at improving health both here in the USA and abroad. The leadership in fostering HIA demonstrated in Europe, Canada, and Australia provided the basis for ready references to inform our efforts in the USA, and we are very appreciative of that.

Special thanks to Joshua Levin, Anna Harkness, Arthi Vijayanagara Rao, and Angela Angel for their assistance with research. Thanks also to the organizations that granted us permission to reprint case studies, tables, and figures.

Lastly, we thank our families and friends for their unwavering support as we tackled this manuscript. You all teach us daily the value of observing, questioning, documenting, and teaching others. An especially warm thank you to Thomas, Linje, Shani, Murray, Fraser, Eric, Ed, Niara, Andrew, and Nicolas. This work is a reflection of your commitment and grace, working and living with us through the production of this textbook.

Finally, we hope this effort will help enable you, our readers, to realize improved health outcomes in your lives and careers.

Catherine, Marla, and Nisha

Contents

Index of Case Studies

Organization	Title of HIA	Type of proposal assessed	Location	Chapter
Spokane Regional Health District and City of Spokane	Spokane University District Pedestrian/ Bicycle Bridge HIA	Project	Washington	1. The Purpose of HIA
University of Wisconsin, Population Health Institute	Wisconsin Transitional Jobs Program HIA	Program	Wisconsin	1. The Purpose of HIA
Johns Hopkins University's Center for Child and Community Health and the city of Baltimore	Transform Baltimore Health Impact Assessment	Policy	Maryland	1. The Purpose of HIA
Center for Quality Growth and Regional Development (CQGRD) at the Georgia Institute of Technology; Centers for Disease Control and Prevention (CDC)	Atlanta BeltLine HIA	Plan	Georgia	5. US Case Studies
Human Impact Partners	Health Impact Assessment of the Healthy Families Act of 2009: Maine Addendum	Policy	Maine	5. US Case Studies

Organization	Title of HIA	Type of proposal assessed	Location	Chapter
Child Health Impact Working Group	A Child Health Impact Assessment of Energy Costs and the Low Income Home Energy Assistance Program (The Unhealthy Consequences: Energy Costs and Child Health HIA)	Policy	Massachusetts	5. US Case Studies
California Department of Public Health	Health Impact Assessment of a Cap and Trade Framework: The California Global Warming Solutions Act of 2006	Policy	California	5. US Case Studies
IMPACT Group (University of Liverpool, UK); Institute of Public Health (Ireland); RIVM (Netherlands); IOEGD (Germany)	Policy HIA for the European Union: A Health Impact Assessment of the European Employment Strategy Across the European Union	Policy	European Union	6. International Case Studies
NewFields	HIA of the Nacala Dam Infrastructure Project	Project	Mozambique	6. International Case Studies
Manukau City Council	Wiri Spatial Structure Plan HIA	Plan	New Zealand	6. International Case Studies
Center on Human Needs, Virginia Commonwealth University	The Potential Health Impact of a Poultry Litter-to-Energy Facility in the Shenandoah Valley, Virginia	Project	Virginia	8. Scoping
Habitat Health Impact Consulting	Health Impact Assessment (HIA) of Mining Activities Near Keno City, Yukon	Project	Canada	8. Scoping

Organization	Title of HIA	Type of proposal assessed	Location	Chapter
The Kohala Center	Health Impact Assessment 2010 Hawai'i County Agriculture Development Plan	Policy	Hawai'i	8. Scoping
Health Impact Project, University of California Los Angeles	Health Impact Assessment of Sacramento Safe Routes to School	Policy	California	9. Assessment
San Francisco Department of Public Health	A Health Impact Assessment of California Assembly Bill 889: The California Domestic Work Employee Equality, Fairness, and Dignity Act of 2011	Policy	California	9. Assessment
Australian Indigenous Doctors' Association and the Centre for Health Equity Training, Research and Evaluation, University of New South Wales	Health Impact Assessment of the Northern Territory Emergency Response	Policy	Australia	9. Assessment
Kansas Health Institute	Potential Health Effects of Casino Development in Southeast Kansas	Policy	Kansas	9. Assessment
NewFields Companies	Draft Wishbone Hill Mine Draft Health Impact Assessment	Project	Alaska	10. Recommendations
Upstream Public Health	Oregon Farm to School Policy HIA	Policy	Oregon	10. Recommendations 11. Reporting
Human Impact Partners	Rapid Health Impact Assessment of the Proposed Farmers Field Development	Project	California	10. Recommendations

List of Figures

List of Tables

List of Boxes

Part I
Context for HIA: Integrating Public Health, Planning and Policy Development

Chapter 1
The Purpose of HIA

Abstract This chapter examines the value of conducting health impact assessment (HIA) in the context of the current disease burden in the USA and the lack of consideration given to the impact of policies on health. It introduces the concept of HIA, including what HIA is and how it may be useful in furthering public health goals and decision making in projects, programs, and policies. The chapter discusses the origins of HIA and presents a timeline contextualizing its development in the setting of key social and historical circumstances that led to the birth of HIA as a practice. It presents various rationales that local, regional, or federal agencies have given for promoting or engaging in HIA, and describes the level of interest shown by different organizations in funding, commissioning, or conducting HIA for different topic areas and in different US regions. The chapter ends with a discussion of how HIA can "move the dial" on health issues, and the ways in which it can and does relate to the larger policy- and decision-making context. The chapter concludes that HIA is critical to identifying, comprehending, conveying, and evaluating many of the urgent health issues facing the USA today.

Keywords National Environmental Policy Act (NEPA) · Health challenges · Healthy public policy · Health impact assessment · Grant funding · Projects · Programs · Purpose of HIA · Healthy decision making · Pew Charitable Trusts · Types of HIA

HIA: An Introduction

What is the Problem?

The major health challenges facing the USA today, including obesity, climate change, reduced physical activity, safety concerns, and healthy food access, are complex. They are also generally attributable to multiple factors, including our social, environmental, and economic environments. It is widely accepted that the health of individuals and communities is shaped by external influences such as the environments where we live, work, learn, play, and worship; social conditions; economic policies; and public services. These issues extend far beyond the world of health care, the function of which is generally limited to curing a disease after it develops. In fact, the greatest opportunity rests with a comprehensive approach to the prevention of disease and poor health. "Physical activity, nutrition and smoking are three of the most important areas to target for prevention and, community based programs can generate a significant return both in terms of health and financial savings" (Trust for America's Health 2009). The ability to combat health challenges requires the identification of decisions and practices that contribute to adverse health outcomes. However, there has been a lag in the development of analytic tools that can evaluate how these external conditions affect people's health and well-being and can guide decision making in a way that supports the promotion of healthy populations.

Health impact assessment (HIA) has developed as a method over the past 15 years and is a proven and accessible approach that can inform health-related decision making. Its origins are in Europe, with recent introduction and practice in the USA.

What is HIA?

HIA is an approach to assessing the risk factors, diseases, and equity issues that create poor health outcomes in the USA (Committee on Health Impact Assessment, National Research Council 2011). The World Health Organization defines HIA as "a combination of procedures, methods and tools by which a policy, program or project may be judged in terms of its potential effects on the health of a population and the distribution of those effects within the population" (European Centre for Health Policy 1999). HIA is at its core a mechanism to examine policies, programs, or projects in a way that makes more evident their potential health risks and benefits and helps promote "healthy" decision making. It is most often applied to policies, programs, and projects that do not have effects on health as their primary target, but that impact health nonetheless; for example, those intended to affect the economy, agriculture, transportation, or energy production.

The primary output of HIA is a set of evidence-based recommendations for how to modify the project, policy, program, plan, or strategy in order to minimize potential adverse health outcomes, maximize beneficial health effects, and reduce any impacts on health equalities (Mindell et al. 2008). To accomplish this task, HIA practice relies on a combination of public health expertise and the collaboration of multidisciplinary groups of experts and affected community members. It pulls from a wide range of methodologies including the fields of epidemiology, environmental impact analysis, risk analysis, cost–benefit analysis, systematic reviews and community, and urban planning, among others (Cole and Fielding 2008, Bhatia and Wernham, 2008). Three brief real-world examples of HIA are shown in Table 1.1, representing a project, a program, and a policy, respectively.

Where Did HIA Come From?

Developments in the environmental movement (McHarg's *Design with Nature,* Carson's *Silent Spring*), planning theory (activism, advocacy), and concern for the

Table 1.1 Examples of HIA

What was examined	What the HIA did
Project	The city of Spokane and the Spokane Regional Health District collaborated on the *Spokane University District Pedestrian/Bicycle Bridge HIA*, conducted to inform decision-makers of potential health impacts associated with the development of a pedestrian bridge in the university district. The HIA assessed the impact of the bridge on both the current and projected future population living, working, or enjoying recreational activities within a quarter-mile radius of the bridge. The primary result of the HIA was the conclusion that the bridge would contribute positively to health in the study area. Explicit recommendations were based on prioritizing cost, impact on health, and impact on reducing vehicle miles traveled
Program	The Wisconsin legislature was facing a decision: whether to renew, modify, or eliminate the Transitional Jobs Demonstration program in its 2013–2015 budget. The program provided low-income Wisconsin residents with job training, experience, and support in reentering the workforce, and had at that point assisted around 3,900 low-income people. The *Transitional Jobs Program HIA* was undertaken to help inform the legislative decision, since the program had not been analyzed for its potential effects on the health of program participants, their families, and their children. The HIA found that the renewal of the program had the potential to improve a number of critical health determinants, including income, social capital, family cohesion, and child maltreatment, and there was mixed evidence for the program's effect on diet and alcohol/tobacco use
Policy	The *HIA of the Transform Baltimore Comprehensive Zoning Code Rewrite* was conducted jointly by Johns Hopkins University's Center for Child and Community Health and the city of Baltimore. The goal was to influence the final version of Baltimore's new zoning code by providing information informing stakeholders and decision-makers of the new zoning code's potential to create healthy communities and decrease health disparities as well as by providing recommendations on how to increase health-promoting outcomes of the new zoning code

environment on the part of public and nongovernmental agencies prompted the passage of the National Environmental Policy Act (NEPA) in 1969. This marks the origin of environmental impact assessment (EIA) as an "operational tool to guide planning and decision making having an impact on the quality of environment and the health and safety of the people" and as a legal tool to enforce environmental sensitivity in policy decisions (Caldwell 1988). EIA also brought together a systematic method of bridging planning, systems thinking, and human health.

As reflected in the legislation's original objectives, NEPA was designed to look at impacts on human health. However, the way in which this has been operationalized through EIAs has been incomplete. In practice, EIAs rarely incorporate broad measures of health, or focus too narrowly on exposure to environmental toxins. In response to this gap, alternative assessment methodologies were developed to more fully incorporate the examination of social impacts and the health consequences of policy decisions. These concerns were grounded in social determinants of health, "which recognizes that the factors which determine health outcomes can be environmental, social, economic and Institutional," and health equity (Harris-Roxas et al. 2012). These supplemental methodologies include both HIA and social impact assessment (SIA), further discussed in Chap. 3, "HIAs, EIAs, SIAs, and Other Assessment Tools" (see Table 1.2).

Table 1.2 HIA milestones

Year	Milestone
1901	• New York City passed the **Housing Tenement Acts** focused on improved lighting and ventilation for dwelling units. This public health Act was passed to promote the health, safety and welfare of people through improvements to their living conditions.
1916	• New York City writes the first **comprehensive zoning ordinance** to alleviate adverse health and safety conditions in urban life.
1930	• *Ambler Realty Company v. Village of Euclid* permitted segregated land uses and partially based its opinion on public health nuisance laws, concluding that separation of uses aids the health and safety of the community.
1969	• **National Environmental Policy Act (NEPA)** includes 'community health and welfare' in its purpose, and **Environmental Protection Agency (EPA)** is founded.
1972	• **Clean Water Act (CWA)** becomes federal law regulating point source pollutants.
1974	• **Safe Drinking Water Act (SDWA)** becomes federal law to protect health by regulating public drinking water
1986	• The World Health Organization (WHO) conducts the first International Conference on Health Promotion, producing the **Ottawa Charter for Health Promotion** and outlines steps for "Health for all by 2000."
1997	• WHO conducts the 4th International Conference on Health Promotion and produces the **Jakarta Declaration**, naming HIA as a priority for 21st Century and recommending health promotion be implemented among all sectors and levels of government.
1999	• The San Francisco Department of Health (SFDH) completes the **first HIA in US** on a proposed policy to increase San Francisco's minimum wage for city contracts. • WHO releases the **Gothenburg Consensus Paper** to produce a common definition and values for HIA.
2000s	• **HIA integrated into EIA legislation** in Australia, Canada, New Zealand and Thailand. • **HIA incorporated into Strategic Environmental Assessment** in Europe and Canada.
2001	• The International Health Impact Assessment Consortium (IMPACT) publishes the **Merseyside Guidelines for HIA.**
2002	• The **Centers for Disease Control and Prevention (CDC)** first hosts a **workshop to discuss HIA in the US**.
2003	• San Francisco Department of Public Health (SFDPH) conducted an HIA on the Trinity Plaza Apartments demolition proposal. **The HIA influenced the EIA process** by revising its scope to include residential displacement and indirect health impacts.
2006	• **"Use of Health Impact Assessment in the US: 27 Case Studies, 1999-2007"** is published in the *American Journal of Preventive Medicine*.

Table 1.2 (continued)

	• International Association of Impact Assessment (IAIA) publishes *Health Impact Assessment International Best Practice Principles* • A federal bill, **The Healthy Places Act of 2006**, is introduced to congress proposing HIA legislation, but was not enacted.
2007	• The Alaska Inter-Tribal Council successfully advocated for the formal **inclusion of HIA into a federal EIA** for a proposed oil and gas development in the National Petroleum Reserve of Alaska's North Slope region. • The **Healthy Development Measurement Tool (HDMT)** created by SFDPH, later renamed the **Sustainable Communities Index** measures livable, equitable and prosperous cities.
2008	• **27 HIAs completed in US** • The North American HIA Practice Standards Working Group outlines the First *Practice Standards for HIA.* • The Washington State Senate Bill 6099 requires an **HIA on the replacement of Route 520 Bridge.**
2009	• Montgomery County, Maryland adopts a Board of Health Resolution **requiring HIA for four new road projects.** • CDC funding create programs for HIA training and technical assistance in four states including Wisconsin and Minnesota. • First Annual **HIA of the Americas Workshop** held in Oakland, CA.
2010	• Robert Wood Johnson Foundation's Health Impact Project funds 13 demonstration HIAs in 2010 • Second edition of *HIA practice Standards: Minimum Elements and Practice Standards for Health Impact Assessment.* • The White House Task Force on Childhood Obesity **recommends local governments conduct HIAs before building new developments.**
2011	• An American Planning Association survey of practicing planners finds that **27% of comprehensive plans address public health**. Less than **4% utilize HIA in their comprehensive planning process.** • National Research Council releases *Improving Health in the United States: The Role of Health Impact Assessment* as a guiding document for the nation on HIA. • **The Society of Practitioners of Health Impact Assessment (SOPHIA)** established.
2012	• First Annual **National Health Impact Assessment Meeting** held in Washington, DC.
2014	• **240 HIAs completed in the US**

Major Actors, Institutions, and Professions

In the USA, HIAs have largely been conducted by public health departments and educational institutions, with a smaller number conducted by private organizations and nonprofit or community groups. Although the uptake of HIA is gaining momentum, its application remains sporadic, with regional concentration seen in California and the South (primarily in Atlanta, largely due to the presence of the Centers for Disease Control and Prevention, CDC) (see Fig. 1.1). Further, the scales of projects

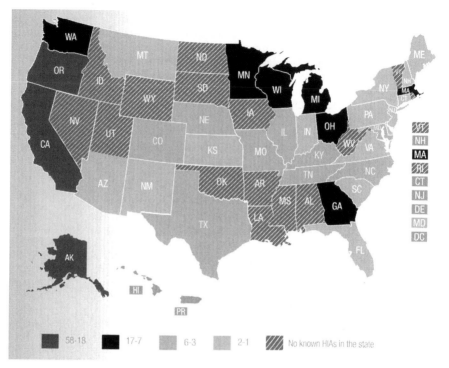

Fig. 1.1 Number of HIA's by state

assessed have been small, with an increasing trend towards larger scales (regional). It is encouraging, however, to note that decision-makers are using HIA at different levels (local, county, state, and federal) (Dannenberg et al. 2008). Figure 1.2 shows the distribution of topics that have comprised HIA practice. The data are drawn from the Health Impact Project, a collaboration of the Robert Wood Johnson Foundation and The Pew Charitable Trusts, which has collated the most complete list of HIAs completed in the USA to date.

Increasingly, prominent US organizations—including those both with and without a health mandate—are calling for HIAs to be more widely conducted or institutionalized. Table 1.3 presents excerpts from recent reports published by influential organizations, recommending HIA as a tool for achieving national health goals and objectives. Some of the key reasons cited for promoting HIA are:

- To proactively provide evidence about potential risks and benefits of policies or programs
- To systemically build health consideration into decision making in non-health sectors
- To improve outcomes for vulnerable groups or individuals
- To reduce environmental injustice or health disparity

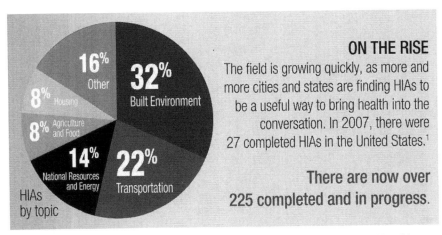

Fig. 1.2 Sector-wise distribution of completed and ongoing HIAs as of April 2013. (Graphic courtesy of the Health Impact Project, a collaboration of the Robert Wood Johnson Foundation and The Pew Charitable Trusts)

Who Funds HIA and How Much Does It Cost?

HIAs are funded at multiple scales and the grant amounts depend on the scope of the work. Costs and grant amounts also vary depending on whether the HIA is stand-alone or integrated into the EIA process. HIAs can cost anywhere from a few thousand to a few hundred thousand dollars. Typically, the lower amounts fund individual project-level HIAs. Larger funding amounts are granted to HIA programs that go beyond individual assessments and develop systems and structures for long-term HIA integration and capacity building.

In the USA, HIAs have been funded predominantly by a small number of organizations: the Robert Wood Johnson Foundation, The Pew Charitable Trusts, The California Endowment, the CDC, and local governments (Dannenberg et al. 2008). The Pew Charitable Trusts and the Robert Wood Johnson Foundation collaboratively fund HIAs through the Health Impact Project, which has to date funded more HIAs than any other source. This sponsorship ties into the Health Impact Project's mandate, which is to promote the use of HIAs as a decision-making tool for policymakers. Private health foundations such as the California Endowment work collaboratively with the Health Impact Project to support the development of a self-supporting HIA program within a specific region (in this case, the state of California). The CDC has worked collaboratively with local agencies within the State of Georgia as well as with agencies from other states, such as the University of California at Los Angeles, in conducting HIAs. *Local agencies fund HIAs on a smaller scale; these agencies have included county-level health authorities, nongovernmental organizations, community groups, and state health departments.*

Table 1.3 Justification for promoting the use of HIA

Organization and report name	Rationale for promoting HIA
Institute of Medicine *Living Well with Chronic Illness: A Call for Public Health Action* (*2012*)	The committee also recommends a health in all-policies approach, with HIAs as a promising practice to be piloted and evaluated for a set of major federal legislation, regulations, and policies for its impact on health, health-related quality of life, and functional status for individuals with chronic illness and relevant efficiencies
US Department of Health and Human Services (HHS), 2012 HHS Environmental Justice Strategy and Implementation Plan	HIAs can be used to evaluate potential health effects of development projects and land-use decision. As an emerging field of practice in the USA, the HIA methodology incorporates potential public health impacts into the decision-making process for plans, project, and policies that traditionally fall outside of the public health arena
	HIA helps decision-makers avoid adverse health consequences and costs and improve health. HIA may also reduce environmental injustices by characterizing opportunities to improve the relationship between affected vulnerable groups and the policy or project. The reinvigorated 2012 version of the strategic plan aims to further ensure that environmental justice factors into the federal decision-making process
HHS Priority Areas for Improvement of Quality in Public Health (2010)	The concept of HIA should be considered as a method for institutionalizing systems thinking in public health… HIA assessments of programs and policies at the federal, state, and local levels ensure that public health has a voice in proposed activities of disciplines that impact health (e.g., agriculture, transportation, education, economic development) and can proactively reduce any potential risks or advance health-promoting benefits
The National Prevention, Health Promotion, and Public Health Council The National Prevention Strategy: America's Plan for Better Health and Wellness (2011)	Assessments and audits (e.g., HIAs) can be used to help decision makers evaluate project or policy choices to increase positive health outcomes and minimize adverse health outcomes and health inequities. …Health impact assessments can inform policy makers of likely impacts of proposed policies and programs on health disparities
National Research Council of the National Academies of Science Improving Health in the United States: The Role of Health Impact Assessment (2011)	HIA has arisen as an especially promising way to factor health considerations into the decision-making process. It has been used throughout the world to evaluate the potential health consequences of a wide array of proposals that span many sectors and levels of the government. International organizations, such as the World Health Organization and multilateral development banks, have also contributed to the development and evolution of HIA and countries and organizations have both developed their own guidance on conducting HIA. This report presents a six-step framework for conducting HIA of proposed policies, programs, plans, and projects at federal, state, tribal, and local levels, including within the private sector

Table 1.3 (continued)

Organization and report name	Rationale for promoting HIA
White House Task Force on Childhood Obesity *Solving the Problem of Childhood Obesity Within a Generation* (2010)	HIAs can be used to focus decision-makers' attention on the health consequences of the projects and policies they are considering, particularly how land-use decisions may impede or improve physical activity. Local communities should consider integrating HIAs into local decision-making processes and the Federal government should continue to support the development of an HIA approach, tools, and supporting resources that promote best practices
Secretary's Advisory Committee on National Health Promotion & Disease Prevention *Healthy People 2020: An Opportunity to Address Societal Determinants of Health in the U.S.* (2010)	HIAs may be an important source of "promising practices" that point to early successes before a large body of evidence can be compiled through comprehensive literature reviews. At the state and local levels, such data can be used to convince decision-makers of the need to undertake policies, programs, and projects that will improve population health
Secretary's Advisory Committee on National Health Promotion & Disease Prevention *Evidence-Based Clinical and Public Health: Generating and Applying the Evidence* (2010)	HIAs offer another tool for gathering the best available information to inform decisions that will impact health. HIAs are a practical tool for building health considerations into policy decisions in other sectors, i.e., through a "health in all policies" approach

HIAs are also valuable as leverage for additional funding of health-related research and consideration within other public health- and planning-related efforts. The Atlanta BeltLine HIA demonstrates this concept well; the HIA has garnered the support of Kaiser Permanente for researching and implementing trail systems along the route. To date, Kaiser Permanente has contributed US$ 2.5 million towards the construction of the Eastside trail. An additional US$ 2.5 million was contributed towards the trail by a private donor. Kaiser has also funded evaluation studies to assess the impact on health of these infrastructure improvements. As a result of the HIA, the Environmental Protection Agency (EPA) awarded US$ 1 million to the BeltLine to clean up brownfields (Ross et al. 2007). In the city of Decatur, Georgia, an HIA conducted as part of the municipality's Community Transportation Planning process helped to increase funding for several health-related programs and to solidify the programs' presence in an institutional capacity. These included the hiring of a director for the Active Living Division and establishing a more sustainable path for the future of the Safe Routes to School Program.

HIA in a Policy Context

Although HIA can be conducted on policies, programs, or projects, it is often best at "moving the dial" on health when taken up at a regional or federal policy level, because of the broad reach that these large-scale policies can have. Recognizing this important potential, the following section provides a closer examination into the role of HIA within the context of public policy.

Introduction to Public Policy

Public policy refers to legislation, regulations, strategies, or plans developed and implemented by governments to produce desired outcomes. Generally, policy is used to encourage conditions that support the well-being and welfare of the populations under the jurisdiction of that government. Policy can be developed for many areas: education, food production and distribution, land use, urban design, transportation, income security, economic development, housing, energy, health, and many more.

It should be noted that health policy is often different from healthy public policy. The World Health Organization (World Health Organization 2013) defines healthy policy (or healthy public policy) as referring to "decisions, plans, and actions that are undertaken to achieve specific health care goals within a society." That is, healthy policy would encompass any policy actions resulting in the promotion of health across the population. However, the health policy that dominates the public conversation in America does not refer to the improvement of health and wellness among individuals or populations, but rather to the structure and function of the health-care system. This clinical perspective disregards the value of maintaining health and focuses only on curing diseases.

Public policy is usually developed through an iterative cycle that consists of identifying a problem; developing policy options; deciding on a specific course of action; implementing the new policy; and evaluating results. HIA has the most potential, and is most likely to be helpful, if it is timed to coincide with the part of the policy-making cycle when options are being considered. This creates opportunities to make adjustments before decisions are entrenched or the policy is implemented.

How Are Other Jurisdictions Using HIA for Public Policy?

Over the past 20 years, HIA has been successfully established at a national policy level in a number of jurisdictions worldwide. The approach to public policy HIA in these jurisdictions varies widely, with differences in the level of government responsible for undertaking HIA, the model used for commissioning and conducting HIA, the supporting tools and frameworks, the degree of accountability, and the funding mechanisms.

In England, Ireland, The Netherlands, Poland, Slovenia, Switzerland, and Wales, budgets for HIA have been allocated at a national level. In Canada, the province of Quebec institutionalized HIA for public policy decisions through the Public Health Act of 2002, and at the federal level, Canada's Senate Subcommittee on Population Health has recommended that the feasibility of integrating HIA into the framework of federal policies be examined (D'Amour and Pierre 2009; Keon and Pepin 2009).

In New Zealand, the mandate to require the consideration of health in the development of new policy is entrenched in specific acts such as the Local Government Act, the Gambling Act, the Land Transport Management Act and the Building Act. HIA is the common tool in each. In Australia and Thailand, the use of HIA is mainly voluntary, except when paired with an EIA.

Within the USA, several jurisdictions, including California and Alaska, are increasing the role of HIA in decision making for a limited set of circumstances. The mandated use of HIA in public policy planning is typically included under the umbrella of EIA, as defined at the federal level by the NEPA laws. In the USA, 20 states and territories have now enacted regional versions of NEPA laws. Each year more than 500 environmental impact statements are completed at the federal level, as are thousands of similar assessments under state-level environmental assessment laws (Humboldt State University Library 2013).

The increasingly widespread application of HIA at both the national and international levels creates the opportunity to integrate health considerations into public and private actions alike. This heightened focus on HIA occurs at a time when the health status of the population is characterized by alarming increases in chronic diseases affecting the youngest and oldest members of society.

The Value of HIA

The earlier sections of this chapter give a brief description of what HIA is, where it came from, who is using or advocating it, and how it fits into healthy public policy. The following list presents a number of potential benefits that can stem from the use of HIA:

1. HIA *supports decision making*. HIA does not make project, program, or policy decisions; it provides information in a clear and transparent way for the decision-makers.
2. HIA makes explicit the *potential impacts of projects, programs, and policies on health*. Where possible, HIA quantifies or characterizes health impacts such that decision-makers are able to understand the potential "trade-offs" when considering policy options. This assists organizations in strategically directing investments towards projects, programs, and policies that are the most likely to have beneficial effects and away from those that are likely to create adverse health effects.
3. HIA focuses on both *positive and negative health impacts*. It not only highlights negative health effects, but also identifies opportunities for projects, programs, and policies to maximize potential positive effects on health.
4. HIA *generates and elucidates health evidence*. It strengthens the links between research and projects, programs and policies, by providing decision-makers with the best available evidence from both qualitative and quantitative sources.
5. HIA helps to *improve health and reduce health inequities*. It can assist in improving the overall health status of the population. It helps to assure that projects, programs and policies do not produce adverse effects on health. HIA can attempt

to minimize the extent to which projects, programs, and policies exacerbate or continue existing inequalities.
6. HIA supports improved *coordination and integration of project, program, and policy development* across different sectors. HIA's multi-sectoral approach contributes to more comprehensive integrated development.
7. HIA helps policy-makers incorporate principles of sustainability and resiliency in project, program, and policy development, in addition to explicit health considerations.
8. HIA can help reduce the *financial impact* of ill health.
9. HIA supports *community engagement,* enabling both project decision-makers and citizens to become more informed and invested in promoting positive health outcomes and limiting negative health exposures.

References

Bhatia R, Wernham A (2008) Integrating human health into environmental impact assessment: an unrealized opportunity for environmental health and justice. Environ Health Persp 116(8):991–1000
Caldwell LK (1988) Environmental impact analysis (EIA): origins, evolution, and future directions. Rev Policy Res 8(1):75–83
Cole BL, Fielding JE (2008) Building health impact assessment (HIA) capacity: a strategy for Congress and government agencies. Partnership for Prevention. http://www.prevent.org/data/files/initiatives/buildignhealthimpactassessmenthiacapacity.pdf. Accessed 18 June 2013
Committee on Health Impact Assessment, National Research Council (2011) Improving health in the United States: the role of health impact assessment. The National Academies Press, Washington, DC
D'Amour R, St. Pierre L et al (2009) Discussion workshop on health impact assessment at the level of provincial governments. National Collaborating Centre for Healthy Public Policy, Montreal. http://www.ncchpp.ca/docs/Interprovincial_Report_EN.pdf. Accessed 18 June 2013
Dannenberg AL, Bhatia R, Cole BL et al (2008) Use of health impact assessment in the U.S.: 27 case studies, 1999–2007. Am J Prev Med 34(3):41–256
European Centre for Health Policy (1999) Gothenburg consensus paper. World Health Organization Regional Office for Europe, Brussels
Harris-Roxas B, Viliani F, Harris P et al (2012) Health impact assessment: the state of the art. Impact Assess Proj Appraisal 30(1):43–52
Humboldt State University Library (2013) Website: Environmental Impact Assessment Reports. http://library.humboldt.edu/infoservices/FEIRsandEISs.htm. Accessed 18 June 2013
Keon WJ, Pepin L (2009) A healthy, productive Canada: a determinant of health approach, final report of the Senate Subcommittee on Population Health. Senate of Canada: Ottawa
Mindell J, Boltong A, Forde I (2008) A review of health impact assessment frameworks. J Public Health 122(11):1177–1187
Ross C, Leone de Nie K, Barringer J et al (2007) Atlanta BeltLine health impact assessment. Center for Quality Growth and Regional development, Georgia Institute of Technology, Atlanta
Trust for America's Health (2009) Prevention for a healthier America: investments in disease prevention yield significant savings, stronger communities. http://healthyamericans.org/reports/prevention08/Prevention08.pdf. Accessed 18 June 2013
World Health Organization (2013) Health policy. Website. http://www.who.int/topics/health_policy/en/. Accessed 18 June 2013

Chapter 2
Public Health and Community Planning 101

Abstract This chapter provides an integrated introduction to the history and current practice of two linked fields: public health and planning. The fields of public health and planning have common historical roots, and there is a significant resurgence recognizing this commonality in both theory and practice. This chapter describes the methods, study designs, activities, and results of both public health and planning in the USA; highlights current persistent health and planning issues; and identifies emerging issues for future research and analysis. The chapter includes a case study on obesity and the built environment, highlighting links between urban planning and health. The chapter pinpoints five primary issues in research and analysis requiring greater attention in order to smooth the road for effective interdisciplinary work on health impact assessments (HIAs). It then concludes by identifying key emerging directions for community planning and public health, for which HIA has a direct role.

Keywords American Institute of Certified Planners (AICPs) · American Planning Association (APA) · American Public Health Association (APHA) · Biomedical model · Case-control studies · Chronic disease · Climate change · Cohort studies · Disease outbreaks · Germ theory · Healthy People 2020 · Infectious disease · Natural experiments · Noncommunicable disease · Obesity · Preventive strategies · Public health infrastructure · Public health interventions · Randomized control trials (RCTs) · Sanitary Reform Movement · Sustainability

Public Health: An Introduction

The American Public Health Association (APHA) defines public health as "the practice of preventing disease and promoting good health within groups of people, from small communities to entire countries." As implied in this definition, health encompasses more than just the absence of illness, and also refers to aspects of social and mental well-being. Public health professionals work to protect, promote, and improve health through population-focused preventive strategies.

C. L. Ross et al., *Health Impact Assessment in the United States,*   15
DOI 10.1007/978-1-4614-7303-9_2, © Springer Science+Business Media New York 2014

Public health has been an important discipline and practice since the first civilizations, and many public health initiatives that remain important today have their origins in initiatives thousands of years old. For example, aqueducts, public toilets, and swamp drainage as public health interventions can be traced back at least as far as the ancient Romans.

As the field progressed, public health improvements became, in many ways, synonymous with development and greater quality of life. Prior to the twentieth century, the burden of disease worldwide consisted primarily of acute infectious diseases and public health efforts were focused on facing these important problems. Since the early 1990s, however, chronic and, particularly, noncommunicable diseases have grown in importance and are now the most significant global cause of death worldwide (World Health Organization 2012; Institute of Medicine 2003). As a result, the field of public health has also undergone a major shift and public health interventions now focus on the conditions associated with chronic disease, such as lifestyle, behavior, social, and environmental factors.

History and Evolution of Public Health

Throughout its history, the USA has generally experienced four periods or phases of public health practice. The first, running from the 1700s to approximately 1850, focused on battling epidemics and widespread outbreaks of infectious diseases such as cholera, smallpox, typhoid, tuberculosis, and yellow fever. The public health response often focused on quarantining individuals or infected areas until the disease subsided.

The second period spanned the years 1850–1949. During this time, influences from Europe—including Edwin Chadwick's 1837 *Report on an Inquiry into the Sanitary Conditions of the Laboring Population of Great Britain* and John Snow's use of mapping techniques to demonstrate cholera's link to specific water sources in London—led public health champions to develop infrastructure- and state-based responses to disease outbreaks. This phase saw the development of state and local health departments and the application of government power over taxation, regulation of commerce, and zoning in order to promote health. To enable these advances, public health officials were charged with ensuring sanitation, controlling communicable infection, educating the masses on personal hygiene, and preventing and diagnosing disease.

Public health infrastructure and the number of actors identified to provide these services expanded during the third period, from 1950 to 1999. This was the result, in part, of society coming to accept government provision of medical services for those in need, beginning in the 1930s. This period also saw a rise in social unrest, race riots, and the view of cities as being somehow toxic. The federal government was seen as an important service provider to address the urban and rural problems facing the nation, since the resources and coordination necessary to address these large-scale influences were not available at the local level.

Public health in this present-day, fourth period has focused on morbidity and mortality from chronic diseases such as heart disease, diabetes, hypertension, obesity, cancer, and respiratory disease; and the behavioral, social, and environmental risk factors that may lead to them.

One of the most significant issues facing public health today is addressing the inadequate provision of health services to a nation with widening wealth and income disparities, significantly divided along race lines. The large population of poor and disenfranchised people without access (real or perceived) to healthcare creates major challenges for public health. The results can be seen in global health rankings; the USA ranks at number 37 out of 191 nations according to its performance, despite spending a higher portion of gross domestic product (GDP) on health than any other country (Murray and Frenk 2010). This failure is due, in part, to the US health model being based on high-cost procedures and medical service delivery systems, rather than prevention or "health care." As a result, in public health, thought is now shifting from a focus primarily on medical care to the inclusion of examining social, economic, and physical changes to the built environment.

Healthy People 2020

As referenced above, the scope of public health includes not only biomedical outcomes but also the social, economic, environmental, and infrastructure "determinants" that influence those outcomes. Reflecting this expanded perspective, the US Department of Health and Human Services published *Healthy People 2020*, a comprehensive set of disease-prevention and health-promotion objectives for the nation to achieve by the year 2020. It defines success in terms of improved health status, diseases prevented, scarce resources preserved, and improved quality of life. The overall goals of *Healthy People 2020* are:

1. To attain high-quality, longer lives free of preventable disease, disability, injury, and premature death
2. To achieve health equity, eliminate disparities, and improve the health of all groups
3. To create social and physical environments that promote good health for all
4. To promote quality of life, healthy development, and healthy behaviors across all life stages

In order to achieve these goals, the document identifies 42 specific objective areas for public health improvement (Box 2.1).These objectives span diseases, prevention areas, health-promotion opportunities, and response.

Box 2.1 *Healthy People 2020* public health improvement priorities. (HealthyPeople.gov 2012)

1. Access to health services
2. Adolescent health
3. Arthritis, osteoporosis, and chronic back conditions
4. Blood disorders and blood safety
5. Cancer
6. Chronic kidney disease
7. Dementias, including Alzheimer's disease
8. Diabetes
9. Disability and health
10. Early and middle childhood
11. Educational and community-based programs
12. Environmental health
13. Family planning
14. Food safety
15. Genomics
16. Global health
17. Health communication and health information technology
18. Healthcare-associated infections
19. Health-related quality of life and well-being
20. Hearing and other sensory or communication disorders
21. Heart disease and stroke
22. HIV
23. Immunization and infectious diseases
24. Injury and violence prevention
25. Lesbian, gay, bisexual, and transgender health
26. Maternal, infant, and child health
27. Medical product safety
28. Mental health and mental disorders
29. Nutrition and weight status
30. Occupational safety and health
31. Older adults
32. Oral health
33. Physical activity
34. Preparedness
35. Public health infrastructure
36. Respiratory diseases
37. Sexually transmitted diseases
38. Sleep health
39. Social determinants of health
40. Substance abuse
41. Tobacco use
42. Vision

Public Health Infrastructure

The public health infrastructure of the USA today is composed of governmental and nongovernmental organizations providing essential public health services. Service providers such as managed care organizations, hospitals, nonprofit corporations, schools, faith organizations, and businesses are an integral part of the public health infrastructure in many communities. Public health professionals play a variety of roles, from promoting vaccinations at local health departments to advising health legislation on Capitol Hill.

Health care providers and state and local health agencies are the most prominent actors in the public health realm, but there is a wide range of stakeholders. The federal government, through the work of the Centers for Disease Control and Prevention (CDC), plays a large role in public health activities, assuming primary responsibility for public health, regulating private actors, providing economic incentives for health-promoting behavior, and disincentives for risky

Table 2.1 Masters of public health core competencies. (Adapted from Calhoun et al. 2008)

Competency	Definition
Biostatistics	The development and application of statistical reasoning and methods in addressing, analyzing, and solving problems in public health-, health-care-, biomedical-, clinical-, and population-based research
Environmental health sciences	The study of environmental factors including biological, physical, and chemical factors that affect the health of a community
Epidemiology	The study of patterns of disease and injury in human populations and the application of this study to the control of health problems
Health policy and management	A multidisciplinary field of inquiry and practice concerned with the delivery, quality, and costs of health care for individuals and populations. This definition assumes both a managerial and a policy concern with the structure, process, and outcomes of health services including the costs, financing, organization, outcomes, and accessibility of care
Social and behavioral sciences	The study of behavioral, social, and cultural factors related to individual and population health and health disparities over the life course. Research and practice in this area contributes to the development, administration, and evaluation of programs and policies in public health and health services to promote and sustain healthy environments and healthy lives for individuals and populations

behavior. Communities are often involved through public participation and grass-roots initiatives. Businesses are also involved as community members, corporate sponsors or funding sources, and employers. Increasingly, the media plays a major role in public health, educating the public, and providing links between citizens and other entities. The APHA plays a leading role in this realm, as the oldest and largest organization of public health professionals in the world. Academic institutions under the umbrella of the Association of Schools of Public Health (ASPH) are also central to the field, informing it with evidence and training its workers in five key areas including: biostatistics, environmental health sciences, epidemiology, health policy and management, and social and behavioral sciences (see Table 2.1).

Public Health Study Designs

There are three main stages of studies in public health: surveillance, descriptive studies, and analytic studies.

Surveillance refers to the ongoing collection, recording, analysis, interpretation, and dissemination of data in order to identify or profile the current health status of a specific community or population. Surveillance activities may focus on vital statistics (e.g., births, deaths, fetal deaths) or particular diseases of interest (e.g., H1N1 influenza or HIV infection), effect (e.g., risk and incidence rates, differences, and ratios), and attributable fractions. Surveillance activities attempt to gather information about all members of a population, rather than just from a representative sample and are usually established by government agencies or other organizations that have the mandate to care for the health and welfare of their population. *Descriptive studies* are used to describe patterns of disease or other existing measures of health status across a population at a specific point in time; for example, obesity in the state of Georgia in 2011. Descriptive studies follow three primary designs: ecological, case series, or cross-sectional. Ecological studies characterize exposures and outcomes of groups across populations: for example, rates of diabetes in the USA versus France or in Texas versus California. Case series studies are made up of multiple individual patient case reports. For example, a case series may describe the clinical experience of 100 patients who were admitted to the hospital with a "new" disease. Finally, cross-sectional studies gather information from a representative selection of individuals within a defined population at a specific time, for the purpose of extrapolating the findings to the larger group. For example, a cross-sectional study may survey 1,000 individuals in Massachusetts about their weight and their consumption of fried foods, with the idea that the findings may be representative of all Massachusetts residents. Descriptive studies can be useful for generating hypotheses or for informing policy/program development. However, they are unable to demonstrate causality between an exposure and an outcome of interest (e.g., fried foods and overweight).

Finally, *analytic studies* measure associations between exposure and outcome in order to determine cause. Analytic study types include cohort studies, case-control studies, and randomized control trials (RCTs). Cohort studies follow groups of individuals, exposed or unexposed, over time—prospective, retrospective, or ambidirectional—and measure multiple outcomes and incidence. Case-control studies select subjects based on their having a particular health outcome (such as lung cancer) and look at past exposures to assess what factors may have led to the development of disease. RCTs are considered the "gold standard" of clinical research studies. In RCTs, the exposure (such as the use of a particular drug or the use of a smoking cessation program) is assigned randomly to study participants by the researcher, and the outcome (such as tumor reduction or success in quitting smoking) is assessed between groups with a different exposure. Analytic studies can help determine whether exposures and outcomes are linked; however, they are expensive, time-consuming, and result generalizability is limited.

In addition to these study types, public health practitioners are occasionally presented with *natural experiments*. Natural experiments are frequently referred to as emerging opportunities in built environment and health research. Natural experiments are cohort studies where the assignment to experimental groups is a function of nature rather than of a researcher. Examples of two well-known natural experiments include John Snow's 1854 finding of cholera contamination of London's Broad Street pump (Snow 1860) and Taylor's study of the impact of viewing green space on children's self-discipline (Taylor et al. 2002). In each study, the exposed and unexposed groups were naturally randomized, by housing choice in London or by the Chicago public housing agency, so comparisons could be made on the outcomes of cholera and behavior, respectively.

Community Planning: An Introduction

The American Planning Association (APA) defines planning as a "dynamic profession that works to improve the welfare of people and their communities by creating more convenient, equitable, healthful, efficient and attractive places for present and future generations." Planners work closely with governments and the public to help communities create short-term and long-term plans for growth and change. Planners objectively advise communities on how to best utilize their land as well as natural and cultural resources to solve community challenges. Typical products of the planning process include land-use plans, facility and infrastructure plans, and transportation plans. Policy recommendations, in addition to regulatory and financial development strategies, form less physically concrete but equally common variations of plan-making.

As shown in Table 2.2, typical specializations in the planning profession include land-use planning, transportation planning, urban design, planning law, environmental planning, and economic development. Planners work at varying scales ranging from the community or neighborhood to the city, county, state, and regional levels.

The APA/American Institute of Certified Planners (AICP) 2010 Planners Salary Survey indicated that 70% of planners work in public agencies and 23% in private consulting firms. The Bureau of Labor Statistics (BLS) of the US Department of Labor found that local governments employed approximately 66% of urban and regional planners. The BLS also projected a job growth of 19% between 2008 and 2018, which is stated to be faster than average. This boom is in response to rapidly increasing urbanization and the corresponding pressures that cities and regions will face with respect to transportation, environment, housing, employment, and land use.

The two most critical challenges of the twenty-first century, (1) globalization and the economic crisis and (2) climate change, put planners in the forefront of the quest for a sustainable world. Globalization has led to economic competitiveness and in the USA this has meant the loss of several traditional employment sectors including manufacturing and information technology services. As a result, a number of cities (Detroit, Pittsburgh) are losing population, and planners are increasingly called upon to revitalize these previously thriving communities. One of the greatest consequences of the economic crisis has been the housing market collapse and resulting foreclosures. As a result, planners have been asked to lend their expertise to guide newly emerging real-estate and economic-development trends.

Climate change is another area in which planners are increasingly lending their expertise. Planners contribute to this conversation by championing smart growth principles as an antidote to suburban sprawl and other resource-consumptive land-use patterns that consequently increase greenhouse gas production and cause secondary public health impacts. Other emerging fields include the study of urban heat islands and other climatological phenomena that might be specifically caused by the way cities are planned.

Table 2.2 Planning discipline specializations defined. (Adapted from Association of Collegiate Schools of Planning 2013)

Specialization	Definition
Land-use planning	Land-use planning is the most traditional kind of planning. These planners do a range of jobs including encouraging or discouraging growth, conducting long-range comprehensive plans, developing or administering local regulations, and evaluating the impact of proposed residential or commercial development and suggest alternative responses.
Environmental planning	Environmental planning focuses on enhancing the physical environment and minimizing the adverse impacts of development. This includes both addressing scientific and technical questions and developing policies and programs to clean up, protect, and manage natural resources.
Economic development planning	Economic development planning focuses on improving a community or region by expanding and diversifying the economic activities that support the families living there. Such actions include developing plans, finding financing, and addressing regulatory and other barriers to attract new business, enhance community features (like tourism or recreation), or retain current businesses.
Transportation planning	Transportation planning serves to address the current and future transportation needs of families and businesses, locally and across a region. The scope includes technical analysis of transportation needs, addressing the social and economic aspects of movement across space, and focus on specific or multiple modes (cycling, public transit, etc.).
Housing planning	Housing planning focuses on strategies to improve the supply of affordable housing and expand home ownership among low-income or disadvantaged groups. Mixed-use and mixed-income developments are often used to realize success.
Social and community-development planning	Social and community planning focuses on improving multiple aspects of often distressed neighborhoods in an effort to increase the overall quality of life. This requires combining skills from other planning specialization areas and working with housing, landuse, and transportation planners. Such actions may include improving transit services or providing better public health facilities in low-income neighborhoods.

Ultimately, several critical planning issues of today fall under the umbrella of *sustainability*. Seen as systemic equilibrium between environmental, economic, and social dimensions framed around equity, sustainable planning signals an altered approach to comprehensive planning. Armed with an environmental ethic, the theme of sustainability might be the unifying substantive and normative goal to inform the urban planning of today and the future.

History and Evolution of Planning

Historically, planning has been a primarily public enterprise. The planning profession emerged at the turn of the twentieth century in response to the "physical squalor and political corruption of the emerging industrial city" (Klosterman 1996). As with public health, planning has gone through several distinct phases as the American society has evolved. Rational planning, also known as synoptic or comprehensive planning, emerged in the 1930s and dominated the first half of the century. It was considered the planning model appropriate for decision-making and the most efficient allocation of resources, formalized by research done at the University of Chicago's School of Sociology on sociology, economics, urban environments and political science. The rational planning model has come under heavy criticism since the 1960s, blamed for several social injustices that can be witnessed in cities today. The demolition of low-income inner-city communities and their subsequent relocation into housing projects, under the guise of "urban renewal," created concentrations of poverty and crime. Sprawling land-development patterns as well as social and environmental injustices are now attributed to segregated zoning, a product of rational planning. Today, a new emphasis on public participatory processes, as well as collaborative and communicative planning, has transformed land planning into a more democratic process of deliberation and negotiation. Planning processes of the future aspire to be more inclusive, based on a shared or collective understanding for a pluralistic society.

Contemporary physical planning involves problem identification and goal setting, information gathering and analysis, design of alternatives, and synthesis (Malizia 2005). The process usually involves extensive public participation and community approval in order to increase community buy-in, raise constituent support, and bring about solutions encouraging more sustainable communities.

Historical Connections between Planning and Public Health

The profession of urban planning is rooted in nineteenth century medical theories of disease and the quest for salubrious landscapes. Disease was seen as a result of effluvium (miasma) released from certain pathogenic sociological (crime, "loose" morals) and environmental (industry, poor housing conditions, improper sanitation, marshes, cemeteries) elements that characterized urban living. The sanitary reform movement marks the first formal collaborative effort between city planning and public health, both from an ideological and methodological perspective. Housing reform, urban parks, rural cemetery movement, zoning, and the later City Beautiful movement represented physically deterministic interventions to public health problems (Corburn 2007; Duhl and Sanchez 1999).

The germ theory redefined the origins of disease in the early part of the twentieth century. The knowledge that disease was caused specifically by microbes led to the public health paradigm of specific immunization and other biomedical models. These biomedical models led to the divergence between urban planning and public health and a concurrent separation between social and medical causes of disease (Corburn 2007; Duhl and Sanchez 1999). Planners continued to contribute indirectly to healthy urban planning, however, in areas such as community and environmental safety (building codes, roadway design, pollution control), zoning codes (building setbacks and height regulations enabling adequate exposure to sunlight), and sanitation and infrastructure planning.

> Health is a state of complete physical, mental and social wellbeing and not merely the absence of disease or infirmity. The enjoyment of the highest attainable standard of health is one of the fundamental rights of every human being without distinction of race, religion, political belief or economic and social condition. (World Health Organization 1948)

The new definition of health as put forth by the constitution of the WHO, coupled with a resurgence of ecosocial epidemiology,[1] heralded a renewed connection between health and the social, cultural, and physical context of the individual. The inability of the biomedical model to explain disease and mortality due to social and community factors prompted this reconsideration of the established notions of health and disease.[2] The limitations of the biomedical model, as well as the realization that health is affected by a multitude of social, environmental, and economic factors, have made the pursuit of good health an interdisciplinary enterprise.

The interconnected disciplines of public health and urban planning parted ways in the mid-twentieth century, but Kochtitzky et al. (2006) report that a reintegration of the two professions is evident both in academic (Botchwey et al. 2009) and professional circles. Their research findings report that public health and medical journals such as the *American Journal of Public Health* (AJPH) and *The Journal of the American Medical Association* (JAMA) have several articles featured in the top 50 most-cited/read list that are of common interest to planners and public health professionals alike. Topics include social capital, effect of housing on health, neighborhood-level effects on health, and others. Other collaborative efforts have included transportation planning and air quality improvement, urban sprawl and health, and the encouragement of physical activity in order to combat obesity. The CDC and other public health agencies have also begun to employ planners to create an integrative approach to better health.

Of particular significance to the reconnection of public health and urban planning (health and built environment) is the concept of the human being as an "embodiment" of the physical and psychosocial environment. The interpretation of the body as an incorporation of the material and social world provides us with the understanding of health as a "continual and cumulative interplay between exposure, susceptibility and resistance," all of which occur at multiple scales and domains of the built environment (Corburn 2004).[3]Socio-ecological models define health as a

---

[1] Ecosocial epidemiology was first coined by Nancy Krieger in 1994 and "fully embraces a social production of disease perspective while aiming to bring in a comparably rich biological and ecological analysis" (Krieger 2001).

[2] The nonspecific immunization phase in public health (1980–present) reflects on causes of death due to suicide and crime, which lie outside the realms of traditional disease causation (Duhl and Sanchez 1999).

[3] Ecological systems theory, a contextual approach to studying human development, was developed by UrieBronfenbrenner in the 1970s. He placed the individual within four hierarchical nested systems—the microsystem (e.g., the home or classroom of a child); the mesosystem (two interacting microsystems, e.g., the effect of the home on the classroom); the exosystem (external environments which indirectly influence development, e.g., the mother's place of work); and the

multidisciplinary and multilevel endeavor, bridging individual health and population health (the basic tenet of complexity theory being that the whole is greater than the sum of its parts)[4] and situates health within "place," explaining distributive aspects of health within populations.

Socio-ecological models of health encourage multidisciplinary research efforts and draw from fields as diverse as psychology, anthropology, urban planning, social work, engineering, psychiatry, nursing, education, criminal justice, epidemiology, and/or public health (Lounsbury and Mitchell 2009). A recurrent theme in the literature is the study of obesity in relation to elements in the built environment such as landuse, walkability, and green space (see Box 2.2).

Box 2.2   Obesity and the built environment: Links between urban planning and health

A study of obesity and the built environment provides an interesting example of how public health and planning remain connected today.

Overweight and obesity constitute perhaps the most important health challenge of the day. Childhood obesity has tripled in the past 30 years. It is referred to as "the gravest and most poorly controlled public health threat of our time" (Hammond 2010). Two-thirds of Americans are now considered overweight, and over one-third of US adults are obese (see Fig. 2.1).

The exponential growth of obesity over the last 25 years has significant implications for public health, as obesity is a primary risk factor for diseases such as hypertension, type 2 diabetes, certain kinds of cancer, arthritis and heart disease, as well as premature mortality (Flegal et al. 2010; Ogden et al. 2007).

The reasons why obesity rates have risen so dramatically and remain uncontrolled are complex. It may be partially due to the multifactorial nature of obesity, which is affected by a combination of genetics, neurobiology, psychology, family and social environment, physical environment, economic markets, economics, and public policy (Ogden et al. 2007). However, the role of the built environment and the way in which people act within it appear to be paramount. The CDC state that America has become an "obesogenic" nation, a country that has built into its structure factors that tend to make people obese.

---

macro system (the larger socioeconomic cultural context). By applying socio-ecological systems concepts to health, we can deduce that health can be a state produced by the constant interaction and mutual influences between the individual as agent and his or her surrounding environments.

[4] Arah (2009) discusses the inaccuracies of making deductions between individual health and population health within the biomedical model of epidemiology. Biomedical models do not explain the dynamic relationships between the cumulative health effects of an individual embedded in an intricate social and environmental web, and the larger health of the population. The socio-ecological model offers an alternative by attempting to understand those connections.

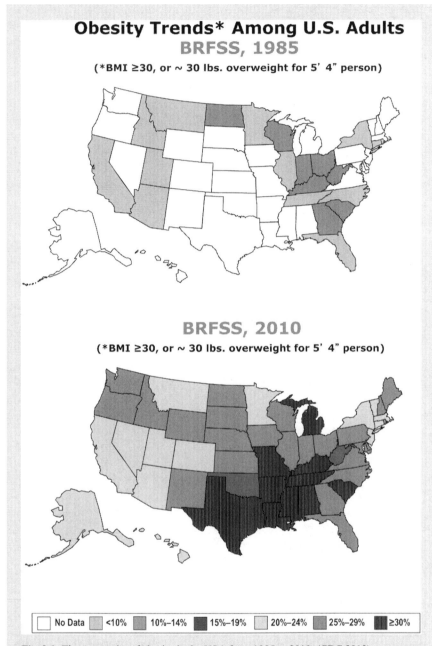

Fig. 2.1 The geography of obesity in the USA from 1985 to 2010. (CDC 2012)

In a review of 63 studies on the built environment and obesity, Feng et al. (2010) identified physical activity potential, landuse/transportation conditions, and food environments as primary domains of the built environment that impact obesity.

Physical activity potential: The built environment includes factors that can enhance or diminish the likelihood for physical activity and exercise. These include both *personal barriers* and *environmental barriers*. *Personal barriers* are subjective considerations that influence an individual's motivation or ability to exercise like lack of time, disabilities, and lack of social support. *Environmental barriers* are objective conditions that dissuade physical exercise such as lack of infrastructure like sidewalks, bike lanes and pathways, unsafe distances between vehicles and pedestrians, obstructions, lack of physical activity-related facilities, and unequal access to these features for all segments of the population.

Land use/transportation: It refers to the way in which cities, towns, or regions are structured, including elements such as density, sprawl, and connectivity, often regulated through zoning codes. Low-density patterns, or sprawl, are often associated with decreased walking and bicycling rates and increased automobile dependence. These in turn are associated with decreased physical activity and increased overweight and obesity (Frank et al. 2004).In addition, increased car use results in higher per capita emissions of volatile organic compounds (VOCs) and other pollutants that decrease air quality and increase risks of respiratory and cardiovascular disease, thereby creating secondary impediments to physical activity (Frank et al. 2006; Lopez-Zetina et al. 2006; Frank et al. 2007; Samimi et al. 2009).

Food environment: It is defined as the availability, quality, health, and accessibility of food options in a given area. The specifics of one's food environment have strong implications for health, particularly concerning obesity/overweight, coronary heart disease, and other chronic conditions. The literature has established a link between unhealthy lifestyles and fast-food restaurants (Li et al. 2009) as well as convenience stores (Morland et al. 2006). Various interventions in the food environment have been effective, including the introduction of farmers' markets (Larsen and Gilliland 2009).The interactions taking place in food environments are complex; for example, Cummins et al. (2005) found that while introducing a large supermarket into a neighborhood did not increase fruit and vegetable consumption, it did have a positive effect on the community's psychological health. Recently, the dominant model for describing areas with poor access to healthy food options, which are disproportionately low-income neighborhoods and/or neighborhoods of color, has been that of the "food desert."Some have begun to criticize this framework, proposing new ways of looking at food environment inequities, such as the emerging idea of the "food hinterlands" (Leete et al. 2012).

Proposed interventions to address the obesity problem
As shown above, research has determined that the built environment influences individual behaviors, such as levels of physical activity and dietary choices. Interventions in the built environment provide a population-based strategy to improve social and physical contexts that can be supportive of healthy lifestyles. A population-level preventive intervention may extend health benefits to both the obese and nonobese population and further reduce the prevalence of obesity (Flegal et al. 2010).

Form-based interventions: Form-based interventions for healthier communities advocate common principles of denser, mixed-use environments, and gridded streets for better connectivity, collectively promoting walkability. These include: Traditional Neighborhood Development (TND), Transit-Oriented Development (TOD), New Urbanism, and Transect Planning.

Policy-based interventions: Interventions based in economic policy include federal- and state-funding opportunities that promote smart growth as well as greater quality and availability of public transit. Some approaches include the Obama Administration's *Partnership for Sustainable Communities Initiative*[5], Growth Management (anti-sprawl), and both environmental impact assessment (EIA) and HIA methods.

In order to address and solve the current built environment and health concerns faced today, both the community planning and public health fields will need to include more cross-disciplinary work. The use of HIA to facilitate these interactions is an effective means of collaborating to create a healthier community. Five primary issues in research and analysis require greater attention in order to smooth the road for effective, more interdisciplinary work on HIAs. These include the following:

1. *Unclear evidence in the link between compact urban form and healthful outcomes*
   Lopez-Zetina et al. (2006) state that "ecological studies suggest rather than provide definitive answers for the associations among complex factors related to the urban environment." For example, all studies evaluating the correlation of obesity with multiple environmental attributes stop short of confirming causation,

---

[5] A promising policy initiative. A federal interagency partnership between the Environmental Protection Agency (EPA), Department of Housing and Urban Development (HUD), and Department of Transportation (DOT), it is guided by six livability principles: *provide more transportation choices, promote equitable, affordable housing, enhance economic competitiveness, support existing communities, coordinate and leverage investment,* and *value communities and neighborhoods* (*EPA-HUD-DOT* 2010).

and it is also unclear how much the built environment affects body mass index (BMI).

2. *Inconsistencies in measuring and modeling the built environment make results difficult to interpret.* Built environment metrics are numerous and range from single measures such as density to composite measures like the sprawl index. Metrics are also created from a variety of data sources and computational methods. Standardized metrics, environmental attributes and scales will help strengthen associations between the built environment and obesity as well as increase comparative opportunities between studies (Feng et al. 2010).

3. *Models tend to measure quantitative variables.* Variables included in the data are often constrained by data availability. Often, variables such as accessibility to parks or sidewalks and qualitative variables such as climate, topography, and crime are excluded from models, as are some important health outcomes such as quality of life and mental well-being. Most models also do not take into account personal preferences for physical activity and dietary choices (Ewing et al. 2003).

4. *Better understanding of place.* Space and place are as much cultural constructs as measurable areas determined by predefined political boundaries. Feng et al. (2010) state that the greatest challenge in health and place research is the use of "administratively defined spatial units and acknowledgement of their limitations as surrogates for more sociologically valid places". These units include counties, census tracts, census blocks, etc. Thus, future studies need more context-specific definitions of place that can provide less generic explanations of local phenomena.

5. *Greater number of longitudinal studies required.* Most studies in health and place research are cross-sectional at a defined point in time. More longitudinal studies are required, for example, to examine changes in land use and corresponding changes in obesity prevalence over time. Additionally, more quasi-experimental research design such as pre- and posttest methods that study the impacts of policy (zoning regulations) or projects (smart growth, sidewalk construction) on physical activity and obesity are required.

There are also three *emerging directions* for community planning and public health. These involve the significant demographic shifts in the USA that are already changing the way we live, the role of local organizations in promoting health, our access to food and tensions in promoting walking while working to decrease pedestrian injuries.

1. *Aging, health, and the built environment.* Cities in the USA are dealing with increasing aging populations. Public health, particularly environmental health, sets thresholds for environmental toxins based on its most vulnerable populations (children). Likewise, sustainable cities need to accommodate their most vulnerable populations (the elderly, children, people with disabilities, etc.).Principles of universal design are being employed in communities to provide equal access to all demographic groups, with differing health status and disability levels. "Aging in place" is another important concept currently being integrated within

the principles of smart growth, new urbanism, and redevelopment. Its aim is to create multi-generational communities offering appropriate living environments for families in different phases of the lifecycle.

2. *The role of community institutions such as hospitals, churches, and community health organizations in promoting community health.* Local-, state-, and federal-level planning processes increasingly require citizen input in decision making. Additionally, the value of individual experiences in guiding the diagnosis, recommendation, and implementation of public health approaches, especially for the most vulnerable, is of growing importance. Unfortunately, citizens with the least access, typically low-income and minority residents, are left with little capital to influence these planning and health-promoting processes. Local institutions like churches, schools, and community organizations are best positioned to understand and speak on behalf of these communities (Martin et al. 2004). Their institutional capital serves as a proxy for residents who are politically, socially, and economically disenfranchised. As a result, they meet the needs of the most vulnerable populations while adding their valuable voices to shape interventions (Botchwey 2007).

3. *Food access, land use and socioeconomic factors.* Research has found that obesity rates are directly associated with access to retail food. Lower-income and minority communities have poor access to high-quality food products as retailed at supermarkets and chain grocery stores. These communities also have higher concentrations of fast-food restaurants. Current urban planning practices enable residential segregation by income and ethnicity, making it easier to create poor access to healthy food. The HIA of the Atlanta BeltLine provided clear evidence of these inequities: Unequal access to nutritious food promotes health disparities (Ross et al. 2012).

Public health and community planning, as disciplines, have taken different historical paths but arose out of similar attitudes and concerns. The resurgence of socioecological approaches to health, as well as a renewed interest in interdisciplinarity on the part of both fields, has opened up dialogues on how best to work together in tackling the enormity of today's challenges. Emerging fields such as planning for "aging in place" and healthy food access necessitate the engagement, cooperation, and knowledge bases of community planning and public health professionals in pursuit of positive outcomes. Each field has much to teach the other and as society undergoes a number of swift and significant demographic changes, successful interventions will increasingly depend on our ability to break down professional silos.

References

Arah OA (2009) On the relationship between individual and population health. Med Health Care Philos 12(3):235–244

Association of Collegiate Schools of Planning (2013) Guide to undergraduate and graduate education in urban and regional planning, 19th ed. Tallahassee, Florida.

Botchwey N (2007) Religious sector's presence in local community development. J Plan Educ Res 27(1):36–48

Botchwey N, Hobson S, Dannenberg A et al (2009) A model curriculum for a course on the built environment and public health: training for an interdisciplinary workforce. Am J Prev Med 36(Supp 2):S63–S71

Calhoun JG, Ramiah K, McGean Weist E, Shortell SM (2008) Development of a core competency model for the Master of Public Health degree. Am J Pub Health 98(9):1598–1607

Centers for Disease Control (CDC) (2012) Overweight and Obesity. http://www.cdc.gov/obesity/data/adult.html. Accessed 16 July 2013

Corburn J (2004) Confronting the challenges in reconnecting urban planning and public health. Am J Public Health 94(4):541–549

Corburn J (2007) Reconnecting with our roots. Urb Aff Rev 42(5):688–713

Cummins S, Petticrew M, Higgins C, Findlay A, Sparks L (2005) Large-scale food retailing as an intervention for diet and health: quasi-experimental evaluation of a natural experiment. J Epidemiol Comm H 59:1035–1040

Duhl LJ, Sanchez AK (1999) Healthy cities and the city planning process: a background document on links between health and urban planning. World Health Organization Regional Office for Europe, Denmark

EPA-HUD-DOT (2010).Partnership for Sustainable Communities. http://www.whitehouse.gov/sites/default/files/uploads/SCP-Fact-Sheet.pdf. Accessed 18 June 2013

Ewing R, Schmid T, Killingsworth R et al (2003) Relationship between urban sprawl and physical activity, obesity and morbidity. Am J Health Promot 18(1):47–57

Feng J, Glass TA, Curreiro FC et al (2010) The built environment and obesity: a systematic review of the epidemiologic evidence. Health Place 16(2):175–190

Flegal KM, Carroll MD, Ogden CL et al (2010) Prevalence and trends in obesity among us adults, 1999–2008. JAMA 303(3):235–241

Frank L, Andersen MA, Schmid TM (2004) Obesity relationships with community design, physical activity and time spent in cars. Am J Prev Med 27(2):87–96

Frank L, Sallis JF, Conway TL et al (2006) Associations between neighborhood walkability and active transportation, body mass index, and air quality. J Am Plann Assoc 72(1):75–87

Frank L, Saelens BE, Powell KE, Chapman JE (2007) Stepping towards causation: do built environments or neighborhood travel preferences explain physical activity, driving, and obesity. Soc Sci Med 65(9):1898–1914

Hammond RA, Levine R (2010) The economic impact of obesity in the United States. Diabetes Metab Syndr Obes 3:285–295.

HealthyPeople.gov (2013) 2020 Topics & objectives—objectives A-Z. http://www.healthypeople.gov/2020/topicsobjectives2020/default.aspx. Accessed 11 May 2012

Institute of Medicine (2003) The future of the public's health in the 21st century. National Academies Press, Washington, DC

Klosterman RE (1996) Arguments for and against planning. In: Campbell S, Fainstein SS (eds) Readings in planning theory. Blackwell, Malden, pp 86–101

Kochtitzky CS, Frumkin H, Rodriguez R et al. (2006) Urban planning and public health at CDC. Morb Mortal Wkly Rep 55(2):34–38

Krieger N (2001) Theories for social epidemiology in the 21st century: an ecosocial perspective. Int J Epidemiol 30(4):668–677

Larsen K, Gilliland J (2009) A farmer's market in a food desert: evaluating impacts on the price and availability of healthy food. Health Place 15(4):1158–1162

Leete L, Bania N, Sparks-Ibanga A (2012) Congruence and coverage: alternative approaches to identifying urban food deserts and food hinterlands. J Plan Educ Res 32:204–218

Li F, Harmer P, Cardinal P, Bosworth M, Johnson-Shelton D (2009) Obesity and the built environment: does the density of neighborhood fast-food outlets matter? Am J Health Promot 23(3):203–209

Lopez-Zetina J, Lee H, Friis R (2006) The link between obesity and the built environment. Evidence from an ecological analysis of obesity and vehicle miles of travel in California. Health Place 12(4):656–664

Lounsbury DW, Mitchell SG (2009) Introduction to special issue on social ecological approaches to community health research and action. Am J Commun Psychol 44(3–4):213–220

Malizia EE (2005) City and regional planning: a primer for public health officials. Am J Health Promot 19(5): Suppl 1–13

Martin M, Leonard AM, Allen S et al (2004) Commentary: using culturally competent strategies to improve traffic safety in the black community. Ann Emerg Med 44(4):414–418

Morland K, Diez Roux A, Wing S (2006) Supermarkets, other food stores, and obesity: the atherosclerosis risk in communities study. Am J Prev Med 30(4):333–339

Murray CJ, Frenk, J (2010) Ranking 37th—measuring the performance of the U.S. health care system. N Engl J Med. 362:98–99

Ogden CL, Yanovski SZ, Carroll MD et al (2007) The epidemiology of obesity. Gastroenterology 132(6):2087–2102

Ross C, Leone de Nie K, Dannenberg A et al (2012) Health impact assessment of the Atlanta Belt-Line. Am J Prev Med 42(3):203–213

Samimi A, Mohammadian A, Madanizadeh S (2009) Effects of transportation and built environment on general health and obesity. Transport Res D 14(1):67–71

Snow, J. 1860. On the mode of communication of cholera, 2nd ed. John Churchill (Facsimile of 1936 reprinted edition by Hafner, New York, 1965), London

Taylor AF, Kuo FE, Sullivan WC (2002) Views of nature and self-discipline: evidence from inner city children. J Environ Psychol 22:49–63

World Health Organization (1948) Preamble to the Constitution of the World Health Organization as adopted by the International Health Conference, New York, 19–22 June, 1946; signed on 22 July 1946 by the representatives of 61 States (Official Records of the World Health Organization, no. 2, p 100) and entered into force on 7 April 1948.

World Health Organization (2012) A comprehensive global monitoring framework including indicators and a set of voluntary global targets for the prevention and control of noncommunicable diseases. World Health Organization, Geneva.

Chapter 3
HIA, EIA, SIA, and Other Appraisals

Abstract This chapter places health impact assessment (HIA) in the context of the historical development of impact assessment processes in the USA and globally. It begins by summarizing and comparing the largest families of impact assessment: environmental impact assessment (EIA), social impact assessment (SIA), and HIA, highlighting similarities and key topical differences. The relationship between EIA and HIA is discussed, US legal standards for EIA are described, and the use of HIA and SIA to address weaknesses in the EIA process is highlighted. Other impact assessment types, including integrated assessment and strategic environmental assessment, are also discussed. The chapter then contrasts HIA with other health research study types, including human health risk assessment, occupational health risk assessment, epidemiologic studies, health program evaluation, and cost–benefit analysis—approaches that may superficially resemble HIA but are in fact quite different. This chapter highlights the unique contributions that HIA can lend to this diverse array of impact assessment and health research methodologies.

Keywords International Association for Impact Assessment (IAIA) · Impact assessment · Social impact assessment (SIA) · Environmental impact assessment (EIA) · Health impact assessment (HIA) · Integrated assessment (IA) · National Environmental Policy ACT (NEPA) · Ecosystem functioning · Pollutants · Council on Environmental Quality · Strategic environmental assessment · Human health risk assessment · Occupational health risk assessment · Epidemiologic studies · Health program evaluation · Cost–benefit analysis (CBA)

Health impact assessment (HIA) has developed in the context of a number of complementary assessment types either used to understand the potential impacts of projects, plans, or policies or used for health research. In this chapter, we discuss two intersecting categories: the family of impact assessments and the family of health assessments.

Impact Assessments

Impact assessments are evaluations specifically designed to identify the potential consequences or impacts of a current or proposed action. The International Association for Impact Assessment defines impact assessment as "a structured process for considering the implications, for people and their environment, of proposed actions while there is still an opportunity to modify (or even, if appropriate, abandon) the proposals," and "is applied at all levels of decision making, from policies to specific projects" (IAIA 2012). Impact assessment is different from many other types of evaluation in that it attempts to make predictions about future effects, rather than evaluating the effects of an already-implemented policy or plan.

EIA, SIA, and HIA

All impact assessment modalities or types have a common goal: to prospectively identify the potential impacts of a proposed project, policy, or program in order to minimize potential harms and maximize potential gains.

The three main impact assessment types currently in wide use are: environmental impact assessment (EIA); social impact assessment (SIA), also known as socioeconomic impact assessment; and HIA. All follow a similar approach in terms of methodology: They determine the scope of the potential impacts to be examined, gather data to understand the current context, predict changes to conditions resulting from the project or policy, and make recommendations for how to improve the proposed project or policy in order to minimize harm and maximize gain.

A primary difference among the assessment types lies in the content area that each focuses on. EIA examines effects on the biophysical environment, SIA examines effects on social and economic environments, and HIA examines impacts on community health. This is shown in Fig. 3.1.

In practice, the divisions between the content areas addressed by EIA, SIA, and HIA are not always clear-cut. There are a number of areas of overlap—topics that transcend more than one integrated assessment (IA) modality because they are relevant for more than one discipline. These overlapping areas are also shown in Fig. 3.1. For example, topics that are relevant to both SIA and HIA include the effects of the proposed project or policy on employment, income, housing, or the capacity of local services such as police or fire departments. However, the relevance of these topics for an SIA and an HIA differ somewhat, and the assessment approach would be different for each. An SIA practitioner might investigate how a project would impact direct, indirect, and induced employment, community revenue, housing availability, or the capacity of police services. In contrast, a practitioner of HIA may be more interested in how changes to these variables might affect health outcomes such as overall morbidity (from employment and income), respiratory disease transmission (from crowded or low-quality housing), or injury rates (from crime and violence). Similarly, impacts on air quality may be of interest to both EIA

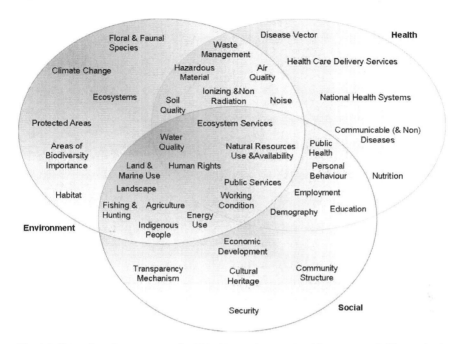

Fig. 3.1 Examples of content areas for EIA, SIA, and HIA. (Graphic courtesy of Filippo Uberti, Eni S.p.A.)

and HIA practitioners, but would be treated in different ways. The EIA practitioner might attempt to understand how the project or policy would change levels of specific air contaminants such as particulate matter, nitrous oxides, or sulfur oxides, while the practitioner of HIA may be more interested in developing predictions about changes in respiratory disease patterns and other chronic disease outcomes resulting from the air quality changes.

The predominant type of impact assessment currently in use both in the USA and internationally is EIA.[1] Legislated into US practice by the National Environmental Policy Act (NEPA) of 1969, EIA was the earliest of the impact assessment practices to be developed and therefore has served as a template for the development of subsequent methodologies.

The environmental impact categories that are included in an environmental impact statement (EIS) are dependent on the project or activity and consider both pollutants and ecosystem functioning. Categories that may be covered include air quality, water quality (surface and groundwater), noise, biological resources

---

[1] In addition to environmental impact assessment (EIA), the terms environmental assessment (EA) and environmental impact statement (EIS) are also commonly used. There are variations in how these terms are used—and they are not always used consistently across jurisdictions—but all generally refer to the process of prospectively identifying potential impacts of a proposed project or policy, with particular focus on impacts on the biophysical environment.

(vegetation, wildlife), cultural resources (architectural, historical, and archaeological), visual resources, and socioeconomic environment. Guidelines for the content of an EIS are available from the Council on Environmental Quality (CEQ) (1973).

Box 3.1 describes the way in which human health impacts are addressed in the NEPA process, and Box 3.2 reviews the sequence of steps that comprise the environmental assessment (EA) process under NEPA.

Box 3.1 Human Health Impacts as Addressed in EIA

The inclusion of a robust, systematic approach to public health is supported by NEPA, the regulations issued by the Council on Environmental Quality (CEQ), the agency in the Executive Office of the President charged with overseeing implementation of NEPA, Executive Orders 12898 and 13045, and available guidance on NEPA and environmental justice.

Congressional Intent In using the term "human environment," Congress signaled that the protection of human communities was a fundamental purpose of the legislation. In the debates leading to NEPA's enactment, Senator Henry Jackson stated: "When we speak of the environment, basically, we are talking about the relationship between man and these physical and biological and social forces that impact upon him. A public policy for the environment basically is not a public policy for those things out there. It is a policy for people."

Health in NEPA NEPA mentions health a total of six times. Among NEPA's fundamental purposes is: "promote efforts which will prevent or eliminate damage to the environment and biosphere and stimulate the health and welfare of man" NEPA § 102 [42 USC § 4321]. NEPA is intended, furthermore, to: "assure for all Americans safe, healthful, productive, and aesthetically and culturally pleasing surroundings" [42 USC § 4331].

And finally to: "attain the widest range of beneficial uses of the environment without degradation, risk to health or safety, or other undesirable and unintended consequences" [42 USC § 4331].

Health in the CEQ Regulations Several general provisions of CEQ's NEPA regulations support the inclusion of health. First, agencies respond to substantive public concerns in the draft environmental impact statement (DEIS) [40 CFR § 1503.4]. When, therefore, an agency can anticipate substantive health concerns based on scoping, it is sensible to include these issues for analysis in the DEIS.

Second, in determining whether an effect may be significant (and therefore require analysis in the EIS) one of the factors that agencies should consider is "the degree to which the effects on the human environment are likely to be highly controversial" [40 CFR § 1508.27 (b) 4]. Commonly, health often figures among the strongest concerns expressed by affected communities.

The CEQ regulations also specifically define health as one of the effects that must be considered in an EIS or an EA. In defining "effects," the regulations state that: "Effects" includes ecological, aesthetic, historic, cultural, economic, social, or health, whether direct, indirect, or cumulative" [40 C.F.R. § 1508.8]. And, the regulations instruct agencies to consider "the degree to which the proposed action affects public health or safety" in determining significance [40 C.F.R. § 1508.27].

Health in Executive Orders Executive Order 12898 instructs agencies to: "make achieving environmental justice part of its mission by identifying and addressing, as appropriate, disproportionately high and adverse human health or environmental effects of its programs, policies, and activities on minority populations and low-income populations in the United States."

Similarly, Executive Order 13045 states that agencies must: "make it a high priority to identify and assess environmental health risks and safety risks that may disproportionately affect children; and...shall ensure that its policies, programs, activities, and standards address disproportionate risks to children that result from environmental health risks or safety risks."

Statements relevant to NEPA-based health analysis in Federal Guidance CEQ guidance on implementing Executive Order 12898 contains several suggestions relevant to public health analysis, including:

- Lead agencies should involve public health agencies and clinics.
- Agencies should review relevant public health data (as for any other resource).
- Agencies should consider how interrelated cultural, social, occupational, historical, or economic factors may contribute to health effects of the proposed action and alternatives. (Wernham and Bear 2010)

Box 3.2 The Environmental Assessment Procedure Under NEPA in the USA

Once the NEPA process is initiated by a federal project, the agency or agencies involved conduct an analysis to determine whether to go forward with authoring an EA, which provides a concise estimation of the project's environmental impact. At this stage, public participation is at the discretion of the agency and not necessarily warranted. The conclusion of the EA process leads to either a Finding of No Significant Impact (FONSI) or the completion of an EIS if there appears to be the potential for significant environmental impact.

An EIS follows a sequence of basic steps. First is the *Notice of Intent (NOI) and scoping* stage. At this point, the process is made transparent, and

NOIs are accessible to the general public. The scoping process lays out the course of the rest of the assessment by identifying the most relevant issues, gathering important data, and inviting the participation of affected stakeholders, among other actions. The medium or method of public engagement is flexible and can vary based on need and suitability.

Next, the agency submits a *DEIS*, which it opens up to public comment for a minimum of 45 days. A key aspect of an EIS is the identification of the project's "purpose and need," and an exploration of ways to meet that other than the way the project initially proposed. One option that must always be analyzed in the alternatives section is the "no action alternative," similar to the "no build scenario" in planning—a scenario in which no new project is undertaken. At this stage, the agency is also able to indicate its preferred alternative, at its discretion.

Following the draft is the *final EIS*. This last version of the document must consider commentary and opinions given by the public in response to the DEIS. At this point, the agency must also select one alternative as preferred. Finally, building on the EIS, the agency produces a *Record of Decision (ROD)*. This publicly available document looks back analytically on the EIA process.

Ultimately, the provisions outlined by NEPA are not binding in terms of outcome. While their completion is required, compliance with final recommendations is optional. EIA as prescribed by NEPA is not an enforcement mechanism but rather an assurance that institutional actors will be well informed in their decisions.

While the EIA process represents an important step towards providing protection for important environmental considerations relevant to people, a number of shortcomings have been identified over the years (Canter 1996; Lawrence 2003). Among these are: the EIA being treated as an end in itself, rather than a means for safeguarding people and the environment; limited public input into the impact assessment and decision-making processes; insufficient attention to social impacts; insufficient attention to human health; and inequitable and unfair treatment of the least-advantaged populations.

In a partial response to these perceived problems, several complementary areas of impact assessment have been developed to try to fill the gaps.

SIA, also called socioeconomic impact assessment, arose in the 1970s as a method for explicitly examining the likely social effects of a given program. In general, SIA is tasked with looking at the full range of ways "in which people and communities interact with their socio-cultural, economic and biophysical surroundings" (IAIA 2003). In the USA, an SIA usually takes the form of the social component *within* an EA process. Thus, SIA exists more as an orientation than as a formal framework itself. Internationally, however, SIA is often used as a stand-alone process or is given equal (or nearly equal) weight to the EIA in a combined assessment.

The concept of HIA first emerged in the late 1980s in response to an identified gap in evaluating the health impacts of large-scale infrastructure projects. Although it was first deployed for projects in the developing world, HIA quickly dispersed to developed nations as well, once the tool's potential to bring a crucial new perspective to assessment was recognized (Forsyth et al. 2010). While many aspects of HIA are descended from experiences with EIA, as Harris-Roxas et al. (2012) point out, there are also aspects of health assessment that are distinct, drawing specifically from the public health profession. The USA was one of the later nations to embrace HIA, with the first US assessment conducted as recently as 1999. However, in the decade following, 54 were completed nationwide and to date, more than 200 HIAs have been completed in the USA.

Like SIA, HIA in the USA can be undertaken either as part of an EA process or as a stand-alone assessment. While HIA is not explicitly mandatory within the NEPA process, it brings critical information and perspective that might not otherwise be considered. For example, the draft environmental impact statement for one transit project in Baltimore detailed a number of likely environmental effects of the proposed project, yet mentioned nothing about the impacts on the surrounding communities' health. Based on these concerns, the city's department of transportation went forward and conducted an HIA to add to the final statement. The resulting HIA unearthed a number of health impacts that would otherwise have gone ignored (Salkin and Ko 2011).

The emergence of HIA in the past decades of the twentieth century reflects the changing challenges faced by decision makers in the present era, confirming the major significance of the built environment as a health determinant and the need to formally address these issues in the project or policy development process.

Integrated Assessment

A growing trend in the world of impact assessment is that of IA. also referred to as environmental, social, and health impact assessment (ESHIA). IAs use an interdisciplinary framework to try to arrive at insights that could not be derived through analysis by just one discipline.

Not all EIAs that include social or health analyses can be characterized as IAs. The majority of EIAs comprise discipline-specific analyses that are integrated only in the sense that they are stapled together into one report (Weaver and Sibisi 2006).

IA has been described as a superior method that is able to deliver greater benefits than discipline-specific assessments conducted independently. There appears to be a consensus in the published literature that IA is more efficient, more effective, more relevant for decision makers, and more closely aligned with stakeholder interests and the principles of sustainability. However, the literature also describes some potential drawbacks, including an impractical level of complexity (Lee 2006). From an HIA perspective, a particular strength of using an IA approach is the ability to investigate health outcomes using a larger interdisciplinary framework (Bhatia and Wernham 2008).

Strategic Environmental Assessment

Strategic environmental assessment (SEA) is similar to EIA, but is conducted at a much broader (or more strategic) level. Rather than identifying the impacts of a proposal for a single project, policy, or plan, SEA attempts to identify the effects associated with strategic-level initiatives such as a program of development or government planning strategies in a particular area. SEA is intended to identify important physical, social, and economic parameters that will enable future development to proceed in a sustainable way (Partidario 2012). An example of an SEA conducted in the USA is the Bureau of Land Management's EIS on an integrated activity plan that will direct oil and gas development and land-use planning in the National Petroleum Reserve—Alaska for the next several decades (Bureau of Land Management 2013).

Types of Health Assessment

There are several types of health assessment that are used to look at effects on human health, but that are not identical to HIA. These are important to understand because each has a unique use; but they should also not be mistaken for HIA.

Human health risk assessment (or HHRA) suffers from confusing terminology. It has also been termed health risk assessment, environmental risk assessment, and environmental health risk assessment. This is a type of evaluation that seeks to predict the effect on human health of exposure to chemical contaminants such as particulate matter, sulfur oxides, heavy metals, and other chemical substances. HHRA has a defined methodology that involves identifying potential chemical hazards; profiling the potentially exposed population; evaluating the possible routes of exposure; and developing estimates of changes in disease burden as a result of the predicted exposure (usually limited to certain forms of cancer and select respiratory outcomes). Like HIA, HHRA is usually conducted prospectively to identify the potential outcomes of future actions; it is also commonly used to evaluate the impacts of environmental projects (such as resource development or industrial projects) that are under review by an EIA or that have potential impacts on toxicologic health outcomes. Two major differences distinguish HHRA from HIA: First, its examination of effects is limited to exposure to chemical contaminants, rather than the full range of health effects examined in HIA. Second, HHRA uses a distinct methodology. HIA and HHRA are complementary, and for many projects or policies, it is helpful to conduct a full HHRA, the results of which can be referenced in the HIA.

Occupational health risk assessment is a type of evaluation that is intended to protect a workforce. It involves identifying industrial processes that may be hazardous to exposed workers. These assessments are usually conducted by an occupational or industrial hygienist who conducts a site examination of an industrial facility in order to identify chemical, biological, and physical hazards, and to assess the degree to which workers are exposed to these hazards. Like HIA, occupational health risk assessment examines a wide range of exposures and outcomes; however, occupational health risk assessment looks only at effects on workers "inside the fence," as opposed to HIA's focus on potentially affected communities "outside the fence" (International Council on Mining and Metals—ICMM 2010).

Epidemiologic studies investigate the distribution and causes of disease within a population. They focus on identifying causal risk factors associated with specific health outcomes: for example, tobacco smoking as a risk factor for lung cancer or the association between the risk factor of being overweight and the outcome of type 2 diabetes. Epidemiology researchers rely on several standard study types: cross-sectional studies, which measure risk factors and health outcomes at one point in time; case–control studies, which look at historical risk factor exposure in groups that currently do or do not have disease; cohort studies, which follow a group over time to identify who develops disease; and randomized controlled trials, which assign exposure (to a medication or a set of behavioral conditions such as exercise, for example) to randomly selected groups. Like HIA, epidemiologic studies look at human health outcomes, but that is where the similarities end. An epidemiologic study tries to ascertain whether there is an association between a single risk factor and a single outcome, with all other concurrent risk factors and outcomes treated as "noise" and controlled for; in other words, practitioners try to eliminate the consideration of those factors' effects. In HIA, conversely, practitioners are required to try to make sense out of the chaos—rather than control for multiple influencing factors, they try to describe all of them and identify what the factors' isolated and combined effects will be on multiple health outcomes. In addition, epidemiology generally has a retrospective focus; epidemiologic analysis can only take place after both the exposure and the disease have occurred, whereas HIA, by definition, attempts to make predictions about future health impacts based on exposures that have not yet occurred.

Health program evaluation refers to a wide range of evaluation types that are used to assess the efficacy of health promotion programs to understand if they had the intended effect. For example, a health evaluation may be used to evaluate whether a smoking cessation program actually resulted in a decrease in the smoking rate, improved education about the hazards of smoking, or other results that may have been the intended effect of the program. This is different from HIA in that these evaluations focus almost exclusively on health promotion programs; they look at the results of programs that have already been implemented; and their evaluation of impacts is generally confined to the *intended* outcomes of the program.

Cost–benefit analysis (CBA) is a process used both within health-focused organizations and more broadly. It attempts to monetize the effects—both adverse impacts and beneficial effects—in order to allow a comparison of the relative economic benefit of each. As such, a CBA often does not develop predictions of effects itself; rather, it applies the CBA methodology to outcomes that have already been predicted through other processes, such as an HIA. A CBA can therefore be a useful add-on to an HIA by providing an estimate of the costs associated with adverse health impacts and the cost savings associated with health benefits. In practice, however, there are many health impacts (such as stress and anxiety) that are difficult or impossible to monetize and therefore a CBA is not always a useful complement to HIA.

Finally, it should be noted that there have been a large number of health studies, assessments, or evaluations conducted that examine the impact of a particular decision, project, program, or plan on a selected range of health outcomes or health determinants. While these may be similar in intention to an HIA, they will only be considered an HIA if they meet minimum criteria for such (see Box 4.2 in Chap. 4), which include scoping the full range of potential health effects, informing decision making, and using established HIA methodology.

In this chapter, we have discussed several different assessment modalities that are currently in use. Each is continuing to evolve and may look different in the future. In addition, as societal norms and priorities change, new assessment types that are compatible with HIA are likely to emerge.

References

Bhatia R, Wernham A (2008) Integrating human health into environmental impact assessment: an unrealized opportunity for environmental health and justice. Environ Health Persp 116(8):991–1000

Bureau of Land Management (2013) National Petroleum Reserve—Alaska (NPR-A) Integrated Activity Plan and Environmental Impact Statement. http://www.blm.gov/ak/st/en/prog/planning/npra_general.html. Accessed 18 June 2013

Canter LW (1996) Environmental impact assessment. McGraw-Hill, Boston

Council on Environmental Quality (CEQ) (1973) Preparation of environmental impact statements: guidelines. Fed Regist 38(147):20550–20562

Forsyth A, Schively Slotterback C, Krizek K (2010) Health impact Assessment (HIA) for Planners: What Tools Are Useful? J Plan Lit 24(3):231–245

Harris-Roxas B, Viliani F, Harris P et al (2012) Health impact assessment: the state of the art. Impact Assess Pro Apprais 30(1):43–52

IAIA (2003) Social impact assessment: international principles: special publication series #2. International Association for Impact Assessment, Fargo

IAIA (2012) What is impact assessment? International Association for Impact Assessment, Fargo

International Council on Mining and Metals (2010) Good practice guidance on health impact assessment. ICMM, London

Lawrence DP (2003) Environmental impact assessment: practical solutions to recurrent problems. Wiley, New Jersey

Lee N (2006) Bridging the gap between theory and practice in integrated assessment. Environ Impact Assess 26(1):57–78

Partidario M (2012) Strategic environmental assessment better practice guide—methodological guidance for strategic thinking in SEA. Portuguese Environment Agency and Redes Energéticas Nacionais. http://ec.europa.eu/environment/eia/pdf/2012%20SEA_Guidance_Portugal.pdf. Accessed 18 May 2013

Salkin PE, Ko P (2011) The effective use of health impact assessment (HIA) in land-use decision making. Zoning Practice, October 2011:2–7

Weaver A, Sibisi S (2006) The art and science of environmental impact assessments. Council for Scientific and Industrial Research. http://www.csir.co.za/general_news/2006/TheArtand-

ScienceofEnvironmentalImpactAssessmentsByDrAlexWeaverandDrSibusisoSibisi14_
September_2006.html. Accessed 18 June 2013
Wernham A, Bear D (2010) Public health analysis under the National Environmental Policy Act.
In: Human Impact Partners, Frequently asked questions about integrating health impact assess-
ment into environmental impact assessment. http://www.epa.gov/region9/nepa/PortsHIA/pdfs/
FAQIntegratingHIA-EIA.pdf. Accessed 18 June 2013

Part II
Introduction to Core Concepts and Key Examples of HIA

Chapter 4
HIA: A Methodological Overview

Abstract This chapter describes the overall objectives and methods of health impact assessment (HIA). It presents a range of definitions, along with key features of the purpose, process, and implications of HIA. Three key defining features of HIA are highlighted: informing decision-making; following a structured but flexible process; and examining the full range of potential impacts to health outcomes and health determinants. The chapter then highlights the steps used in an HIA: screening (determining if HIA is required or useful), scoping (planning the HIA approach), assessment (identifying impacts to health and distribution of effects), recommendations (developing strategies to enhance health benefits and minimize harms), reporting (communicating results to decision-makers and stakeholders), evaluation (understanding the effectiveness of the HIA), and monitoring (tracking changes over time). The chapter discusses when in the decision-making cycle HIA can be most effective, who may commission or conduct an HIA, and the variation in approaches and methods that may be used. It also discusses the typology of HIA: An assessment can be rapid, intermediate, or comprehensive. Each type has a different speed, levels of stakeholder involvement, and intensity of data collection, and each occupies a different place within the need for HIA. Ultimately, HIA is a heterogeneous and flexible practice that is tied together by a core set of commonalities and principles.

Keywords Gothenburg Consensus Statement · Decision-Making · Definition · Screening · Scoping · Assessment · Recommendations · Reporting · Evaluation · Monitoring · Stakeholders

Fundamentally, all HIAs have one common objective: to provide decision-makers with sound information on the implications of a particular project or policy for human health. In achieving this objective, the HIA may take any one of several forms or approaches, as discussed in this chapter.

Definitions and Key Features of HIA

The most widely promoted definition of health impact assessment (HIA) comes from the Gothenburg Consensus Statement. It describes HIA as

C. L. Ross et al., *Health Impact Assessment in the United States,*
DOI 10.1007/978-1-4614-7303-9_4, © Springer Science+Business Media New York 2014

a combination of procedures, methods, and tools by which a policy, program, or project may be judged as to its potential effects on the health of a population, and the distribution of those effects within the population. (European Centre for Health Policy 1999).

Other definitions have also been proposed, as shown in Box 4.1.

Box 4.1   Definitions of health impact assessment

A combination of procedures, methods, and tools by which a policy, program, or project may be judged as to its potential effects on the health of a population, and the distribution of those effects within the population. (European Centre for Health Policy 1999)

A means of assessing the health impacts of policies, plans and projects in diverse economic sectors using quantitative, qualitative and participatory techniques. (World Health Organization 2012)

A tool that can help organisations to assess the possible consequences of their decisions on people's health and well-being, thereby helping to develop more integrated policies and programmes. (Welsh Health Impact Assessment Support Unit 2004)

HIA has two essential characteristics:
• It is intended to inform a decision.
• It seeks to predict the health consequences of implementing different options. (Kemm 2007)

A systematic way of working to shed light on the health consequences of proposed policy decisions. (Federation of Swedish County Councils 1998)

Assessment of the change in health risk reasonably attributable to a project, programme or policy and undertaken for a specific purpose. (Birley 1995)

A multidisciplinary process within which a range of evidence about the health effects of a proposal is considered in a structured framework…based on a broad model of health which proposes that economic, political, social, psychological, and environmental factors determine population health. (Lock 2000)

Health Impact Assessment (HIA) aims to identify how development induces unintended changes in health determinants and resulting changes in health outcomes. HIA provides a basis to proactively address any risks associated with health hazards. HIA also addresses health improvement opportunities in development. (Quigley et al. 2006)

Specifically, HIA seeks to provide information that will allow decision-makers to enhance the positive impacts on health of any project, programme or policy, and also reduce (or eliminate) any associated negative impacts. To do this, HIA seeks to produce a set of 'evidence-based' recommendations in a format accessible to, and appropriate for, the decision-makers. (Department of Public Health and Epidemiology, University of Birmingham 2003)

Although these definitions of HIA vary and each emphasizes different elements of the assessment, several key features appear consistently across most definitions and characterize the tool. These are the following:

1. The main purpose of HIA is to inform decision-making
2. HIA follows a structured but flexible process
3. HIA examines the full range of potential impacts to health outcomes and determinants

Because these features are fundamental to what defines HIA, a discussion of each is presented below.

The main purpose of HIA is to inform decision-making The purpose of HIA is to present information during the decision-making process that will promote an enhanced understanding of potential health consequences and, as a result, enable better decisions to be made. *Informing a decision* is one key feature that distinguishes HIA from academic health research. Whereas epidemiologic studies are intended to enhance scientific knowledge as a whole, HIA is intended to inform a specific decision about a particular project, program, or policy.

It is important to note that HIAs are generally conducted on projects or policies that *do not have health effects as their primary objective*—for example, a resource development project, an urban infrastructure project, or an economic policy. While health impacts commonly arise from these types of projects and policies, primarily through changes to the social and environmental determinants of health, but the primary objectives of these projects and policies are to effect changes in other areas. Because HIA brings forward previously unknown or ignored information about health, it is most valuable and most often used in areas outside of health services or policy. Table 4.1 presents examples of different sectors to which HIA has been applied.

In terms of who might use the HIA to inform a decision, this may include people who live in communities affected by the project or policy;[1] the entity proposing the project or policy; the regulatory agency that will review or approve the project or policy; service providers that may experience the consequences of changing health conditions in the local population; and agencies or organizations (such as municipal government) that have a stake in project or policy outcomes.

The value that HIA brings to decision-making may vary depending on the context in which it is used. HIA can provide value by delivering evidence-based predictions about changes in population health status. HIA can also provide value through the process of fostering intersectoral discussion and collaboration on health issues. Many HIAs attempt to include both of these approaches.

HIA follows a structured but flexible process Although every HIA is conducted differently in order to be responsive to local conditions and to be specific to the policy,

---

[1] An HIA can examine a project, policy, program, plan, or strategy. Throughout this book, we refer to "project or policy" for brevity.

Table 4.1 Examples of sectors in which HIA has been applied

Sector	Examples of policies and projects on which HIA has been conducted
Transport	High-speed railway Travel demand management Transportation strategy
Economy	National budget Economic development strategy
Employment	Employment and skills action plan Indigenous worker training program Paid sick day legislation
Housing	New housing developments Housing rental voucher program
Infrastructure	Broadband infrastructure program Airport expansion plans
Energy	Projects involving mining, oil and gas development, hydroelectric power, nuclear power, wind energy New home energy efficiency scheme
Finance	National alcohol strategy
Agriculture	Regional agricultural policy US Federal Farm Bill
Urban development	Regional development programs Urban renewal projects
Community and social support	Family violence strategy Street lighting proposal
Health	Changes to health insurance coverage Siting of new hospitals

program, or project under consideration, there are standardized steps that comprise the HIA method (see Fig. 4.1). These are:

Screening: Screening is the process used to determine whether the HIA is necessary and the approach that is most appropriate for the HIA to take. The decision is based on a number of factors, including the likelihood that the project/policy could affect important determinants or outcomes of health and whether there is an opportunity for the HIA to influence the decision-making process.

In practice, screening is often not performed; rather, most HIAs are undertaken as a result of a political process or a regulatory requirement, because a community organization initiates one or because applicable funding becomes available (Quigley et al. 2005).

Scoping: Scoping contains two important components: issues scoping and setting parameters. Issues scoping is the preliminary process of identifying how the project or policy might affect health determinants and outcomes, so that these linkages can be assessed in the next phase. It provides a "basket" of issues to be considered, some of which may turn out to be important, while others may not. Scoping of issues is usually done by the HIA practitioner in consultation with the local community, project proponent, and other stakeholders. The scoping stage also involves defining

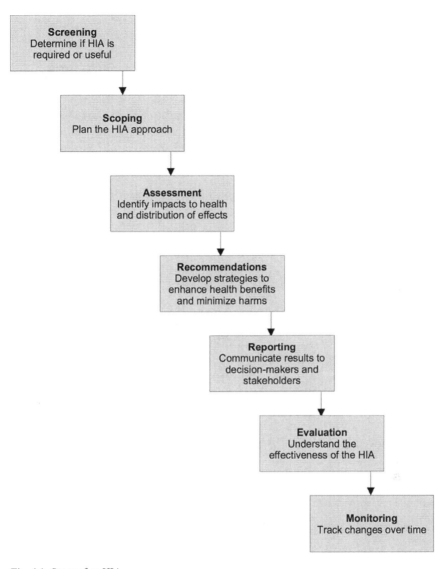

Fig. 4.1 Steps of an HIA

how the HIA will move forward: setting the geographic and temporal boundaries, identifying methods to be used, establishing a steering committee, and establishing terms of reference.

Assessment: Once the relevant health determinants and outcomes have been established through scoping, the next step is to systematically assess whether the project/policy is likely to affect those outcomes and if so, how. The assessment itself relies upon a combination of quantitative and qualitative evidence. Risk is often characterized by factors such as the likelihood, magnitude, duration, frequency, and distribution of impacts within the population.

Recommendations: Developing suitable, evidence-based recommendations is at the heart of HIA. The purpose of conducting the HIA is not merely to quantify risks, but to mitigate potential harms and increase potential health benefits. The development of recommendations may also involve the development of an implementation plan with responsibility and accountability clearly delineated.

Reporting: Results of the HIA are communicated to a variety of stakeholders, such as the proponent of the project or policy, local community groups, local health officials, nongovernmental organizations (NGOs), or other interested external parties.

Evaluation: Evaluation refers to the meta-assessment of the HIA's process and outcomes: whether it was successful in achieving its goals. Was the HIA able to affect decision-making? Did it meet the needs of health stakeholders?

Monitoring: Monitoring refers to the tracking of relevant health indicators after the project/policy has been put into place, in order to understand how health and its determinants change over time. Monitoring is most successful when tied to a plan for action that is based on changes in observed indicators linked to the health determinants and impacts assessed as part of the HIA. Monitoring continues long after the HIA is completed.

These steps are parallel to those found in environmental impact assessment (EIA) and other impact assessment modalities and thus constitute part of a standard framework that lends structure and consistency to the HIA approach.

HIA examines the full range of potential impacts to health outcomes and health determinants Because HIA attempts to be both a balanced and a comprehensive process, the potential health effects examined in any particular HIA include all those that may be affected by the project or policy under consideration. If the assessment is limited to only one or two outcomes of interest (for example, looking only at air quality changes as a result of a new freeway while ignoring potential changes to mobility, injury, and other important outcomes), then the assessment is by definition not an HIA.

Health impacts include changes in biomedical health outcomes (such as injury and disease rates), mental well-being, and health determinants. The HIA will identify potential positive or beneficial health benefits stemming from the policy, as well as potential negative or adverse effects.

While HIA examines impacts to the health of the population as a whole, it also considers differences in how particular subgroups might be affected. This is a dimension of health equity, recognizing that there may be systemic and unfair distribution of potential health risks and benefits across different segments of the population.

In 2010, a consensus document was produced by North American HIA practitioners that attempted to define the minimum essential elements that must be present in order for an assessment to constitute an HIA (North American HIA Practice Standards Working Group 2010). These minimum elements are reproduced in Box 4.2.

Box 4.2   Minimum elements of HIA. (North American HIA Practice Standards Working Group 2010)

A health impact assessment (HIA) must include the following minimum elements, which together distinguish HIA from other processes. An HIA:
1. Is initiated to inform a decision-making process and conducted in advance of a policy, plan, program, or project decision
2. Utilizes a systematic analytic process with the following characteristics:
   1. Includes a scoping phase that comprehensively considers potential impacts on health
   2. outcomes as well as on social, environmental, and economic health determinants, and selects potentially significant issues for impact analysis
   3. Solicits and utilizes input from stakeholders
   4. Establishes baseline conditions for health, describing health outcomes, health determinants, affected populations, and vulnerable subpopulations
   5. Uses the best available evidence to judge the magnitude, likelihood, distribution, and permanence of potential impacts on human health or health determinants
   6. Rests conclusions and recommendations on a transparent and context-specific synthesis of evidence, acknowledging sources of data, methodological assumptions, strengths and limitations of evidence and uncertainties
3. Identifies appropriate recommendations, mitigations, and/or design alternatives to protect and promote health
4. Proposes a monitoring plan for tracking the decision's implementation on health impacts/determinants of concern
5. Includes transparent, publicly accessible documentation of the process, methods, findings, sponsors, funding sources, participants, and their respective roles

When Should HIA Be Undertaken?

The decision-making process for both policies and projects (shown in Fig. 4.2) follows a cycle that involves the identification of a problem, the development and analysis of alternatives, the selection of a preferred solution, the implementation of that solution, and the evaluation of the results. Although this cyclical representation has been most often linked to public policy development, it is similar to the process used for developing programs and major projects. HIA is most effective when done as part of the development and analysis of alternatives, once the parameters of possible solutions have become clear, but before final decisions are made or implementation takes place.

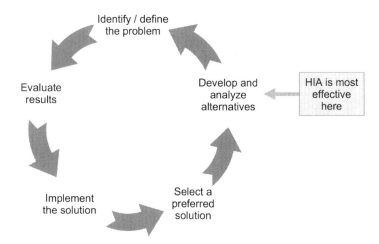

Fig. 4.2 Timing of HIA in the decision-making cycle

Who Conducts HIA?

HIAs are conducted in response to either regulatory or social demand. The types of organizations that commission or coordinate HIA are those that respond to this demand, and include government (federal, state, county, and tribal government agencies have all commissioned HIAs within the USA), academia, NGOs or community organizations and private-sector companies. These entities may request and pay for an HIA, may form a steering committee to provide oversight, or may create terms of reference describing the requirements that the assessment must meet.

The actual conduct of the HIA is almost always a team effort that brings together the expertise of public health professionals (who may have training in epidemiology, clinical medicine, community health, or other public health specialties) with other discipline experts such as regional and urban planners, transportation planners, sociologists, economists, toxicologists, air or water quality specialists, or others. This team is in charge of conducting the HIA, engaging stakeholders, undertaking analyses, and writing up the results.

HIA Typology

Although all HIAs follow the overall stepwise approach described above, there is considerable flexibility in how this can be accomplished. The approach can vary in terms of the intensity level and time allotted, as well as whether the HIA is conducted as a stand-alone process or integrated into other assessments.

Levels of Intensity The level of intensity or effort that is put into the HIA will depend on factors such as the decision-making timeline around the policy or project

Table 4.2 Typology of HIA based on effort and timeline

Rapid	Intermediate	Comprehensive
Very quick (2 days to 6 weeks)	4 weeks to several months	Several months to several years
Requires few resources	Requires moderate amount of resources	Requires significant resources
No stakeholder involvement	Some stakeholder involvement	Significant stakeholder involvement
No new data collection	Some new data collection; often relies on existing data banks	Usually involves collection of primary data

being assessed, the relative complexity of potential health impacts, and the financial and human resources available to conduct the assessment.

An HIA may be carried out in as few as 1 or 2 weeks; on the other hand, some have been known to take years. Based on the level of effort and length of time put into them, HIAs have been classified as rapid (also known as desktop), intermediate, or comprehensive. As shown in Table 4.2, a rapid HIA is conducted in days or weeks, relies only on existing data, and involves essentially no stakeholder engagement. At the other end of the spectrum, a comprehensive HIA takes months to years, requires the collection of a significant amount of new data, and involves significant stakeholder engagement. An intermediate HIA lies between the rapid and the comprehensive extremes.

Approach to Integration Many HIAs are conducted as stand-alone processes. That is, the assessment is undertaken in isolation from other studies concerning the policy or project under review. A separate HIA report is developed and submitted to decision-makers and other key stakeholders that provides health-specific analyses and recommendations.

HIA can also, however, be conducted as part of an integrated process alongside EIA or socioeconomic impact assessment. Where the integration is strong and balanced, these combinations are often referred to, holistically, as an integrated assessment (IA), an integrated impact assessment (IIA), or an environmental, social, and health impact assessment (ESHIA). Where there is less balance, usually tending towards a particularly strong focus on the natural environment, the HIA may be included as one chapter or subsection of an EIA or an environmental impact statement (EIS). These concepts are discussed further in Chap. 3.

HIA Subtype Several different "subtypes" of HIA have been developed, the most common of which are health equity impact assessment (HEIA) and mental health impact assessment (MHIA).

Equity is a core value of HIA, and the consensus among HIA practitioners is that equity should be considered in every assessment (Douglas and Scott-Samuel 2001, North American HIA Practice Standards Working Group 2010). There has, however, been a historical lack of practical guidance on how to operationalize a focus on health equity (Harris-Roxas et al. 2004). This has resulted in inadequate attention being given to equity within most published HIAs. HEIA uses the standard stepwise approach to HIA, but the assessment is framed in terms of how the project or policy being examined may create health inequities between groups (Mahoney et al. 2004). Similarly, MHIA adopts a lens that focuses on the potential impacts of a project or policy on mental health and well-being (Cooke et al. 2011).

In summary, HIA has been defined in diverse ways and one of its strengths is the flexibility of approach that allows the HIA practitioner to tailor methods to specific project and population contexts. The HIA process can function as a stand-alone procedure or as one that can be easily integrated with environmental, social impact, and other assessments. In addition, HIA offers a broad umbrella under which professionals from many disciplines can bring their methods and procedures to inform the assessment. Several consistent elements, however, allow for HIA to be defined differently from other types of evaluations and health studies and to provide a distinct and valued product.

References

Birley M (1995) The health impact assessment of development projects. Her Majesty's Stationery Office, London

Cooke A, Friedli L, Coggins T et al (2011) Mental well-being impact assessment: a toolkit for well-being, 3rd ed. National MWIA Collaborative, London

Department of Public Health and Epidemiology, University of Birmingham (2003) A training manual for health impact assessment. http://www.apho.org.uk/resource/item.aspx?RID=44927. Accessed 18 June 2013

Douglas M, Scott-Samuel A (2001) Addressing health inequalities in health impact assessment. J Epidemiol Comm H 55:450–451

European Centre for Health Policy (1999) Gothenburg consensus paper. World Health Organization Regional Office for Europe, Brussels

Federation of Swedish County Councils and the Association of Swedish Local Authorities (1998) HIA: how can the health impact of policy decisions be assessed? Informationsavdelningen, Stockholm

Harris-Roxas B, Simpson S, Harris E (2004) Equity focused health impact assessment: a literature review. Centre for Health Equity Training Research and Evaluation, University of New South Wales, Sydney, Australia

Kemm J (2007) More than a statement of the crushingly obvious: a critical guide to HIA. West Midlands Public Health Observatory, Birmingham

Lock K (2000) Health impact assessment. BMJ 320(7246):1395–1398

Mahoney M, Simpson S, Harris E et al (2004) Equity focused health impact assessment framework. Australasian Collaboration for Health Equity Impact Assessment

North American HIA Practice Standards Working Group (2010) Minimum elements and practice standards for health impact assessment, version 2. http://hiasociety.org/documents/PracticeStandardsforHIAVersion2.pdf. Accessed 18 June 2013

Quigley R, Cave B, Elliston K et al (2005) Practical lessons for dealing with inequalities in health impact assessment. National Institute for Health and Clinical Excellence, London

Quigley R, den Broeder L, Furu, P et al (2006) Health impact assessment: international best practice principles. Special publication series no. 5. International Association for Impact Assessment, Fargo

Welsh Health Impact Assessment Support Unit (2004) Improving health and reducing inequalities: a practical guide to health impact assessment. Cardiff Institute of Society, Health and Ethics, Cardiff

World Health Organization (2012) Health impact assessment: promoting health across all sectors of activity. http://www.who.int/hia/en. Accessed October 31, 2012

Chapter 5
US Case Studies

Abstract This chapter reviews four case studies, discussing the methods and outcomes associated with each. These case studies represent comprehensive health impact assessments (HIAs) conducted in the USA, each of which has had significant policy implications. The first case study is an HIA of the Atlanta BeltLine, an ambitious redevelopment plan intended to transform Atlanta, Georgia into a city connected by transit, trails, and green space, with substantial potential health benefits. This HIA demonstrates the importance of interdisciplinarity and collaboration, as well as key factors relating to projects' timeframes. The second case study describes an HIA assessing the potential health implications of federal legislation (the Healthy Families Act of 2009) for the state of Maine. The assessment drew on peer-reviewed and empirical research, applied analysis of available statistics, and used a public involvement process that included focus group interviews. The third case study is an HIA that examined the federally funded Low-Income Home Energy Assistance Program (LIHEAP) and assessed the potential health impacts of rising energy costs on children living in low-income households. It incorporated, among other components, an extensive review of the literature and interviews with key stakeholders, and ultimately identified a number of key causal pathways between energy prices and health risks. The final case study is an HIA of California's 2006 Global Warming Solutions Act. The HIA incorporated both quantitative and qualitative methodologies and made substantial recommendations for monitoring and adaptive management.

Keywords Atlanta BeltLine · Redevelopment · Infrastructure · Trails · Transi ·
Active living · Comprehensive HIA · Healthy Families Act of 2009 · Paid sick leave
· California Global · Warming Solutions Act of 2006 · Greenhouse gas emissions ·
Low-Income Home Energy Assistance Program (LIHEAP) · Weatherization ·
Freight railway corridor · Green space · Centers for Disease Control and Prevention ·
Tax Allocation District · Carbon offset programs

The majority of health impact assessments (HIAs) conducted in the USA to date have examined the potential health effects of policies and projects in the realms of planning, transportation, and housing. The four case studies presented in this chapter demonstrate the vast differences in scope, complexity, public input, and analytical frameworks that characterize the ways in which HIA has been conducted

C. L. Ross et al., *Health Impact Assessment in the United States,*   57
DOI 10.1007/978-1-4614-7303-9_5, © Springer Science+Business Media New York 2014

in the USA. The selected case studies are also excellent examples of the ways in which the HIAs have influenced policy outcomes and decisions.

The first case study is a comprehensive HIA that examined the effect of the Atlanta BeltLine, a major redevelopment project in central Atlanta, on physical activity and other health outcomes. The Atlanta BeltLine was a proposed project that involved the construction of a 22-mile loop of trails and transit on old railway lines, with a selection of new parks, in the heart of the Atlanta to promote active living and redevelopment. The Atlanta BeltLine HIA was one of the first comprehensive HIAs conducted in the USA.

The second case study is an HIA that analyzed the Healthy Families Act of 2009, a legislation that guaranteed workers the right to paid sick days. The HIA was conducted to demonstrate the potential of the legislation in reducing direct and indirect negative health impacts arising from the inability of certain categories of workers to access paid sick leave.

The third case study is an HIA that analyzed the California Global Warming Solutions Act of 2006. Preliminary data collected under the requirements of the act were examined to determine the potential positive and negative health benefits of legislation to reduce greenhouse gas emissions.

The fourth case study is an HIA that assessed the impact of The Low-Income Home Energy Assistance Program (LIHEAP), a federally funded program created in 1981 to provide heating, cooling, and weatherization assistance to low-income households that spent a high proportion of their income on energy costs. The purpose of the HIA was to evaluate the impact of rising energy costs on children living in these households.

Case Studies

Title:	**Atlanta BeltLine HIA**	Case Study
Author:	Center for Quality Growth and Regional Development (CQGRD) at the Georgia Institute of Technology and the Centers for Disease Control and Prevention (CDC)	
Year:	2007	
Location:	Atlanta, Georgia	

Project, program, or policy being assessed The Atlanta BeltLine is a former freight railway corridor around the core of Atlanta. The BeltLine redevelopment project proposed to change a 22-mile span of the corridor into a transit and trail loop surrounded by parks and residential and commercial development. This ambitious redevelopment, once realized, was intended to transform Atlanta into a city connected by transit, trails, and green space, as shown in Fig. 5.1.

Proposed BeltLine Parks, Existing Parks, and BeltLine Trail

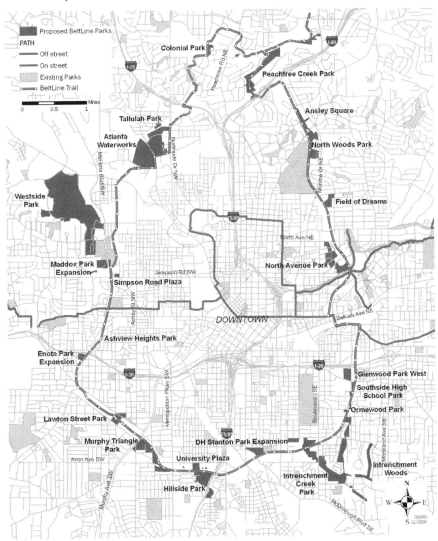

Fig. 5.1 Proposed BeltLine parks, existing parks, and BeltLine trail. (Ross et al. 2007)

Purpose of the HIA The HIA was intended to identify the impact of the proposed BeltLine redevelopment on health outcomes and health determinants, including green space and transit, and to determine which segments of the population and which communities would most benefit, and which would experience adverse impacts.

Affected population Residents of the city of Atlanta and visitors to the city.

Methods The HIA was conducted by an interdisciplinary team composed of researchers, physicians, and public health professionals from the Centers for Disease Control and Prevention (CDC) and the Center for Quality Growth and Regional Development (CQGRD) at the Georgia Institute of Technology and was funded by the Robert Wood Johnson Foundation. The HIA followed the standard steps of screening, scoping, assessment, development of recommendations, and reporting.

Outreach (local stakeholder engagement) was carried out as part of the scoping process. Four stakeholder groups were identified: decision-makers, implementers and experts (public agencies, private developers), study area residents and businesses, and academic practitioners. The main goals of the outreach process were to announce the project, to educate and inform attendees on HIA and health, to identify potential health impacts, to collect information and data (largely qualitative), and to develop recommendations.

Assessment results The research team appraised changes in equitable access to health supports, in particular access to parks and trails, transportation, healthy housing, and healthy food. Specifically, the HIA focused on assessing probable impacts on the following health determinants:

- *Access and social equity* (access to parks, access to transit and trails, access to healthy housing, access to healthy foods)
- *Safety* (injury, crime)
- *Social capital*
- *Environment* (air quality, water quality, noise, brownfields)

To identify potential effects of the proposal on access to parks, the analysis used existing GIS data to define the existing and proposed parkland, as shown in Fig. 5.2. Researchers estimated the number and percentage of residents who had access to parks at the time and forecasted a projection for the year 2030 and analyzed the composition of residents by age, race, income, poverty or carless status, and planning subarea. The analysis showed that park access would increase for study area residents and for the City of Atlanta. The finding had direct implications for physical activity and positive health outcomes.

In order to assess access to healthy foods, the study team evaluated the location of full-service chain grocery stores, since the literature suggests that access to grocery stores is associated with a healthier diet. As shown in Fig. 5.3, only 53 % of the study area was in walking (0.25 mile) or bicycling (0.8 mile) distance from a grocery store and nonwhite households were underrepresented in this group (50.1 % versus 62.2 % of the entire study area). Based on these analyses, the HIA developed recommendations that emphasized making parks and trails more prevalent, connected, and conducive to pedestrian access, especially in underserved areas; locating housing and businesses near trails and transit; creating programs to support affordable housing and prevent displacement; and ensuring equitable distribution of development and transportation facilities.

Study Area Park Access

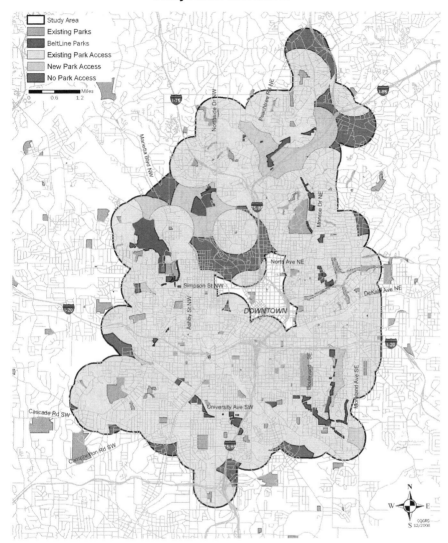

Fig. 5.2 Study area park access. (Ross et al. 2007)

An environmental analysis was conducted for ambient air pollution levels and the number of housing units in local air pollution hotspots. This analysis indicated that the BeltLine could improve ambient air quality by offsetting motor vehicle travel, but that some new buildings could potentially be vulnerable to locally elevated air pollution levels. The HIA recommended monitoring local

Access to Chain Grocery Stores

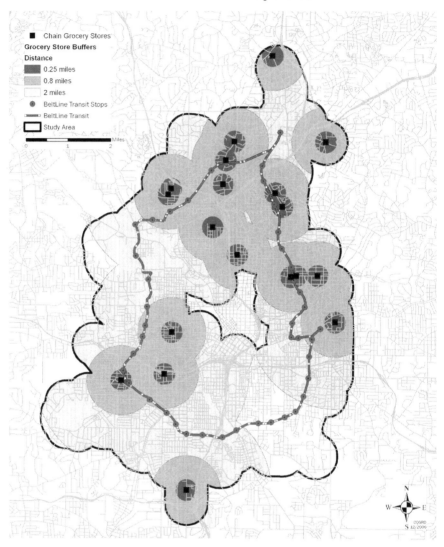

Fig. 5.3 Access to chain grocery stores. (Ross et al. 2007)

pollution levels at suspected hotspots and relocating or mitigating effects on proposed developments there. The HIA identified that the BeltLine had the potential to improve health by remediating and redeveloping brownfields. A primary recommendation included mitigating noise and stormwater runoff from BeltLine property.

The HIA also recommended that the BeltLine plan should promote physical activity by prioritizing pedestrian access to transit; incorporating universal design principles to enable and encourage the elderly, people with disabilities and children to use the facilities; providing lighting and emergency call boxes in order to increase perceived safety of the facilities; and providing a variety of recreational amenities. The HIA recommended appropriate designs for pedestrian and bicycle facilities to reduce the risk of crashes; safe design and maintenance for transit infrastructure; and crime prevention through environmental design (CPTED) principles. In response to redevelopment proposals in BeltLine plans, the HIA report encouraged public participation in planning and collaborative decision-making; public spaces that promote socialization; and strategies to prevent displacement of current residents and businesses.

The HIA has impacted several preliminary policies and processes related to the construction of the BeltLine.

In terms of infrastructure development, the HIA influenced decision-makers to make the construction of green space the foremost priority. As of mid-2011, the first 22 acres of parkland and 5.5 miles of multiuse trails were open for public use and additional parks and trails were under construction. The HIA garnered the support of Kaiser Permanente and others as major supporters of trail systems along the BeltLine. As of 2013, Kaiser Permanente had contributed $ 2.5 million towards the construction of the Eastside trail and an additional $ 2.5 million was contributed by a private donor towards the trail. Kaiser Permanente also funded evaluation studies to assess the impact of these infrastructure improvements on health. As a result of the HIA, the Environmental Protection Agency (EPA) awarded US$ 1 million to the BeltLine to clean up brownfields. In announcing the award, the EPA cited the BeltLine HIA and its finding that "brownfields redevelopment can help reduce urban sprawl and lead to healthier communities by creating more greenspace and walkable areas" (Ross et al. 2007).

On the organizational and policy front, the HIA has influenced the environmental impact statement (EIS) process. The Tax Allocation District Citizen Advisory Committee, a committee which provides oversight on the federal EIS, added a public health professional to their committee and named her chairperson of the Environment Task Force. As a result of the HIA, several health-based metrics are being incorporated into other assessment tools. Connectivity (with respect to transportation services and facilities as well as civic spaces) has been added to evaluation criteria in the federal Georgia environmental assessment processes. The evidence from the HIA provided support for affordable housing and the prevention of displacement. This led to the development of an affordable housing policy for the BeltLine. At the community level, the HIA was used by local residents to guide needs assessment. The actual permeation of health-based priorities into community development at the planning subarea levels will become apparent as the development plans are implemented.

Several key components of the HIA have been identified as contributing to its success. Foremost among these was sufficient time and resources to allow for a full prospective HIA to be conducted and to address unanticipated stakeholder concerns. Collaborative aspects of the work helped increase interdisciplinary knowledge and working capacity. Finally, the conduct of the HIA raised public consciousness around health issues, which was identified as one of the factors that led to more than $ 6 million in additional funds attracted to the BeltLine redevelopment project (Ross et al. 2012).

Title:	HIA of the Healthy Families Act of 2009: Maine Addendum	Case Study
Author:	Human Impact Partners	
Year:	2009	
Location:	Maine	

Project, program, or policy being assessed The Healthy Families Act of 2009 is a federal legislation that would guarantee workers the right to earn paid sick days. Under the proposed law, employees of large businesses (25 or more employees) would accrue 1 hour of paid sick time for every 40 hours worked, while those at small businesses would accrue 1 hour for every 80 hours worked. A bill with similar requirements for the provision of paid sick time was poised to be introduced into the 124th Maine legislature in 2010. More than 40 % of the Maine workforce would be directly affected by the legislation being considered, as almost 250,000 workers in the state had no access to paid sick days.

Purpose of the HIA The HIA was conducted to demonstrate the potential of the legislation in reducing direct and indirect adverse health impacts associated with the absence of paid sick days legislation. Researchers at Human Impact Partners and the San Francisco Department of Public Health had conducted an HIA of the effects of the legislation earlier in 2009 and HIA was carried out at a national level. The addendum specific to the state of Maine focused on assessing the impact of the state level legislation.

Affected population The residents of the state of Maine, particularly workers who do not receive paid sick days through their employer.

Methods The research methodology for both the Maine and the national-level HIA included a literature review of peer-reviewed research; analysis of available statistics on the availability and utilization of paid sick days; data on communicable disease outbreaks and illnesses; a statistical analysis of data from the National Health Interview Survey to determine the relationship between access to paid sick days and use of medical services; and assessment of the burden of illness. The Maine addendum also included local public involvement and focus group interviews of workers in the city of Bangor.

Assessment results The national report contains a descriptive analysis of how the lack of paid sick days impacts health-care utilization and costs. It concluded that delays in diagnosis and treatment of many medical conditions increased the use of hospitals and emergency departments for chronic conditions such as diabetes, asthma, and hypertension. The use of emergency departments for these conditions is expensive, inefficient, and largely avoidable when patients are able to access timely outpatient and primary care. The Maine assessment identified 17% of emergency room visits as avoidable, "delayed care seeking by individuals reluctant to lose time from work who wait until the weekend and then find that they cannot access office-based care." Paid sick days legislation was identified as a way to reduce these numbers.

The potential for the transmission of communicable disease—foodborne illness and respiratory infections such as influenza—was also examined in the HIA. As described in the HIA report, previous research has shown that outbreaks of foodborne illness can be linked to ill food service workers. Ninety-two percent of restaurant workers and 27% of nursing home workers in the USA cannot access paid leave for sick days. The responsibility is primarily on the worker and their employers to recognize signs of the illness and enforce measures (such as staying home) to protect coworkers and the public from infection. However, workers for whom financial burdens are significant lack incentive to stay home. Furthermore, they may delay getting treatment, unknowingly infecting others. Paid sick days might help reduce the transmission of many communicable diseases such as influenza and gastroenteritis in health care, food service, and childcare facilities.

Responses from the focus group interviews corroborated findings from the data analysis. Participants reported that financial and employment repercussions that prevented them from taking sick days led to medical emergencies and escalation of illness. The inability to rest, delayed access to primary care, or inability to take care of sick dependents was stated as the primary reasons. Focus group participants were fully aware that they were jeopardizing their coworkers health by going in to work sick. However, the fear of being penalized or financial repercussions made them choose to work in spite of being cognizant of the risks. Participants also feared employer retaliation, perceived threats, or discrimination when they took time off from work when sick. They also felt a lack of basic human rights and a lack of trust from the employers.

The *HIA of the Healthy Families Act of 2009: Maine Addendum* used a combination of quantitative data and qualitative information to convincingly demonstrate the potential health benefits of enacting paid sick days legislation; benefits that would accrue not only to the workers covered by the legislation, but also to the community at large.

Title:	HIA of a Cap-and-Trade Framework: The California Global Warming Solutions Act of 2006	Case Study
Author:	California Department of Public Health	
Year:	2010	
Location:	California	

Project, program, or policy being assessed California passed the *Global Warming Solutions Act* on September 27, 2006 in response to threats faced by climate change. The aims of the Act were to reduce greenhouse gas emissions to 1990 levels by the year 2020, to maximize public health benefits, and to ensure that low-income communities were not disproportionately affected by measures to reduce emissions. One of the primary regulatory mechanisms outlined in the Act and a focus of the HIA was a "cap-and-trade" program that capped carbon emissions while allowing the sale or trading of emissions credits among corporations or governments.

Purpose of the HIA The Climate Action Team Public Health Workgroup (CAT-PHWG) headed by the California Department of Public Health undertook the HIA to in order to "make visible the potentially significant human health consequences of public decisions." The HIA was intended to supplement other government analyses that focused on air quality or economic implications but did not consider the full range of potential adverse or beneficial effects on human health.

Affected population The potentially affected population varied depending on the health issue being examined. Some affected populations were very localized; for example, specific communities that would benefit from tree planting or reduced fire hazard. For other issues, such as potential impacts on employment, the affected population was very broad and spanned all areas of California.

Methods The HIA followed the well-defined steps of screening, scoping, assessment, and recommendations. The screening and scoping processes involved extensive stakeholder participation to suggest pathways for health impacts and to create a conceptual framework within which to investigate them.

Assessment Results The HIA identified a number of distinct areas of health concern for the analysis, as shown in Fig. 5.4. These were:

- Changes in air pollution levels (assessed separately by the Air Resources Board and not as part of the HIA)
- Changes in employment and income that could result from the legislation encouraging a shift away from certain industries and towards others
- Changes in household energy costs
- Economic, environmental, and health impacts from specific carbon offset programs such as forestry projects and biofuels
- Health effects stemming from community investment funded by revenue generated from carbon emissions trading

Overall, the assessment concluded that no significant health impacts would be expected for any of the areas examined, but that minor negative health impacts could accrue from changes in labor demand and energy costs for low-income populations. Potential minor positive health effects included reduction in occupational injuries due to a shift in employment to safer industries, marginal increase in income, and reduction in residential energy consumption and resulting improvement in air quality. Four different carbon offset programs were examined and all were found to have positive health impacts by reducing greenhouse gas emissions and consequently improving environmental conditions. Figure 5.5 shows the projected effects for one of the carbon offset programs—forestry projects that would encourage the planting of trees and better forestry management on private and public lands. While both posi-

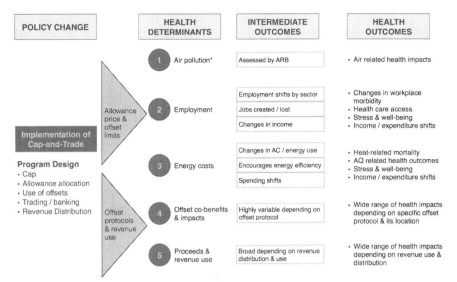

Fig. 5.4 Stakeholder-identified health impact pathways associated with a cap-and-trade program in California. (California Department of Public Health 2010)

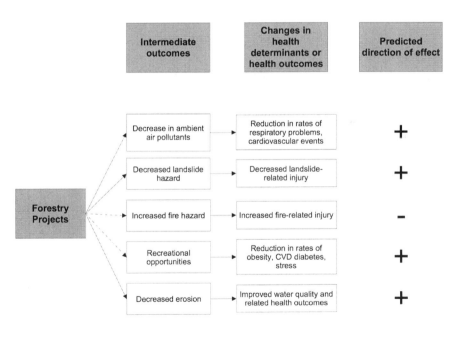

Dotted lines denote more speculative links

Fig. 5.5 Summary of potential health effects from forestry projects to offset carbon emissions. (California Department of Public Health 2010)

tive and negative health effects are predicted, the net effect of the forestry projects was found to be beneficial.

In addition to the state-level analyses described above, assessment at the community level was conducted to address concerns that the benefits from the Act might not be equitably distributed geographically and that emission hot spots might be created in some locations. Three communities—Wilmington–Harbor City–San Pedro (WHCSP), the City of Richmond, and the San Joaquin Valley—were studied in more detail. The first two communities have a long-standing history of environmental injustices characterized by high levels of industrial pollution, poor air quality, and health inequities. All three communities are characterized by populations with increased socioeconomic vulnerabilities. Health impacts were assessed using indicators that measured community health outcomes (mortality, chronic disease prevalence rates), community characteristics and neighborhood resources (access to parks, healthy foods, health care), and environmental quality. Based on this assessment, recommendations were made to put monitoring systems in place, redirect program benefits (monetary and environmental benefits) towards vulnerable communities, and adopt mitigation strategies to stabilize these communities.

The HIA provides a thorough analysis of potential health impacts of the cap-and-trade program at multiple scales and places particular emphasis on vulnerable communities. The resulting recommendations suggest several measures to redirect proceeds from the program towards investments in public health programs, making a direct link between improved health and economic outcomes.

Title:	A Child Health Impact Assessment of Energy Costs and the Low Income Home Energy Assistance Program	Case Study
Author:	Child Health Impact Working Group, Boston	
Year:	2006	
Location:	Massachusetts	

Project, program, or policy being assessed The LIHEAP is a federally funded program created in 1981 to provide heating, cooling, and weatherization assistance to low-income families that spend a high proportion of their income on energy costs. Families qualify based on both financial criteria and whether the household includes vulnerable members of society (young children, disabled adults, seniors). In 2006, approximately 140,000 households in Massachusetts received LIHEAP assistance.

Purpose of the HIA In 2004, a multidisciplinary group of experts, including representatives from the Boston University School of Medicine, Boston University School of Public Health, Brandeis University, Children's Hospital, Boston, Harvard Medical School, Harvard School of Public Health, and University of Massachusetts, Boston, met to develop a Child Health Impact Assessment strategy (CHIA). The objective of the CHIA was to examine implications of policies, regulations, and laws on children's health and well-being, particularly in areas outside of traditional public health and health policy. The CHIA evaluated the health impacts associated with rising energy costs for children living in low-income households and the effects of the LIHEAP program.

Affected population Approximately 400,000 children living in low-income households throughout Massachusetts.

Methods The scoping and assessment process were essentially expert driven, consisting of data collection through extensive literature review and interviews of key stakeholders. The first step in the assessment process was the collection of data to provide quantifiable, objective evidence to policymakers about the potential health impacts of energy costs on child health. Data sources included academic research, government databases, advocacy websites, and key stakeholder interviews. An extensive literature review was conducted on the topics of LIHEAP and the impact of home energy costs on children's basic needs such as access to health care, education, housing, nutrition, and safety. This evidence base was further strengthened through interviews with key stakeholders who had extensive experience, knowledge, and expertise in the energy assistance area. These key stakeholders comprised national and state LIHEAP program officers, community action groups, and energy advocates. Their perceptions and experiences provided a broader understanding regarding the links between health determinants and energy assistance.

Assessment Results Four key causal pathways between health risks and energy prices were described in the HIA:

- Low-income families that spend disproportionately higher amounts on energy costs make household budget trade-offs, compromising other essential needs such as food, health care, or rent/mortgage payments. Associated health outcomes include food insecurity and poor physical and cognitive development. These household budget trade-offs can jeopardize children's health and potentially lead to housing instability.
- Low-income families resort to more hazardous forms of indoor heating when faced with high energy costs. Heat sources such as kerosene space heaters and fireplaces increase risk of burns, carbon monoxide exposure, and deadly house fires, endangering children's well-being.
- High energy costs impose significant budget constraints on low-income families, forcing them to live in cheaper, substandard housing conditions. This could expose children to hazardous environmental health risks from rodents, mold, and lead paint.
- Growing gaps between energy prices and LIHEAP benefits leave more number of families unable to pay their utility bills, risking arrearages and disconnections and further jeopardizing children's health.

The analysis provided clear evidence of potential health consequences of unaffordable energy costs that were preventable through timely policy interventions. Recommendations included guidelines for improving funding, programmatic changes, and systematic data collection.

Funding recommendations included funding the LIHEAP program at the maximum authorized level of $ 5 billion federal, proportionate increase in benefits with increase in participation, and increased benefit levels for vulnerable families in Massachusetts.

Programmatic recommendations included engaging clinicians and health-care settings to monitor children and vulnerable populations for energy-related health risks, increase participation in the LIHEAP program, and reduce waiting times for families already enrolled and awaiting assistance.

Of particular importance is collection of data with regard to trends in arrearages and utility disconnections as well as the effectiveness of LIHEAP programs in providing energy self-sufficiency. The CHIA recommended the use of readily available instruments such as the Home Energy Insecurity Scale Survey developed by the Division of Energy Assistance and The National Energy Assistance Directors Association (NEADA) Template for Arrearage and Disconnection Data Collection to track levels of energy self-sufficiency among vulnerable households as well as to respond appropriately to economic or natural emergencies and their impacts on energy prices.

Overall, the CHIA on energy costs provides a unique example of an assessment on a nontraditional health policy topic and also focuses on children as a smaller subset of vulnerable populations. Strong recommendations are tied closely to the health effects identified in the assessment (Smith et al. 2007).

References

California Department of Public Health (2010) Health impact assessment of a cap-and-trade framework. http://www.arb.ca.gov/cc/ab32publichealth/cdph_final_hia.pdf . Accessed 18 June 2013

Human Impact Partners (2009) A health impact assessment of the Healthy Families Act of 2009: Maine addendum. http://www.humanimpact.org/doc-lib/finish/5/70 . Accessed 18 June 2013

Ross C, Leone de Nie K, Barringer J et al (2007) Atlanta BeltLine health impact assessment. Center for Quality Growth and Regional development, Georgia Institute of Technology, Atlanta

Ross C, Leone de Nie K, Dannenberg A et al (2012) Health impact assessment of the Atlanta BeltLine. Am J Prev Med 42(3):203–213

Smith LA, Flacks J, Harrison E (2007) Unhealthy consequences: energy costs and child health, a child health impact assessment of energy costs and the low income home energy assistance program. http://www.healthimpactproject.org/resources/document/massachusetts-low-income-energy-assistance-program.pdf. Accessed 18 June 2013

Chapter 6
International Case Studies

Abstract This chapter discusses the drivers that have led regional development of health impact assessment (HIA) in Europe, South America, Africa, the Asia-Pacific region, and Canada. For example, a number of European countries were frontrunners in the emergence and development of HIA and now have HIA firmly entrenched into their decision-making frameworks. In South America and Africa, the application of HIA has primarily been driven by major lending banks and is usually integrated into environmental, social, and health impact assessments. In the Asia-Pacific region, countries such as Thailand and Mongolia have been pioneers in building HIA into local environmental impact assessment requirements. The chapter concludes by presenting three case studies of HIAs carried out in the European Union, Mozambique, and New Zealand to highlight the diversity of HIA approaches. The first case study highlights an HIA that assessed the potential health impacts of a pan-European Employment Strategy. The second case study examines effects of a dam redevelopment project in Mozambique's Nampula Province. The final case study examines a land-use framework proposed for a New Zealand suburb, with a strong lens on how the local Maori population would be affected. By looking at these case studies from around the world, we can better understand the role and trajectory of HIA in the USA.

Keywords Regulatory environment(s) · Gothenburg HIA framework · Institutionalized · European employment strategy · Infrastructure project · International finance corporation · Spatial structure · Urban design

Health impact assessment (HIA) has evolved differently in various parts of the world. Several factors drive this divergence, such as variation in regulatory environments, the extent to which health and planning are involved in local policy making, the degree to which health is already included in decision making by way of other processes, and emergent opportunities based on existing personal relationships and unique local conditions.

Some authors have argued that two separate strands of HIA have developed globally (Krieger et al. 2010). The first strand is public-sector HIA. This type is based on national, regional, or local government policies, infrastructure, or programs. Public-sector HIAs evolved out of the 1999 Gothenburg HIA framework and focus on the social determinants of health. They have almost all been conducted in industrialized countries (Erlanger et al. 2007). The second strand is HIA conducted to aid decision making within the private sector. These HIAs are usually performed on large industrial development projects, frequently take place in developing countries, and are often integrated into or harmonized with an environmental impact assessment (EIA).

Other authors, however, have argued that this distinction presents a false dichotomy (Vohra et al. 2010). They put forth that the lines between public- and private-sector HIAs are blurred and that the methodologies are compatible. Harris-Roxas proposes a typology of four different forms of HIA describing current international practice based on commonalities of purpose: mandated HIAs, decision-support HIAs, advocacy HIAs, and community-led HIAs (Harris-Roxas and Harris 2011). More than one type may be present in many jurisdictions. Which dominates, if any, is often determined by the environment in which the HIA is conducted.

The following section describes how HIA has evolved in different parts of the world.

Regional Overview of HIA Development

Europe

Several European nations, notably the UK and the Netherlands, were early pioneers of HIA, and a number of seminal documents that set the stage for public-sector HIA practice, such as the Gothenburg Consensus Paper (European Centre for Health Policy 1999), came from early practitioners across Europe and within the World Health Organization's European offices. HIA is now firmly entrenched in Ireland, Finland, Sweden, Switzerland, Spain, the UK, and the Netherlands. A large number of HIAs have been produced in Europe within the last decade, conducted on both projects and policies, with a strong focus on health inequity, climate change, and sustainability agendas. Within the European Union (EU), EIA and strategic environmental assessment have been mandated, but HIA has yet to be institutionalized within the environmental assessment process. At the national level, HIAs have generally been conducted outside of the environmental assessment process on topics such as urban regeneration/renewal projects, government strategies, transportation policies, and social programs. More recently, several countries including Switzerland and the Netherlands have supplanted a project-based HIA approach with a broader policy-based agenda, focusing on the inclusion of Health in All Policies (HiAP). In Finland, human impact assessment (HuIA) has been developed as a way to combine social and health impacts into one assessment process. Approximately 50 HuIAs had been implemented by social and health authorities as of 2012.

South America and Africa

In South America and Africa, use of HIA has primarily been driven by the major lending banks: the International Finance Corporation (IFC), the Inter-American Development Bank (IADB), the African Development Bank (ADB), and others (IFC 2012; African Development Bank 2003). These lenders have built a requirement for HIA into their lending policies; its implementation, however, is far from universal in funded projects. Those conducted in South America and Africa have tended to be on major resource development and infrastructure projects, such as very large dams or mines. These HIAs are often integrated into environmental, social, and health impact assessments (ESHIAs) or may exist as HIAs conducted in parallel with (although separately from) other environmental or socioeconomic assessment activities. The importance of limiting the spread of infectious diseases such as malaria and HIV, which devastate many local populations and which also have a well-established link to resource development activities, may have provided this initial impetus.

Asia-Pacific

As in South America and Africa, the major lending banks have had an influence on HIA being applied to some large development projects, such as the Nam Theun II Dam in Laos. Several countries, however, have also been developing their own HIA processes independent of external requirements. In Thailand, the National Health Commission instituted an HIA mechanism in 2009 requiring assessment to be performed on many types of resource development project including mines, dams, power plants, and landfill areas (Health Impact Assessment Coordinating Unit 2010). Nonetheless, the requirements were relaxed slightly in 2010, allowing some projects to move forward without requiring an HIA. It is interesting to note that in Thailand, the institution of HIA recognizes culture, spirituality, and history as important aspects of health and well-being, and these determinants have been incorporated into the nation's HIA framework. HIA capacity building has also been undertaken within the governments of Laos, Cambodia, and Mongolia (Harris-Roxas 2011). Australia and New Zealand both have robust practices of using HIA in the assessment of government policy and programs, driven in large part by a concern over health inequities (often within indigenous populations) and healthy urban planning. In both countries, numerous HIAs have been conducted at the national, regional, and local levels. In Australia, the process was first introduced as an integrated component of EIA (Harris and Spickett 2011). HIA has since broadened considerably, and a focus has developed on "policy Health Impact Assessment." Two Australian states, New South Wales and Victoria, have led the development of an approach for HiAP, a technique bringing health into the crafting of government policy at a very early stage by utilizing a collaborative, intersectoral approach.

Canada

Canada has a long track record of HIA, with the practice first being mandated for use in public policy development in 1993 in British Columbia. (See Chap. 16 on organizational capacity for a discussion of why the BC initiative fell apart.) HIA is currently institutionalized at a provincial policy level in Quebec, where the focus of the process is to get health "to the table" with policy makers from other sectors. A similar model is under consideration in several other jurisdictions in Canada.

Case Studies

The three case studies below vary considerably in scope, approach, and focus. They have been selected to represent the diversity of international practice.

The first case study is an HIA that examined an employment strategy in the EU. This case exemplifies some of the challenges of policy-based HIA, here amplified due to the cross-national context in which it was conducted.

The second case study is an HIA applied to a large dam project in Mozambique. This assessment followed IFC guidelines and is in many ways typical of those conducted in the private sector for resource development projects, particularly in developing countries.

The third case study is an HIA that assessed a land-use plan in New Zealand. While the assessment focuses on many of the same health-related issues as land-use plan HIAs in the USA, this case study is interesting in that it used an approach (the Whanau Ora HIA guidance) specifically tailored to New Zealand's significant Maori culture (Ministry of Health 2007).

Title:	HIA of the European Employment Strategy Across the European Union	Case Study
Author:	IMPACT Group (University of Liverpool, UK); Institute of Public Health (Ireland); National Institute for Public Health and the Environment (Netherlands)	
Year:	2004	
Location:	European Union	

Project, Program, or Policy Being Assessed The European Employment Strategy (EES) was developed to increase the employment rate across the EU between 2005 and 2010, while encouraging social cohesion, inclusion, productivity, and quality output at work. This policy was intended to stimulate long-term job creation and encourage entrepreneurship.

Purpose of the HIA This HIA was completed as part of the policy health impact assessment for the EU project, funded by the European Commission. It was intended to pilot what was then the relatively new EU Policy HIA (EPHIA) methodology.

Affected Population This broad policy had the potential to affect all people living and working in the EU, a total population of almost 380 million. The policy was particularly targeted, however, to bolster job conditions and prospects for certain groups underrepresented in the labor market: women, older people, and ethnic minorities.

Methods The HIA was conducted using the standard steps of screening, scoping, assessment, development of recommendations, evaluation, and monitoring. It aggregated information from the following sources:

- Existing data
- Primary data collected from special interest groups and experts
- Analysis of policy documents
- Review of pertinent literature
- Mathematical modeling of the policy's impact on the number of sick days

Assessment Results For this assessment, the authors examined potential health changes associated with three specific objectives of the policy:

- Increasing employment and reducing unemployment
- Increasing the flexible labor market (part-time and contract work)
- Increasing active labor markets (the number of people available to work)

Each of these three areas was linked to specific changes in health outcomes, including mortality, child health, health-related absenteeism, biophysical health outcomes, changes in health-related behaviors (e.g., increases in smoking, reductions in physical activity), mental well-being, use of health services, food insecurity, and social cohesion.

Excerpt from Sample Assessment Section: Increasing Employment and Reducing Unemployment Table 6.1 summarizes the HIA's conclusions on the potential impacts of increasing employment through the EES. The narrative that follows provides additional explanation for conclusions.

Any increase in employment will have positive effects on the health of the population as a whole. Brenner (2002) has forecast a reduction in all-cause mortality in the EU using an unemployment-GDP model with a lag of 2 to 14 years after the increase in GDP and employment. It is believed that this is primarily due to the increase in per capita income resulting from GDP growth. There may also be improvements in mental health. Evidence from the US suggests there may be short and long-term health benefits to the children of families where parents move from unemployment to employment increasing the household income and enhancing the family environment (e.g. Hurston 2003; Morris et al. 2001).

But evidence from the literature, stakeholders and key informants has also shown that not all employment is beneficial for health. Some work characteristics can be as damaging to health as unemployment. Workers in jobs that are of poor quality, including low paid, and precarious (insecure) have similar health scores to the unemployed (Burchell 1996). Evidence from the US also indicates negative impacts on the cognitive, emotional and

Table 6.1 Potential health impacts of an increase in employment due to the European Employment Strategy (EES). (IMPACT Group et al. 2004)

Potential health impacts	Direction/severity	Likelihood
Across the EU		
Reduction in all-cause mortality (2–14-year lag)	Health gain/medium	Probable
Improvement in mental health	Health gain/low	Possible
Short/long-term health benefits for children in employed households	Health gain/low	Speculative
Member states		
Member states will continue to increase employment levels, but some will be at slower rates than others; the EES is unlikely to impact on this maintaining health inequalities between member states	No change	Possible
Women		
The level of women in employment will continue to increase, but there will be a differential increase in employment for women across the EU; the EES is unlikely to impact on this leading to maintaining health inequalities between member states	No change	Possible
Older people	No change	Possible
The level of older people in employment will continue to increase, but there will be a differential increase in employment for older people across the EU; the EES is unlikely to impact on this maintaining health inequalities between member states		
Job quality		
Some indicators of job quality, e.g., injuries from accidents at work, suggest improvements in job quality in the EU leading to improvements in productivity and health outcomes	Health loss/low	Speculative
Other indicators of job quality, e.g., work-related stress, suggest a deterioration in job quality in the EU leading to poor health outcomes	Health gain/low	Speculative
Poor job quality, including low pay, can be as detrimental to health as unemployment; the EES is unlikely to impact on job quality	Health loss/low	Speculative
Social cohesion		
There are many health benefits associated with increased social cohesion: reduction in premature mortality, prevention of illness, increased mental health and well-being	Health gain and health loss/low	Possible

behavioral development of children of families where parents move from unemployment to employment where there is no increase in household income, and the job is of poor quality with few prospects (Hurston 2003; Yoshikawa et al. 2003). Although the EES is also concerned with improving the quality of jobs, some evidence, for example, from trends in the incidence of injuries from accidents at work suggest improvements, some is ambiguous, for example, trends in the incidence of work-related ill-health; whilst others, for example, trends in the incidence of work-related stress, indicates a deterioration. The development of 'job quality' indicators (Commission of the European Communities 2001a) is welcomed. The collective reporting of these, and the development of an overall job quality index, will be important in monitoring improvements in job quality.

(IMPACT Group et al. 2004)

Title:	Nacala Dam Health Impact Assessment	Case Study
Author:	Newfields LLC	
Year:	2010	
Location:	Nampula Province, Mozambique	

Project, Program, or Policy Being Assessed Nacala Dam is the principal water source for Nacala City, Mozambique. Due to the collapse of the dam's bottom outlets, however, the Nacala Dam is not able to meet either the current or the future water needs of Nacala City; an infrastructure project to repair and upgrade the dam was thus proposed. This included rehabilitating and elevating the dam wall; upgrading the spillway; a road deviation; and excavating materials for these activities.

Purpose of the HIA The HIA was conducted to comply with IFC requirements for funded projects, and therefore, used the IFC's specified methodology.

Affected Population People living in the communities near the dam comprised the "potentially affected populations," as they would experience impacts of the dam development activities. These local populations included 17 households that would be resettled as a result of dam development, as well as residents of communities within the dam's footprint and residents of communities downstream from the dam wall.

Methods The HIA incorporated a systematic literature review, review of project documentation, a review of similar projects in other areas, a field visit with key informant interviews and focus groups to help inform the assessment, and the development of recommendations.

Assessment Results In line with IFC guidance (IFC 2009), 12 specific "environmental health areas" were considered for the assessment:

1. Communicable diseases linked to housing design
2. Vector-related diseases
3. Soil-, water-, and waste-related diseases
4. Sexually transmitted infections
5. Food- and nutrition-related issues
6. Noncommunicable diseases
7. Accidents/injuries
8. Veterinary medicine and zoonotic diseases
9. Exposure to potentially hazardous materials, noise, and odors

10. Social determinants of health
11. Cultural health practices/traditional medicine
12. Health systems issues

Excerpt from Assessment Section: Vector-Related Diseases The assessment
section discussing malaria, given below, describes current practices around malaria
(which are described in detail in the report's baseline section); discusses the pathways through which the dam project could increase or reduce malaria incidence
in the local population; presents a matrix characterizing the risk of project-related
malaria both with and without the use of mitigation measures; and proposes recommendations for mitigating the risk of malaria.

> Malaria is endemic in the area and the biggest public health threat. It was the most com-
> mon cause for outpatient consultation in the project area and reported as a significant cause
> of mortality. Knowledge of the disease and health seeking behaviours were adequate, but
> traditional medicine still appeared to play a role which could delay access to appropriate
> treatment. Prevention activities are limited with very poor ownership of bednets. Nacala
> Port has integrated malaria control program activities with indoor residual spray. This has
> not been extended to Nacala-A-Velha. Health care services are adequate.
>
> The project will influence malaria transmission risk in the area with the following
> considerations:
>
> - Construction activities around the dam wall is likely to cause pooling of water through
>   environmental modification and creation of breeding sites in the lay down yards. This
>   will be highly localized.
> - Increasing of the surface area of water through the refurbishment of the dam wall will
>   not play a meaningful role in proliferation of breeding sites compared to the present
>   situation. It may however increase the potential vector range and expose more people to
>   mosquitoes that have emerged from the dam. The extension of the upper reaches of the
>   dam may play a more significant role to communities living in these areas. The flight
>   range of mosquitoes and the potential risk areas from water reservoirs is shown in Fig. 38
>   to describe this [40].
> - There should be minimal change in the vector breeding patterns of the different species
>   of anopheles mosquito linked to the dam. Wetland mashamba's are still likely to pre-
>   dominate as status quo. An increase of emergent vegetation on the banks of the dam and
>   in the upper reaches may increase vector habitats. This is an existing status as shown in
>   Fig. 37.
> - A major study deduced that malaria transmission linked to dam projects in stable malaria
>   transmission areas (project area) have in general not created negative effects, in par-
>   ticular when control programs have been launched simultaneously. The casual web of
>   malaria transmission from this study is displayed in Fig. 39. Based on this relationship
>   if mitigation measures are applied the project can induce significant benefits related to
>   malaria transmission.
> - These benefits can be reduced if large scale in-migration is induced. This is unlikely
>   given the size and time scale of the project. Makeshift housing and poor town plan-
>   ning will increase available vector breeding sites through environmental modification.
>   Limited public services such as waste removal will be compounded. Influx will also
>   potentially increase the malaria parasite burden circulating in the community.

(Newfields 2010)

Significance Statement: Moderate. (Newfields 2010)

Impact	Effect				Total score	Overall signifi-cance	PAC
	Temporal scale	Spatial scale	Severity of impact	Risk or likelihood			
Without mitigation	Short term	Study area	Severe	May occur	9	Moderate	1–2
With mitigation	Short term	Local-ized area	Substantial benefit	Probable	9	Moder-ately benefi-cial	1–2

PAC potentially affected communities

Project Impact Mitigation

- Perform a baseline parasite prevalence survey in the communities. This should ideally occur at the end of the rainy season, and must be followed up at similar times of the year to ensure consistent comparisons. This will determine the burden of disease in the community, and also serve as an indicator to monitor the impact of the disease and interventions.
- Support information, education, and communication (IEC) programs in the communities, schools, and even with traditional healers. This can be supported through community-based peer health educators managed from the local health centre.
- Facilitate the extension of the integrated vector control activities at Nacala Port to the project site to ensure any potential impacts are managed. Engage the National Malaria Control Program as well as Malaria Consortium as an active NGO in the area.
- Develop a malaria workplace policy that incorporates awareness, bite prevention, chemoprophylaxis, and medical management.
- Limited vector control activities should occur at the construction site and lay down yard to prevent vector proliferation. This should include larvaciding and indoor residual spray. Space spray with foggers is not recommended.

(Newfields 2010)

Title:	**Wiri Spatial Structure Plan: Health Impact Assessment Report**	*Case Study*
Author:	The Healthy Cities team from Manukau City Council in partnership with the Urban Design team and with support from Synergia HIA consultants	
Year:	2010	
Location:	Manukau, New Zealand	

Project, Program, or Policy Being Assessed This HIA analyzed the "spatial structure" (i.e., the urban design) proposed for Wiri, a suburb of Manukau City. The spatial structure consisted of a municipal plan for streets, open spaces, and transport corridors. It included a number of land-use changes, such as the construction of a state highway; new development to increase housing units and population density; the construction of a new education campus, train station, hotel, library, and parking lots; and the development of an extensive pathway system to connect communities.

Purpose of the HIA This HIA was initiated by the Manukau City Council in response to its 2007 commitment to improving the well-being of the city's people by creating a social and physical environment that would enhance the health and well-being of all constituent groups.

Affected Population The Wiri area has a quickly growing population of approximately 4,280. A high proportion of residents are ethnically Pacific Islanders (52%, with Maori representing 26%), with smaller proportions of European-descended (22%) and Asian-descended (12%) residents. The population is very young, with slightly over half younger than 25 years old, compared to 35% of the population nationally. Wiri residents suffer high levels of deprivation and unemployment and tend to have low incomes. Almost 80% of the Wiri area's population lives in what is considered to be one of the most deprived neighborhoods in New Zealand.

Methods The HIA followed the standard steps of screening, scoping, appraisal, and reporting. Extensive consultations were held with three special populations that would be particularly affected by the project: the Maori population; children and youth; and the elderly. Throughout the assessment, potential impacts were identified not only for Wiri's population as a whole, but also for these three targeted subsets.

Assessment Results For each of the targeted subsets and for the population as a whole, the HIA assessed potential impacts on four health-related areas:

*   Accessibility
*   Housing
*   Safety
*   Economic potential

Sample Assessment Section: Safety Figure 6.1, reproduced from the HIA report, shows how safety in Wiri would be affected by the new plan. The four circles represent key safety factors that could be impacted: crime, safety issues arising from a car-dominated environment, quality of the urban infrastructure (such as sidewalks and lighting), and design friendly to families and people with disabilities. The words outside the circles indicate elements influencing one or more of these four safety areas. Solid arrows indicate that more of one will lead to more of the next in the chain (e.g., more alcohol leads to a higher level of crime). Dashed arrows indicate that more of one will lead to less of another (e.g., speed controls lead to a reduction of risk in a car-dominated environment).

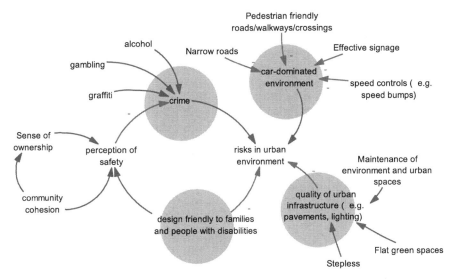

Fig. 6.1 Positive and negative impacts in the Wiri Spatial Structure Plan. (Manukau City Council 2010)

As can be seen in the diagram, the Wiri Spatial Structure Plan has neither a positive nor a negative "net effect" on safety. Different elements of the plan will lead to increases or decreases in level of safety. Part of the HIA's role was to identify where potential harms or benefits might occur so that appropriate mitigation or enhancements could be planned.

Based on the results of the assessment and the participation of stakeholder groups, the HIA featured a number of recommendations to help improve safety in the Spatial Structure Plan. These included:

- Designing for people, rather than cars, first; for example, by creating wide footpaths and narrower streets to slow traffic
- Planning for a mixture of residential and commercial development to ensure activity throughout the day and night
- Encouraging "walking buses" as a safety measure for children on their way to school
- Improving Wiri's cultural relevance as a way to promote pride and ownership and to reduce crime

Suggestions from stakeholders included using creative, colorful, vibrant cultural designs; installing signs in many languages; and incorporating into the built environment a greater acknowledgment of Maori history, all of which were believed to reduce crime rates and incidence of graffiti.

References

African Development Bank (2003) Integrated environmental and social impact assessment guidelines. http://www.afdb.org/fileadmin/uploads/afdb/Documents/Policy-Documents/Integrated%20Environmental%20and%20Social%20Impact%20Assesment%20Guidelines.pdf. Accessed 18 June 2013

Erlanger JE, Krieger G, Singer BH, Utzinger J (2007) The 6/94 gap in health impact assessment. Environ Impact Asses 28(4–5):349–358

European Centre for Health Policy (1999) Gothenburg consensus paper. World Health Organization Regional Office for Europe, Brussels

Harris-Roxas B (2011) Health impact assessment in the Asia Pacific. Environ Impact Asses 31(4):393–395

Harris-Roxas B, Harris E (2011) Differing forms, differing purposes: a typology of health impact assessment. Environ Impact Asses 31(4):396–403

Harris P, Spickett J (2011) Health impact assessments in Australia: a review and directions for progress. Environ Impact Asses 31(4):425–432

Health Impact Assessment Coordinating Unit (2010) Thailand's rules and procedures for the health impact assessment of public policies. National Health Commission Office, Thailand

IMPACT Group (University of Liverpool, UK); Institute of Public Health (Ireland); and RIVM (Netherlands); IOEGD (Germany) (2004) Policy HIA for the European Union: a health impact assessment of the European employment strategy across the European Union. http://ec.europa.eu/health/ph_projects/2001/monitoring/fp_monitoring_2001_a6_frep_11_en.pdf. Accessed 18 June 2013

International Finance Corporation (2009) Introduction to health impact assessment. International Finance Corporation, Washington, DC

International Finance Corporation (2012) Overview of performance standards on environmental and social sustainability, effective Jan 1 2012. International Finance Corporation, Washington, DC

Krieger GR, Utzinger J, Winkler MS et al (2010) Barbarians at the gate: storming the Gothenburg consensus. The Lancet 375(9732):2129–2131

Manukau City Council (2010) Wiri spatial structure plan HIA. http://www.apho.org.uk/resource/item.aspx?RID=101558. Accessed 18 June 2013

Ministry of Health (2007) Whanau Ora health impact assessment. New Zealand Ministry of Health, Wellington

NewFields (2010) HIA of the Nacala Dam infrastructure project. http://www.terratest.co.za/files/downloads/Nacala%20Dam/EIA%20to%20PDF/Appendix%20I/Nacala%20Dam%20Health%20Impact%20Assessment%20-%20%20June%202010.pdf. Accessed 18 June 2013

Vohra S, Cave B, Viliani F, Harris-Roxas B, Bhatia R (2010) New international consensus on health impact assessment. Lancet 376(9751):1464–1465. (author reply 65)

Part III
Applied Learning: Conducting an HIA

Chapter 7
Screening

Abstract This chapter describes screening, the first step in the health impact assessment (HIA) process. The primary purpose of screening is to determine whether or not there would be value in conducting an HIA. Screening consists of a rapid appraisal of the potential adverse and beneficial health impacts of a policy, program, or project and establishes whether there is need for an HIA and what level of effort may be required. Screening can also, as a secondary outcome, provide valuable information to be used in the process of conducting an HIA, or can stand alone in helping to describe the potential impacts of a proposal on health. The incorporation of checklists into the screening process can be an efficient way of conducting this activity. The chapter ends by clarifying distinctions between screening and the next step in HIA, scoping.

Keywords Screening · Resources · Funding · Checklists · Value · Regulatory requirements · Screening report

Purpose of Screening

The primary purpose of screening is to identify projects or policies for which health impact assessment (HIA) is appropriate, useful, and timely and to determine if an HIA is warranted. Screening involves judgments about how an organization's resources should be used and whether the results of the HIA will contribute to stakeholder knowledge or the decision-making process. In addition, screening can establish whether there are likely to be vulnerable populations or areas that need consideration and whether there are important community concerns that should be addressed.

The process of conducting screening is generally fairly rapid, lasting only a few hours. The process involves reviewing the project or policy to develop a preliminary judgment of whether it is likely to affect health determinants or health outcomes (either beneficially or adversely); reviewing the context to determine if the HIA can contribute new knowledge or inform the decision-making process; and reviewing available resources to determine if there is sufficient time, personnel, and funding to conduct the HIA. As shown in Box 7.1, there are situations in which conducting an HIA may not be useful.

C. L. Ross et al., *Health Impact Assessment in the United States,*
DOI 10.1007/978-1-4614-7303-9_7, © Springer Science+Business Media New York 2014

> **Box 7.1   Why or when might an HIA not be useful?**
>
> Sometimes the outcome of screening is the decision that an HIA is not neces-
> sary or useful at a particular time or for a particular project or policy. What
> are some of the reasons that screening might identify for not doing an HIA?
>
> - There is no opportunity to influence the decision-making process—either
>   the amount of time available is too short, or there is no opportunity to
>   move the results into public discussion
> - Limited resources are available and an HIA can only be conducted on one
>   of several possible projects/policies
> - The HIA is unlikely to bring forward new information about health that is
>   not already being discussed
> - The project or policy will not affect health determinants or health outcomes

What Gets Screened?

Any organization interested in conducting an HIA—whether a government agency,
a community group, a nongovernmental organization (NGO), a developer, or otherwise, will have to decide how many and which proposals to review and screen for
consideration for HIA. A number of approaches have been developed to guide this
decision process.

In some jurisdictions—including both Sweden and Quebec—the government
has made the decision that all new public policy should be screened for HIA. This
process of reviewing all material in a particular category is known as "systematic
screening" (Taylor et al. 2003). While systematic screening is comprehensive in
capturing all proposals that would benefit from an HIA, it is a very resource-inten-
sive and time-consuming approach and is most appropriate for very large organizations that both conduct the HIA and are in control of the project/policies being
reviewed.

More commonly, however, screening is carried out on a limited subset of projects or policies that are of interest to a particular agency or organization. How many
HIAs should be conducted will depend both on the appropriateness of the project or
policy and on the amount of resources (personnel, funding, etc.) available to direct
towards conducting the HIA.

In many cases, however, the screening decision is made before the HIA practitioners are even involved. For example, there may be a regulatory requirement to
conduct HIA, or a company may decide to undertake an HIA in order to understand
corporate risk and responsibility. As stated by Quigley et al. (2005), "It is rare for
HIA to begin with a screening exercise—most begin because of a political process;
or because a local champion recommends an HIA; or because funding for an HIA
becomes available."

How Screening is Done

As described in Chap. 4, the objective of an HIA is to examine the unintended health consequences of a proposed project, policy, program, plan, or strategy. The screening process begins by reviewing what is known (the "project description"). This information may be publicly available; however, because the project or policy is often in an early stage of development, the organization interested in conducting the HIA may have to work closely with the organization proposing the project or policy in order to obtain sufficient information.

With information about the project, policy, or program in hand, a small team is assembled to undertake the screening activity. The team responsible for screening may consist of only one person or may include several people; but it is important to make sure that the team has, at a minimum, adequate knowledge of the project's details, including the decision-making process and timeline; how HIA is undertaken; and what resources would be available to conduct an HIA. In some circumstances, the screening team may include representatives from potentially affected communities, persons with particular expertise, or persons having extensive or unique knowledge about the subject of the HIA.

Just as HIA is a flexible but systematic process that can be approached in multiple ways, the screening process can also be undertaken at varying levels of detail and using different approaches.

The use of screening checklists or standardized matrices is fairly common practice in the USA. Checklists and similar tools are useful in that they help to "structure, standardize and document" the decision process (Cole et al. 2005). Two examples are shown below. Figure 7.1 shows a matrix developed by faculty at the School of Public Health at the University of California Los Angeles (UCLA). This matrix walks the user through a series of yes-or-no questions that direct the reader to one of three outcomes: conduct no HIA, conduct a rapid HIA, or conduct a full HIA. Figure 7.2 presents a screening checklist developed by the City Council of Leeds, a city in England. The checklist poses many questions similar to those in the UCLA matrix, identifying whether there are likely to be health impacts, whether the HIA can feed into a decision-making process, and whether there are sufficient resources to conduct the HIA. However, the Leeds screening checklist does not provide a definitive answer as to if and what level of HIA should be conducted; rather, it helps the practitioner identify whether the context tends to support conducting an HIA or not.

In addition to being carried out through the use of checklists or similar tools, screening can also be conducted as a "desk-top" process through the review of relevant literature or epidemiological data by technical experts.

Engagement of Stakeholders in Screening

The early engagement of stakeholders in the screening step is sometimes—though not always—appropriate.

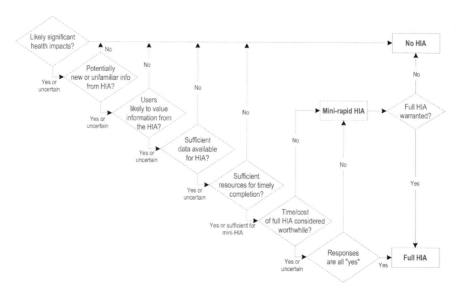

Fig. 7.1 Example of a screening algorithm. (Cole et al. 2005)

Bias towards HIA	To your knowledge:	Bias against HIA
Yes	Are sufficient resources available to conduct the HIA?	No
Yes / don't know	Are the potential −ve health impacts associated with the activity likely to be serious?	No
Yes / don't know	Are the potential −ve health impacts likely to be serious if the activity doesn't proceed?	No
No	Is the activity of relatively short duration?	Yes
Yes	Is there scope to act on the recommendations of the HIA?	No
Yes / don't know	Are the potential −ve health impacts likely to be greater for vulnerable, marginalised or disadvantaged groups?	No
Yes / don't know	Are there community concerns about potential health impacts?	No
Yes	Is there an evidence base to support appraisal of the impacts?	No*
Yes	Is the activity important in the context of corporate & environmental service priorities?	No

Fig. 7.2 Example of a screening checklist. (Swift et al. 2007)

Stakeholder input can be useful in that it provides local knowledge and multiple viewpoints that may otherwise be overlooked, and thus provides a more context-sensitive set of information to guide the conduct of the HIA (Harris et al. 2007). Stakeholders may also provide a deeper narrative of the sociopolitical context within which the HIA is being conducted, and may provide key information on the community's health priorities as well as its perception of relative risks and benefits. This makes the ensuing HIA more appropriate to the particular context, rendering it thus more relevant to policy-making (Joffe 2003; Milner et al. 2003). More introspective questions such as "who decides the purpose of an HIA?" or "who decides which approach is best?" may also be productive to explore through stakeholder engagement (Joffe 2003).

Stakeholder engagement at the screening stage can fulfill a capacity-building role. Training interested stakeholders, community representatives, experts, and decision-makers in the development of specific screening tools and educating them about the screening process brings all constituents to a common reference point early in the process and begins to frame a dialogue (Elliott and Francis 2005).

Which stakeholders should be involved at the screening stage depends on the subject of the HIA and the context in which it is conducted, and may include local residents, NGOs, local government representatives, or project proponents, as well as representatives from the organization funding the HIA. However, it may be useful to keep the number of stakeholders involved at the scoping stage relatively small in order to facilitate a manageable process, and instead engage a wider group of stakeholders at the start of the scoping step.

Engagement of stakeholders in screening is not recommended in all situations; for example, if the organization considering conducting the HIA is not prepared to commit to the screening recommendations on whether or not an HIA should be done, then stakeholder engagement may create unrealistic expectations and be counterproductive rather than empowering.

What Else Does the Screening Step Do?

In addition to fulfilling the main purpose of helping to determine whether or not an HIA should be undertaken, the screening process can serve several other purposes:

First, screening can be used to identify the data and resources needed to conduct an HIA, such as the type and depth of data collection required and the initial human resource needs.

A preliminary identification of health inequities—an integral value of the HIA process—is a part of many screening processes. Differential distributions based on socioeconomic status, ethnicity, gender, geography, or other stratifications can help identify vulnerable populations and guide further assessment procedures to impart a greater focus on these groups (Harris-Roxas et al. 2004).

Second, screening may also help clarify the political context within which the HIA may be conducted. Political considerations such as the degree of transparency that will be allowed, the level of support for the HIA process, and the regulatory environment for the HIA are all vital considerations in determining how an HIA should be conducted and how the results may be incorporated within the decision-making process (Bhatia 2010; Taylor et al. 2003).

Finally, the screening process can help uncover hidden opportunities to incorporate health considerations within the decision-making process. Even if a full HIA is not undertaken, the screening step can be used as an opportunity to identify ways in which the policy/project proposal can be modified in order to improve the likelihood of minimizing potential harms and generating potential health benefits (Harris et al. 2007).

Outputs of the Screening Process

After the screening process is completed, a screening report is written that describes that screening process that was used as well as a recommendation on whether or not to proceed with an HIA. The screening report may also provide additional detail to help guide the ensuing HIA, such as a realistic assessment of the human, data, and financial resources that would be required to execute a good HIA.

As mentioned above, even if the screening process results in the recommendation that an HIA not be pursued, the screening report itself can still be a valuable tool. The screening report can call attention to the potential health impacts of the proposal being examined and can make recommendations for changing the proposal to improve associated health outcomes.

Confusion over Screening vs. Scoping

As a final note, there is often confusion between screening and scoping. Deciding whether or not an HIA is required is the primary purpose of screening; the primary purpose of scoping (as described in the next chapter) is to establish the methods that will be used to conduct the HIA. Many screening processes also give consideration to potential methods—including an initial determination of which health areas should be examined in the HIA—which is what gives rise to this confusion. However, even when the screening process produces more full or robust results than the recommendation of whether or not to proceed with an HIA, this remains the fundamental objective of this step.

References

Bhatia R (2010) A guide for health impact assessment. California Department of Public Health. http://www.cdph.ca.gov/pubsforms/Guidelines/Documents/HIA%20Guide%20FINAL%20 10-19-10.pdf. Accessed 18 June 2013

Cole B, Shimkhada R, Fielding J, Kominski G, Morgenstern H (2005) Methodologies for realizing the potential of health impact assessment. Am J Prev Med 28(4):382–389

Elliott E, Francis S (2005) Making effective links to decision-making: key challenges for health impact assessment. Environ Impact Asses 25(7–8):747–757

Harris P, Harris-Roxas B, Harris E, Kemp L (2007) Health impact assessment: a practical guide. Centre for Health Equity Training Research and Evaluation, University of New South Wales, Sydney, Australia

Harris-Roxas B, Simpson S, Harris E (2004) Equity focused health impact assessment: a literature review. Centre for Health Equity Training Research and Evaluation, Sydney, Australia

Joffe M (2003) How do we make health impact assessment fit for purpose? Public Health 117(5):301–304

Milner S, Bailey C, Deans J (2003) 'Fit for purpose' health impact assessment: a realistic way forward. Public Health 117(5):295–300

Quigley R, Cave B, Elliston K et al (2005) Practical lessons for dealing with inequalities in health impact assessment. National Institute for Health and Clinical Excellence, London

Swift J (2007) Health impact assessment toolkit for public health practitioners—blank worksheets. http://www.apho.org.uk/resource/item.aspx?RID=48983. Accessed 18 June 2013

Taylor L, Gowman N, Lethbridge J, Quigley R (2003) Learning from practice bulletin: deciding if a health impact assessment is required (screening for HIA). Health Development Agency, London

Chapter 8
Scoping

Abstract This chapter describes scoping, the second step of a health impact assessment (HIA). Scoping provides a blueprint for the planning and execution of the HIA while identifying potential hurdles and opportunities. The scoping process involves defining how the HIA will be managed and resourced; identifying which health issues will be carried forward into the assessment; and determining the methods that will be used for analyzing impacts. This chapter concludes by presenting three case studies that demonstrate different aspects of scoping.

Keywords Scoping · Management · Methodological approach · Temporal scope · Geographic scope · Oversight · HIA project team · Steering committee · Terms of reference

Purpose of Scoping

The purpose of scoping is to plan the approach for the HIA in terms of logistics, methods, and contents. Scoping sets the stage for how the rest of the HIA will be carried out. While there is no single template for how scoping should be conducted, most HIA guidelines agree that there is a central core of planning that needs to be undertaken in order for the HIA to proceed smoothly.

The issues to be addressed during the scoping stage fall into three main categories, described below and in Box 8.1:

- **Management of the HIA**—setting up a process that will enable the HIA to move forward smoothly with appropriate resources, and a plan to ensure that the results of the HIA are used in the final decision-making process.
- **Scope of the HIA**—identifying which health issues the HIA will assess and what populations and/or geographical areas will be included.
- **Methodological approach of the HIA**—determining how, specifically, to analyze impacts: where to look for information, how information will be analyzed, how impacts will be characterized, and how stakeholders will be engaged during the process.

C. L. Ross et al., *Health Impact Assessment in the United States,*
DOI 10.1007/978-1-4614-7303-9_8, © Springer Science+Business Media New York 2014

Box 8.1   Issues to be considered in the scoping phase

Management of the HIA
- Who will comprise the steering committee?
- Who will conduct the HIA?
- What personnel and financial resources are available for the HIA?
- What is the timeline for producing the HIA?
- What should be the deliverables or outputs of the HIA process?
- What are the plans for disseminating results?
- How can the results be incorporated into decision making?
- What is the plan for evaluating the HIA process and for monitoring results?

Scope of the HIA
- What health issues will be examined in the HIA?
- What constitutes the geographic scope and potentially affected communities?
- What constitutes the temporal scope (timespan of the potential effects)?
- What are the alternative scenarios that will be assessed?

Methodological approach of the HIA
- What data sources will be used?
- What will be the assessment methodology?
- How will stakeholders be engaged?

Management of the HIA

The early establishment of a well-designed management process is essential for the smooth functioning of the HIA and the successful implementation of results.

Normally, both a steering committee and an HIA project team are established. The steering committee provides high-level oversight and direction to the HIA; the HIA project team is involved in the day-to-day conduct of the assessment.

The steering committee is necessary to ensure that the plan for the HIA adequately represents diverse interests, responds to planning and decision requirements, remains within the mandate and capacity of the organization funding it, and is set up to appropriately address health issues. This committee could include members of the funding organization(s), as well as stakeholders representing municipal or regional government, the local public health agency, the project proponent, community or special-interest groups, or affected residents. Whereas a very small group of people is involved in screening, a larger group is usually brought in as the steering committee; the size and composition should be optimized to provide a diversity of interests and capabilities without the group becoming unwieldy. One of the purposes of HIA is to facilitate diverse partnerships in promoting health. The steering committee provides an opportunity to open communication and develop relationships with other organizations to achieve this goal.

The composition of the HIA project team is also important. The team should include at least one member with knowledge or experience of how to conduct HIA, since the function and structure of an HIA are considerably different from those of most other types of health research or reports. Including at least one team member with experience in stakeholder engagement is important, and the team also needs to have expertise in health-related research and the appropriate collection and analysis of health data. Finally, the team needs to have or be able to access expertise in the specific health areas that will be assessed. For some HIAs, the project team can be assembled from within the sponsoring organization, particularly if the organization is a public health entity. In other cases, HIA expertise is brought by external consultants.

Management of the HIA also includes determining what resources will be available, both in terms of personnel and funding and in terms of the schedule that the HIA should adhere to. This will partially determine whether the HIA needs to be done as a desktop exercise, as an intermediate, or as a comprehensive HIA.

Consideration should be given to what the deliverables or outputs of the HIA process will be. As discussed in Chap. 11, "Reporting and Dissemination," these outputs could comprise written reports, public presentations, or other products. The steering committee can advise on optimal ways (and leverage their resources) to disseminate results among different groups and populations, and should plan for how to effectively get the HIA results to decision makers.

A final management issue to be addressed in scoping is the development of plans for evaluating the HIA process and monitoring the results, as discussed in Chaps. 12 and 13.

Scoping of the HIA

Health issues: One of the central goals of scoping is deciding on the set of issues that will be examined in the HIA. The process of identifying health issues that may be linked to the proposed project/policy is often started in the screening process, as described in Chap. 7. At the screening stage, the identification of potential health impacts is used to inform the decision of whether or not conducting an HIA is warranted. The process of issue identification continues in scoping. At this stage, however, the purpose is to develop a set of issues to be carried through to the assessment.

All potential health effects should be considered for inclusion in the HIA, not only those that support a particular advocacy position.

The issue scoping process starts with identifying the full range of health outcomes and health determinants that could possibly be affected by the project/policy under consideration. At the start of the scoping stage, there is no attempt made to determine whether a particular health impact *will* occur as a result of the proposed project or policy; the point is to identify all the areas in which impacts *may* occur and are therefore appropriate for further consideration and assessment. It is critically important that in the scoping phase, no "cherry-picking" occurs regarding which potential health impacts will be examined in order to promote a certain viewpoint. All potential health effects should be considered for inclusion in the HIA, not only those that support a particular advocacy position. The identification of potential issues is generally completed through a review of literature, input from subject-area experts, input from stakeholders, and the judicious application of professional expertise.

This identification of potential health issues commonly results in a very large number of health issues being put forward—often too many to reasonably include in an HIA. A process needs to be developed to pare the list down to those issues that will be most practical and fruitful in the HIA. Most HIAs tend to focus on between four and twelve primary areas. There is no single or dominant method for refining the list of issues to those ultimately included; however, many HIA guidance documents recommend that the HIA prioritize those issues that are of the greatest importance (Bhatia et al. 2011; WHIASU 2012). Importance could be identified through a number of methods: for example, because the issue has the potential to carry severe health consequences; because the issue is particularly meaningful or important to certain stakeholders; or because the issue has not yet been raised in discourse about the project. The decision regarding which issues are most "important" necessarily involves a value judgment. The HIA practitioner should therefore be mindful of ensuring that the process used to identify which health issues will or will not be included is done transparently, to minimize the appearance of bias.

In addition to identifying those health issues to be included, several other factors need to be considered as part of the scope for the content of the HIA.

Geographical scope and potentially affected communities: The HIA's scope needs to define what the geographic scope of the HIA analysis will be, in terms of the populations or communities that have the potential to be affected. The International Finance Corporation guidance on HIA uses the term "potentially affected communities" (International Finance Corporation 2009). Environmental and socioeconomic impact assessments often refer to Local Study Areas (LSAs) and Regional Study Areas (RSAs), the distinction being that the LSA is more likely to experience direct effects, whereas the RSA is more likely to experience effects indirectly. It should be remembered that not all potentially affected communities may be affected in the same way, and that different health issues may be applicable to each. For example, in the case of the Nacala Dam project described in Chap. 6, "International Case Studies," the families living next to the dam comprised one potentially affected community; they would be directly affected by dam construction activities and the plan to resettle their village. A different set of potentially affected communities were those living downstream from the dam; the impacts relevant to them stemmed from changes in water levels and electricity provision. In order to identify an appropriate geographic scope for an HIA, the project or policy proposal has to be carefully reviewed, as the choice of study area will depend on how and over what distance effects are likely to manifest.

Temporal scope: The temporal scope refers to the time frame over which health effects will be considered; for example, over the following 5 years, or over the following 25. Health effects may persist for a long time, but they are often different in the short term and the long term, and become harder to predict with a longer time horizon. For industrial project proposals, the timeline is often defined as including the construction, operations, and decommissioning phases of the project.

Project alternatives: The HIA needs to respond to the way in which decisions about the project/policy are being made. Generally, by the time the project or policy has reached the proposal stage, the options have been narrowed down to a small number of alternatives. For example, there may be three or four different alternatives being considered for a highway upgrading project; for public policy, there may be a simple yes/no option that is being voted on. The HIA should identify an assessment approach that will allow a comparison to be made between these alternatives.

Some HIAs that have attempted to go outside of previously identified alternative scenarios have met resistance from decision makers, because the results were perceived as unhelpful for the decision being made at the time. Conversely, some HIA practitioners have insisted that they be allowed the freedom to best represent the health interests of stakeholders, whether or not the recommendation fits within the decision framework.

Methodological Approach of the HIA

Finally, the scoping phase needs to plan out the methods that will be used for the assessment. The steps of assessment are described in Chap. 9 and include developing a baseline community health profile, using various evidence sources to appraise or predict impacts to different populations, and characterizing the results. Potential methods will likely include a combination of literature review, key informant input, expert advice, and stakeholder input. An a priori approach should be set for how information will be identified and gathered, how evidence will be weighed or evaluated, and how effects will be characterized. Advance consideration should also be given to the structure of the HIA report and the development of a table of contents.

Input from various stakeholders and key informants comprises a key source of information for the assessment. Stakeholder engagement is reviewed in detail in Chap. 14, but the scoping should include the development of a comprehensive plan for stakeholder engagement: Which affected groups will be invited to participate and how? How will their views be incorporated into the overall HIA and final report? How will key informants from various stakeholder groups be identified and how will their input be solicited?

Outputs of Scoping

The output of the scoping step is usually a stand-alone report. This report acts as a blueprint for the HIA team members to follow during the rest of the time the HIA is being conducted.

The report may be termed a Scoping Report, an HIA Management Plan, or a Terms of Reference. These terms are generally synonymous, although each may carry a slightly different connotation. Terms of Reference is the name most commonly used within an EIA process and often represents the expectations set by a regulatory agency specifying the objectives that the EIA is required to meet.

The creation of the scoping report is important because it documents the decisions that were made, keeps the HIA on track and efficient, serves as an agreement document, and can be used later to help evaluate the extent to which the HIA achieved the goals set at its outset.

In addition to a stand-alone scoping report, a summary of the scoping process and results is commonly included in the full HIA report (see Chap. 11, "Reporting and Dissemination").

Case Studies

Title:	The Potential Health Impact of a Poultry Litter-to-Energy Facility in the Shenandoah Valley, Virginia	Case Study
Author:	Center on Human Needs, Virginia Commonwealth University	
Year:	2013	
Location:	Virginia	

The Shenandoah Valley in northwestern Virginia is a rural area with a strong agricultural base. This HIA examined the potential health impacts of a proposed facility that would use the "litter" from Virginia's poultry industry as fuel in a combustion process to produce energy. The HIA report clearly describes the structure of the research team and the advisory panel and how stakeholders were engaged.

Research Team
The primary entity responsible for the production of this report was the Virginia Common-wealth University (VCU) Center on Human Needs (CHN), an academic research unit that studies issues related to health equity and the social determinants of health. The CHN team at VCU managed the project, organized stakeholder involvement, formed the analytic plan, conducted literature reviews, and wrote the report. CHN collaborated with the VCU Center on Environmental Studies (CES), which was primarily responsible for conducting the air models associated with the assessment phase and providing guidance on environmental issues.

Advisory Panel
In an effort to receive more periodic feedback and meaningfully incorporate a diversity of perspectives from local stakeholders, the research team formed a 10-member advisory panel. They circulated a monthly newsletter—The HIA Chronicle—that gave the panel an update on the analysis and held monthly conference calls to discuss progress in the steps of the HIA process. In addition to community residents, panel members included representatives of the following groups:

- The Virginia Department of Environmental Quality (DEQ)
- The Virginia Department of Agricultural and Consumer Services
- The Chesapeake Bay Commission
- The Shenandoah Valley Network
- The National Park Service
- The Shenandoah Riverkeeper

Stakeholder Engagement
A key component of scoping is identifying and engaging stakeholders that could be impacted by the decision or could influence the outcome, either as advocates or policymakers. The DEQ established an advisory group on poultry litter-to-energy matters in 2011. This panel was composed of members of national and state government agencies, advocacy groups, the major power company of Virginia, a technology company that constructs such facilities, universities, and other stakeholders. They were notified at the beginning of our project that the decision about constructing a poultry litter-to-energy facility was to be the subject of an HIA. The members of the advisory group were invited to a training session on conducting HIAs that was led by Human Impact Partners.
In order to get feedback from a wider audience, a four-hour public meeting was held in New Market, Virginia on March 30, 2012 to hear from concerned community members and organizations about the most important health impacts of a large-scale, poultry litter-to-energy facility. A total of 23 potential research questions on the potential impact of the facility were formed based on the feedback from this meeting. The advisory panel prioritized this list of research questions into a manageable scope for the HIA.

Summary
The research questions that form the basis of this he research questions that form the basis of thi the potential impacts of a proposed poultry litter-to-energy facility and the feedback received by community members and interested parties in the Valley. The research team held a two-day training on HIA methods and practices, and many of those who attended that meeting remained engaged throughout the HIA process as members of an advisory panel. The initial list of research questions was created based on feedback from a community meeting where members of the public articulated their health concerns about the facility. The resulting list was prioritized by the advisory panel. It focused on air quality, water quality, employment in the poultry/agriculture industry, truck traffic, alternative technologies, and the national park.

(Center on Human Needs 2013)

Title:	Health Impact Assessment (HIA) of Mining Activities Near Keno City, Yukon	Case Study
Author:	Habitat Health Impact Consulting	
Year:	2012	
Location:	Yukon, Canada	

The small community of Keno City, Yukon (population less than 20 people), has historically been a silver-mining community and at its peak had a population of more than 600. However, after mining dried up in the area in the late 1980s, the city re-branded itself as a center for outdoor recreation and tourism. A recent resurgence in mining caused a number of residents to become concerned about health effects. Many of these concerns were not addressed in the environmental assessment process overseen by the Yukon Environmental and Socio-economic Assessment Board (YESAB), and as a result the Yukon Department of Health and Social Services decided to commission an HIA. This excerpt describes the different information sources that were used to identify which health topics would be examined in the HIA.

In order to determine what health-related issues were appropriate to include in the HIA, we undertook a scoping exercise. We reviewed a large number of documents, including:

- All submissions on the YESAB Registry for Bellekeno Mine Development and Lucky Queen and Onek Deposit Production including:
  - Submissions from Alexco (the mining operator)
  - Submissions from territorial and federal government agencies
  - Submissions from Keno residents
  - Submissions from concerned individuals and organizations (e.g., David Suzuki Foundation, Yukon Conservation Society)
- Published literature related to the effects of mining in communities in other areas of Canada and globally
- The Human Health Risk Assessment for Residents of Keno City, Yukon (SENES Consultants)

Concerns brought up by residents and other stakeholders during in-person interviews were also considered. A list was compiled of the main issues that emerged; this is shown in the Table 8.1 below. Issues were grouped by common health pathways. This resulted in the selection of seven areas for investigation in the HIA: air- and soil-related health effects, water-related health effects, noise-related health effects, infectious disease, stress and mental well-being, injury, and emergency medical response. These areas comprise the basis for the analysis of effects in this report.

Table 8.1 Health-related issues raised by stakeholders in the Keno, Yukon, mining HIA. (Habitat Health Impact Consulting 2012)

AREA OF HEALTH CONCERN	YESAB REGISTRY SUBMISSIONS			Resident Interviews	Professional Judgment (see note)
	Alexco (mining company)	Residents	Other		
AIR- AND SOIL-RELATED HEALTH EFFECTS					
dust from mine/mill operations	*		3,4	*	
dust from drystack tailings	*	*	3,4		
dust from industrial traffic	*		3,4		
WATER-RELATED HEALTH EFFECTS					
potential drinking water contamination from acid metal leaching from waste rock storage facility		*	2,3,4,5,7,8		
contamination of ground (and surface) water from drystack tailings			5	*	
potential contamination from the spill of toxic substances (lead and zinc concentrate) transported by truck		*			
NOISE-RELATED HEALTH EFFECTS					
Noise	*	*	3,4,9	*	
INFECTIOUS DISEASE					
respiratory illnesses					*
sexually transmitted infections					*
gastrointestinal illnesses	*				*
STRESS/MENTAL WELL-BEING					
economic impacts	*	*	4,10	*	
community change	*	*		*	
perceived contamination		*		*	
INJURY					
accidents and malfunctions at the mine and mill sites	*		2,3,6	*	
industrial traffic on public roads	*	*	2,4,6	*	
EMERGENCY MEDICAL RESPONSE					
availability of ground ambulance			3		

Note: 'Other' refers to: 1 - Village of Mayo; 2 - First Nation of Na-Cho Nyak Dun; 3 - Health and Social Services, Yukon Government; 4 - Tourism and Culture, Yukon Government; 5 - Environment, Yukon Government; 6 - Energy, Mines and Resources, Yukon Government; 7 - Safe Environments Directorate, Government of Canada; 8 - Fisheries and Oceans, Government of Canada; 9 - International visitors; 10 - individuals representing the film industry.

Note: "Professional judgment" refers to the inclusion of health areas that have been found to be associated with similar developments elsewhere, but that were not initially raised as a concern by any of the stakeholders consulted for this project.

(Habitat Health Impact Consulting 2012)

Title:	Health Impact Assessment: 2010 Hawaii County Agriculture Development Plan	Case Study
Author:	The Kohala Center	
Year:	2012	
Location:	Hawaii, USA	

Table 8.2 Sample scoping questions from the Hawaii County Agriculture Development Plan HIA. (The Kohala Center 2012)

Policy: Increased institutional procurement (and serving in K-12 school meals) of locally produced FFVP by Hawaii Department of Education

Relevant health issues	Indicators	Existing conditions and data needed	Questions for HIA	HIA research methods and tasks	Sources of data
Food security/ hunger:	Food security measures (CPS-FSS)	What is the current rate of food insecurity on Hawaii? For adults? For children?	Would this policy impact children's food security?	Locate existing data on HI food insecurity and relationship to income and geographic area	CPS-FSS (USDA)
Academic performance Behavioral issues		What are the contributing factors to food insecurity on Hawaii?	Would this policy affect adult food security?	Determine how increased local FV in school meals will affect childhood food security	CDC literature review
		Which populations are disproportionally affected by food insecurity?	How would schools buying local FFVP impact the retail value of local FFVP in local markets?		
Obesity (over-nutrition)	Prevalence of childhood obesity	Relationship of family income to family diet quality and obesity	Would this policy impact (through increased FV consumption) prevalence of childhood obesity?	Literature research re: FFV consumption in early years to impact childhood and adult obesity	CDC literature review
	Prevalence of adult obesity	Which populations are disproportionally affected by obesity and related diseases in Hawaii?		How does a decrease in obesity affect life expectancy?	
	Lower levels of obesity and diabetes?			How would a decrease in childhood obesity affect the state's cost of providing health care? How would a decrease in obesity affect business costs, 10 years down the road, for obese adults?	

FFVP Fresh Fruit and Vegetable Program, *CPS-FSS* (USDA) Current Population Survey Food Security Supplement (US Department of Agriculture), *CDC* Centers for Disease Control and Prevention

This project is described as a "Health Impact Assessment detailing the potential impacts of increasing local commercial food production, promoting farm to school procurement and supporting school, community and home food production." Specifically, the HIA comments on three policy recommendations that formed part of the Hawai'i County Agriculture Development Plan: institutional purchasing of locally produced food; commercial expansion of food agriculture; and the expansion of home, community, and school gardens. The HIA examined potential effects in five critical health areas: (1) Hunger (food security) and diet quality (nutrition security); (2) obesity; (3) food-borne illness; (4) economy; and (5) well-being and cultural connectedness. As part of the scoping process, the HIA team developed tables to guide their methodology, identifying the questions they would try to answer, the research methods they would use, and the data sources they would access. An example is shown in Table 8.2, which describes these parameters for the outcomes of food security/hunger and obesity in relation to the policy recommendation of increased institutional procurement.

References

Bhatia R, Gilhuly K, Harris C et al (2011) A health impact assessment toolkit: a handbook to conducting HIA, 3rd edn. Human Impact Partners, Oakland. http://www.humanimpact.org/doc-lib/finish/11/81. Accessed 18 June 2013

Center on Human Needs, Virginia Commonwealth University (2013) The potential health impact of a poultry litter-to-energy facility in the Shenandoah Valley. Virginia. http://humanneeds.vcu.edu/page.aspx?nav=217. Accessed 18 June 2013

Habitat Health Impact Consulting (2012) Health impact assessment (HIA) of mining activities near Keno City, Yukon. http://www.hss.gov.yk.ca/pdf/hia_keno.pdf. Accessed 18 June 2013

International Finance Corporation (2009) Introduction to health impact assessment. International Finance Corporation, Washington, DC

The Kohala Center (2012). Health impact assessment of the 2010 Hawai'i county agriculture development plan. http://kohalacenter.org/pdf/HIAFullReportFinalWeb.pdf. Accessed 18 June 2013

WHIASU (2012) Health impact assessment: a practical guide. Wales Health Impact Assessment Support Unit, Cardiff

Chapter 9
Assessment

Abstract This chapter describes the process of assessment (or appraisal) of impacts. The assessment process begins by characterizing baseline conditions in the potentially affected populations. A number of helpful resources are provided within the chapter to guide the reader through acquisition of health-related data that may be relevant for baseline conditions. The next step in assessment focuses on determining the likely impacts or predicting how baseline conditions might change as a result of the proposed project or policy. Logic frameworks, explaining the potential health effect pathways between the proposed project or policy and health outcomes, are used as a means of organizing the information and ensuring that assumptions are transparent and validated. The last step in assessment, effect characterization, focuses on conveying the relative importance, likelihood, and magnitude of potential health effects. The chapter concludes with a sampling of case studies excerpting *health impact assessments* that demonstrate a range of approaches to assessment, illustrating the principles and questions introduced earlier.

Keywords Assessment · Appraisal · Baseline · Community profile · Impacts · Logic framework · Research ethic · Evidence · Effect characterization · Likelihood · Data collection

What is Assessment?

Assessment is the third phase of the health impact assessment (HIA) process. Its purpose is to identify whether impacts are likely to occur and then to quantify or characterize the predicted impacts.

Throughout this book and in this chapter in particular, we focus on health *impacts*. While the word "impact" often carries a negative connotation, the health impacts examined in an HIA may be either adverse (negative) or beneficial (positive). *Impact* should thus be viewed as a neutral term, synonymous with "effect." However, it is important to note that in some disciplines—most notably among environmental impact assessment (EIA) professionals—the term *impact* almost invariably refers to a negative outcome.

C. L. Ross et al., *Health Impact Assessment in the United States,*
DOI 10.1007/978-1-4614-7303-9_9, © Springer Science+Business Media New York 2014

Assessment Process

Assessment is a complex and difficult component of HIA and may vary the most in terms of how it is approached. However, it usually follows several distinct and standardized steps that include developing a community profile or baseline, assessing or appraising the impacts, and characterizing the effects. Each of these steps is described in detail below.

Step 1: Develop a Health Baseline or Community Profile

The first step is to create a baseline profile that describes current conditions relevant to health in the potentially affected communities. A health profile serves several primary purposes:

- To identify health vulnerabilities, challenges, and opportunities in the potentially affected population in order to ensure that the proposed project or policy does not exacerbate problems and, where possible, leverages the opportunity to improve health
- To identify the current status of health conditions such that predictions can be made about the extent of change
- To identify potentially vulnerable subsets of the population
- To create a reference point for measuring or gauging future change in health status

Some HIA practitioners have made a distinction between a baseline and a community profile. Under this distinction, a community profile is intended to provide an overall picture of community health to help the practitioner and readers of the HIA to better understand the health context of affected populations. A baseline, in contrast, is intended to collect a limited set of replicable data indicators that will be monitored over time to identify change related to a specific project/policy. Whether a baseline or a community profile is more appropriate will depend on the intended use of the data. Currently, most HIAs appear to favor the community profile approach, but use the term "baseline" nonetheless. The rest of this chapter therefore uses that terminology as well.

In a baseline health profile, the following types of information are generally collected:

- Demographic information such as population size and distribution of age, sex, income, and education levels
- Information on health outcomes such as life expectancy, self-rated health, chronic disease rates, acute disease rates, and injuries
- Information on health-related behaviors such as smoking, physical activity, and diet
- Information on social, environmental, or institutional health determinants such as housing, exposure to airborne and waterborne contaminants, and access to health-care services

The information to be gathered should be specific to the health issues identified in the scoping stage in order to avoid a scattershot approach that presents irrelevant data points. Data for the baseline may be available from preexisting secondary sources, such as census information or data from the Behavioral Risk Factor Surveillance System (see Table 9.1); it may be available in published or "grey" literature; or it may need to be collected from key municipal or health system informants or directly from community residents via surveys or focus groups.

In some HIAs, there are distinct populations that may be affected differently by a proposed project or policy. For example, in the *Nacala Dam* case study (Chap. 6), 17 families in the immediate vicinity of the dam would be displaced from their homes. The health effects felt by these 17 families would likely be very different from the health effects experienced by residents of downstream communities who may be the beneficiaries of electricity from the dam. Because the health effects would be vastly different for these two groups, it is appropriate to develop a separate health baseline or profile for each.

As with any exercise in data collection and presentation, it is important to balance the researcher's need to collect data with ethical considerations relating to individual and community privacy. Primary data collection should only occur with a strong rationale for how and why it is essential and with external ethical review, if possible (for example, from the researcher's academic institution, which typically has an Institutional Review Board). If primary data are provided by individuals, protocols must be in place to ensure anonymity, confidentiality, and appropriate use of information. In many jurisdictions, health privacy laws govern the way in which consent must be obtained and data must be collected, stored, and handled.

Step 2: Assess the Likely Impacts

Assessment—also termed *appraisal* or *analysis*—is the act of predicting what health changes will occur as a result of the project or policy, identifying the extent to which the changes will occur and determining how different population subsets will be affected.

In the scoping stage, a preliminary identification is made of the health issues to be examined in the assessment. The next step is to develop an understanding of the health effect pathways that link specific attributes of the project/policy to those health issues and, ultimately, to health outcomes. This can be a daunting task. It is a critical one, however, because the purpose of HIA is not to provide general information about factors that can influence health, but rather to conduct an examination of how a specific project or policy is likely to affect health in a particular context.

A *logic framework* is helpful for organizing this information. A logic framework is a structured diagram that illustrates the potential pathways linking project or policy components to health outcomes. The structure of a logic framework in HIA often consists of four columns: *Project/Policy Attributes, Proximal Impacts, Intermediate Outcomes, and Health Outcomes* (UCLA HIA Project, year not stated).

Table 9.1 National-level data sources relevant for HIA

Data source/who owns it	Type of data available
Surveillance Epidemiology and End Results (SEER)/National Cancer Institute (NCI)	Site-specific cancer incidence, death, survival, and prevalence rates
American Fact Finder/US Census Bureau	Demographics, income, employment, education, behavior and lifestyle, housing, business, and industry statistics
Behavioral Risk Factors Surveillance System (BRFSS)/Centers for Disease Control and Prevention (CDC)	Statistics on health risk behaviors (e.g., smoking), preventive health practices (e.g., physical activity, cancer screenings), and health-care access statistics mainly related to chronic disease and injury. Mortality and hospitalization data available for major chronic diseases
Youth Risk Behavior Surveillance System (YRBSS)/Centers for Disease Control and Prevention (CDC)	Data on health risk behaviors related to injury and violence, pregnancy and sexually transmitted disease, alcohol and drug use, tobacco use, unhealthy dietary behavior, and inadequate physical activity in youth
US Census/US Department of Commerce	Demographics, education, housing, income, and business statistics
County Health Rankings and Roadmaps/Robert Wood Johnson Foundation and University of Wisconsin Public Health Institute	County-level data on mortality, morbidity, health behaviors, clinical medical care, and environmental and social health determinants
Data Finder/US Environmental Protection Agency (USEPA)	Data on air quality, climate change, health risks (exposure, health assessment, toxicity), pollutants and contaminants, waste and water
Child Stats/Federal Interagency Forum on Child and Family Statistics	Summary reports on demographics, family and social environments, economics, physical environment and safety, health care, behavior, education, and health with a focus on children and families. Data are provided at national level
Data Resource Center for Child and Adolescent Health/Child and Adolescent Health Measurement Initiative	State-level data on children's health. Topics include: overall health status, insurance, and access to health care, family and social content, health conditions, health disparities and health-care system performance and quality
Bureau of Justice Statistics/Office of Justice Programs	Statistics on crime and corrections. Includes data on Native American populations
Research and Innovative Technology Administration/US Department of Transportation	Transportation statistics by mode, region, and subject (e.g., economy and finance, energy and environment, infrastructure, etc.)
Education Data Community/US Government	Data on education across all learning categories (e.g., K–12, special education, vocational and adult, etc.)
Bureau of Labor Statistics/US Department of Labor	Statistics on inflation and prices, spending, unemployment, employment, pay and benefits, productivity, workplace injuries. International comparisons available

1. *Project/policy attributes* are distinct aspects or components of the project/policy, such as creating jobs, building roads, or constructing a new facility.
2. *Proximal impacts* are those effects that stem directly from the project/policy attributes. For example, creating jobs may lead to increased income; building roads may lead to changes in traffic patterns; construction may lead to noise.
3. *Intermediate outcomes* follow directly from the proximal impacts. These are often framed as determinants of health (see Chap. 2 for discussion of determinants of health).
4. *Health outcomes* are the ultimate biophysical outcomes experienced by individuals such as respiratory illness, diabetes, injuries, or mental health.

This logic framework is depicted in the example in Fig. 9.1, which shows the health effect pathways related to a Safe Routes to School policy intended to reduce traffic around school facilities and encourage greater numbers of students to walk or bike to school. The pathways follow specific components of the policy—for example, adding crossing guards and building improved infrastructure for cyclists and pedestrians—through to the health outcomes that could be expected.

The logic framework is flexible; in practice, logic framework can be modified in any way to best explain the potential relationships in the particular HIA, for example by adding columns or by positioning effects between columns as in Fig. 9.1. The strengths of the logic framework are that it is transparent and easy to understand and that it presents assumptions about potential impacts in a way that makes it possible to validate their accuracy. However, logic frameworks can also easily become overly complex if not managed properly.

A preliminary logic framework can be developed either during the scoping phase or at the start of the assessment, depending on the preferences of the HIA team. When the logic framework is initially created, it should capture the *potential* health effect pathways between the proposed project/policy and health outcomes; that is, it should document assumptions about how the pieces may fit together.

The next step is to generate evidence that will validate or invalidate each pathway and will help the HIA practitioner better understand the nature of the impacts. To do this, he or she looks to a variety of evidence sources. Evidence is defined very broadly in HIA and can come from a wide variety of sources, including:

- Systematic reviews and meta-analyses
- Peer-reviewed literature
- Published or grey literature reports from government or other organizations
- Quantitative models
- Previously published HIAs
- Academic subject-area expert opinion
- Key informant interviews (interviews with a person who is particularly well informed about a particular topic)
- Stakeholder/resident opinion, gathered through focus groups, one-on-one interviews, community workshops, etc.

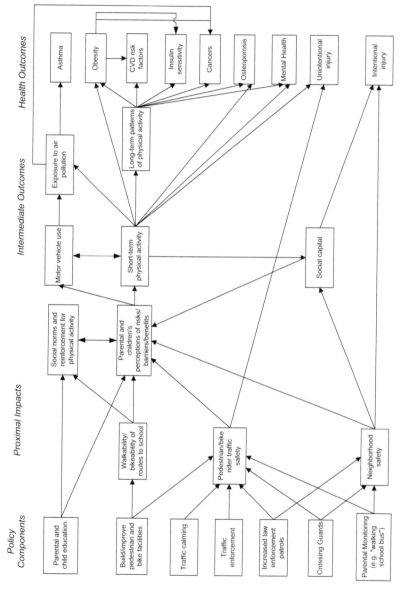

Fig. 9.1 Example of a logic framework—Sacramento Safe Routes to School HIA. (UCLA Health Impact Assessment Project 2004)

The *Minimum Elements and Practice Standards for Health Impact Assessment* states that the "best available" evidence should be used (North American HIA Practice Standards Working Group 2010). What comprises best-available evidence will depend on the health impact being examined. For areas where strong epidemiologic evidence exists, systematic reviews can be an excellent source of information if they are applicable to the specific context of the HIA. As an example, published epidemiologic evidence and population-level modeling would be appropriate to use in gauging the potential impact of a known change in air quality on respiratory outcomes. However, published information is unlikely to be available for all the health impacts being examined, or may not be applicable to the population, location, policy, or project. In this case, a different type of evidence is likely to be more appropriate. As an example, if one is trying to determine the impact a particular project is likely to have on the capacity of the local waste treatment system, appropriate evidence is most likely to come from discussions with people who are in charge of that waste treatment facility, rather than from academic literature. While academic literature can provide excellent information on the general workings of waste treatment facilities or problems that may arise in them, only local key informants can provide information on the history of problems at that particular facility, plans to upgrade the facility, how close it is to running at maximum capacity, or other details that may be relevant in the context of changing local conditions. No matter what type of information is used, it is important to remember that the HIA should not "cherry pick" information to support a given conclusion.

The evidence from these different sources is combined with information about the proposed project/policy and the baseline/community profile information to help the HIA practitioner describe what the likely impacts will be for each of the health areas under consideration. In this description, it is important to present not only the impacts that are likely to be experienced by the majority of the population, but also how impacts may be differentially experienced by different subsets, such as vulnerable subgroups.

For some health impacts, it is possible to develop a quantitative assessment that gives a numerical prediction of the predicted change in health outcomes. This type of quantitative assessment is often relished by readers—numbers are easy to compare, can be persuasive, can form the basis of an economic argument, and have a ring of scientific "truth" (despite the fact that models are often based on numerous assumptions and quantitative estimates may be highly erroneous). Where it is possible to develop a numerical or quantitative characterization of impacts, this option should be strongly considered. However, there are currently very few health outcomes in HIA that are amenable to quantitative estimation.

For health effects where quantitative assessment is not possible, it is important to provide a very strong qualitative narrative. This description should clearly explain (1) what the health impact is likely to be, (2) who will be affected, (3) how strong the effect will be, and (4) what sources of evidence have been used to arrive at this conclusion. Several examples of this are presented in the case studies at the end of this chapter.

Table 9.2 Examples of common effect characterization parameters

Parameter	Meaning
Direction	Beneficial or adverse
Likelihood	How likely it is that the exposure or effect will occur
Severity	How severe the potential health effects may be
Magnitude/geographic extent	How widely the effects would be spread within a population or across a geographical area
Frequency/duration	How often or for how long the exposure will occur
Vulnerable populations	Distribution of the effects among vulnerable populations
Latency	Amount of time after exposure before effects would be visible
Ability to adapt	The resiliency of the affected population to adapt to the change
Certainty of evidence	The degree of certainty that exposure or effects will occur, based on available evidence

Step 3: Characterize/Summarize the Health Impacts

Finally, it is important to provide a summary characterization of predicted impacts in order to allow readers to compare the relative importance of different health effects. For example, the HIA may determine that the project or policy will have effects on six or seven health areas such as traffic-related injury, diet quality, stress and anxiety, and exposure to air contaminants. The summary effect characterization enables stakeholders, including decision-makers, to more easily identify which of these effects is potentially most important or most likely to occur and should be prioritized in terms of channeling resources towards mitigation. This comparison can be challenging but is especially important if the impacts being compared are conceptually very different, such as contaminant exposure and mental well-being.

Effect characterization is generally done by using standardized parameters such as *likelihood, severity,* and *duration* to characterize impacts. Table 9.2 lists a number of effect characterization parameters that have commonly been used in HIAs. Generally, somewhere in the range of three and six parameters are used within any one HIA to consistently characterize all health effects analyzed. The parameters are chosen to best fit the particular effects being described in the HIA.

For each of these parameters, definitions need to be created a priori to characterize an effect as "high," "medium," or "low" (or whatever other categories are appropriate). An example from the Alaska HIA technical guidelines is shown in Box 9.1. These definitions should be reported as part of the HIA methods—this transparency will allow readers to understand the rationale for an effect being characterized as "high" severity, rather than moderate or low. The definitions used for the specific levels in each parameter may need to change from one HIA to another HIA, in order to fit the specific context.

Effect characterization using standardized parameters such as those above is a useful and transparent way to evaluate the relative importance of different effects and to communicate the results to stakeholders. Other options exist, such as translating the projected health effects into dollars or disability adjusted life years (DALYs), and may be used if appropriate. However, this relies on additional information, such

Box 9.1   Example of *severity* ratings from Alaska HIA technical guidance. (State of Alaska HIA Program 2011)

Low: Effect is not perceptible.
Medium: Effect results in annoyance, minor injuries, or illnesses that do not require intervention.
High: Effect resulting in moderate injury or illness that may require some intervention.
Very high: Effect resulting in loss of life, severe injuries, or chronic illness that requires intervention.

as cost, that is often not available and has not been treated frequently in HIAs to date.

Case Studies

Three case studies have been chosen to demonstrate a range of approaches to assessment within an HIA. Brief excerpts from the assessment section of each are presented below. Appendix 3 provides the full assessment section from which this is taken and the full HIAs can be found online among the resource material for this book. We urge readers to refer to the full assessment section for each of these HIAs; while these excerpts give a flavor for how an analysis looks, the full version enables a much better understanding of what an HIA analysis can consist of and how it might be structured.

Title:	Potential Health Effects of Casino Development in Southeast Kansas	Case Study
Author:	Kansas Health Institute	
Year:	2012	
Location:	Kansas	

Project/policy assessed by the HIA In 2011 and 2012, a number of bills were introduced in the Kansas legislature that were intended to stimulate the building of casinos in the state and specifically in the Southeast Kansas Gaming Zone, with the hope of creating jobs and boosting an economically depressed region of Kansas.

Sample assessment The HIA conducted by the Kansas Health Institute examined how the presence of a casino might affect health, both in terms of potential risks such as exposure to secondhand smoke, traffic accidents, gambling addiction, divorce, and suicide and in terms of potential benefits such as job creation, tourism, state and local revenue increases, and health insurance. Previous discussions around the issue of casino development had been limited to potential economic benefits and pathological gambling; this HIA attempted to broaden the discussion on health. The HIA draws on three sources of evidence: qualitative information from the potentially affected community, published literature on health effects, and data from a casino that had been built elsewhere 2 years previously (the Boot Hill Casino in Dodge City, Kansas). It provides an excellent example of describing impacts using a logic framework and a clear effect characterization matrix. The following excerpt reproduces the summary of health effects associated with potential employment at the casinos.

Summary: Health Implications for the Southeast Kansas Gaming Zone
Based on literature review and labor market data for Ford County (which has no nearby casinos) and the Northeast Kansas Gaming Zone, the addition of a SEKGZ casino is likely to increase local employment by 300 to 350 jobs. Furthermore, overall local employment levels can be expected to rise once casino construction begins. Literature review shows that building a casino in SEKGZ would likely result in a lower local unemployment rate because rises in employment are usually offset by an increase in population, meaning that there are more jobs dispersed among more people. In addition, the literature review shows that the impact of a casino on the local unemployment rate depends on the extent that newly hired employees relocate or commute from elsewhere, other changes in the local labor market or population, and how other economic conditions affect the local labor market.

In general, stakeholders noted that a casino could bring economic benefits, including "a little more business support of the community" and "jobs and money in the community." However, stakeholders were somewhat divided in their views about a casino's potential health impacts. Some stakeholders thought a casino would improve access to health care and result in health benefits associated with increased income. Other stakeholders raised concerns about the negative impacts of a casino on the financial stability of families if people spend their money on gambling rather than essentials. Stakeholders also noted a number of factors that are likely to influence the degree to which a SEKGZ casino actually improves the health of residents; for example, whether a casino provides health insurance for its employees and their families.

Based on findings from the literature review, data analysis and stakeholder opinion, new casino jobs may increase income for residents of Cherokee and Crawford counties as well as offer insurance to full-time employees. Increased income and access to health insurance may improve access to health care services and healthy foods, thus improving the health (e.g., reducing mortality and morbidity, increasing quality of life and life expectancy, reducing BMI) of SEKGZ casino employees and their families. As noted earlier, employment, insurance and income have strong, positive links to health. In order to achieve these positive health impacts, it is important to address potential negative effects of casino employment, such as shift work and exposure to secondhand smoke, which can lead to increased risk of morbidity and mortality, lung cancer and heart disease.

(Kansas Health Institute 2012)

Title:	A Health Impact Assessment of California Assembly Bill 889: The California Domestic Work Employee Equality, Fairness, and Dignity Act of 2011	Case Study
Author:	San Francisco Department of Public Health	
Year:	2011	
Location:	California	

Project/policy assessed by the HIA The *Domestic Work Employee Equality, Fairness, and Dignity Act of 2011* proposed to make a number of labor protections already enjoyed by many other workers similarly applicable to domestic workers. These included the right to overtime pay, annual cost of living pay increases, meal and rest breaks, 8 h of uninterrupted sleep under adequate conditions, paid vacations and sick leave, coverage by state Workers' Compensation and Division of Occupational Safety and Health, and other provisions.

Sample assessment The HIA assessment focused on two areas of the Bill integral to human health: health effects associated with sleep deprivation and health effects associated with providing Workers' Compensation coverage. The excerpt given below presents the HIA's analysis of the health effects of uninterrupted sleep. The analysis demonstrates a strong review of the literature, connects the policy provisions to specific health outcomes, and summarizes the findings using an effect characterization table that is likely to be useful and understandable to the HIA's various audiences.

> **What is the likelihood, certainty, and magnitude of health effects resulting from the legislative changes to sleep requirements?**
> In summary, based on the available evidence, understanding of the domestic worker population and their socio-economic and work-related vulnerabilities, we predict that the passage of a sleep requirement for domestic workers would protect the health of a sizable and growing subset of domestic workers in California.
> Table 9.2 provides a summary judgment of the likelihood, intensity, and magnitude of the health effect and the uncertainties related to limits of available evidence. A quantitative estimate of the magnitude of health effects related to sleep is not possible due to the lack of data on the following factors:
>
> • the number of domestic workers working 24 hours or more or working as live-in workers
> • the current distribution of sleep hours for domestic workers impacted by the law. (Fig. 9.2)

(San Francisco Department of Public Health 2011)

Title:	Health Impact Assessment of the Northern Territory Emergency Response	Case Study
Author:	Australian Indigenous Doctors' Association and the Centre for Health Equity Training, Research and Evaluation, University of New South Wales	
Year:	2010	
Location:	Australia	

Project/policy assessed by the HIA The Northern Territory Emergency Response (NTER) was a series of emergency policy measures proposed by the Australian national government to reduce violence and child abuse in the Northern Territory of the country. The emergency measures outlined in the legislation included changes to the government's approach to welfare payments to indigenous families, alcohol

(San Francisco Department of Public Health 2011)

Table 12: Summary Assessment of Expected Effects of Sleep Protections on Health							
Health Outcome	Likelihood	Intensity / Severity	Who Impacted DW	CR	GP	Magnitude	Uncertainties related to limited evidence
Mortality	▲ ▲ ▲	High	+			Small	Studies on health effects of sleep not specific to domestic work population
Chronic Disease & Obesity	▲ ▲	Mod	+			Small to Moderate	
Stress & Mental Health	▲ ▲	Mod	+	?		Small to Moderate	Limited information on current sleep patterns in affected population
Cognitive & Motor Performance	▲ ▲ ▲	Mod	+	+		Moderate	
Work Errors & Injuries	▲ ▲ ▲	High	+	+		Moderate	Baseline health status in affected domestic work population
Traffic Accidents	▲ ▲ ▲	High	+	+	+	Uncertain	
							Data on utilization of protections

Explanations:
- Likelihood refers to strength of research/evidence showing causal relationship between sleep and the health outcome: ▲ = limited evidence, ▲ ▲ = limited but consistent evidence, ▲ ▲ ▲ = causal relationship established. A causal effect means that the effect is likely to occur, irrespective of the magnitude or severity.
- Intensity/Severity reflects the nature of the effect its affects on function, life-expectancy and its permanence (High = very severe/intense, Mod = Moderate)
- Who impacted refers to which populations are impacted by the health outcomes associated with proposed sleep requirements. DW = Domestic Workers, CR = Care Recipient, GP = General Population.
- Magnitude reflects a qualitative judgment of the size of the anticipated change in the health effect (e.g. the increase in the number of cases of disease, injury, adverse events).

Fig. 9.2 Summary assessment for expected effects of sleep protections on health

and pornography bans, health checks on indigenous children and allowing access to indigenous land. The NTER was highly controversial due to the lack of consultation with communities and the appearance of being patronizing and discriminatory.

Sample assessment The HIA, which was itself controversial, described potential health impacts from proposed changes to external governance, compulsory income management, alcohol restriction, the prohibition of certain materials, mandatory checks on child health, and reforms for housing and education. The following excerpt focuses on housing and is a good example of the use of the voices from impacted communities as a source of qualitative evidence. The full version of this assessment section is presented in Appendix 3; several quotations from the community are omitted in the excerpt below.

Positive Impacts
The main positive impact on housing related to the significant investment promised by governments for housing, and higher number of housing repairs occurring.

There's money been promised for houses which is great. I mean there are 4000 dwellings need to be constructed right now. They've earmarked it.
Non-Aboriginal Senior Bureaucrat

Negative Impacts
Most of the community responses to the housing measures promised in the Intervention were restatements of the serious, pre-existing housing problems that the Intervention promised to address. Although there was grave concern about the transference of leases to Australian Government control, many people welcomed the thought of there being, finally,

a serious effort to provide the housing they need. However, after 12 months the Intervention had, it seemed, disappointed people who had hoped and expected that action would be quicker, particularly in terms of improved maintenance.

Concern was also expressed at the priorities for building houses with most of the new houses being allocated to Business Managers, police and health staff so that there was no impact on the quality of housing and overcrowding among community families. Also there was a perception that if you lived close to existing infrastructure you were given greater priority and also able to negotiate for more flexible arrangements on the ways in which the projects were implemented.

Housing has got to be one of the most corrupt and incompetent areas of Indigenous affairs. We're looking at houses that you build for $ 100 000 costing $ 4 to $ 5 to $ 600 000 to build and it's just nonsense and they're not, and a lot of them are falling down within a few years. We must look at the type of housing, the material we're using and look at how we can reduce the cost 'cause that is just a bizarre situation. You cannot tell me just because it's in a remote area, or it's in a rural area that it's going to cost that amount of money to build that type of housing.
Aboriginal Leader

Overcrowding and poor housing affects everyone in the community including Aboriginal Health Workers.

There are fifteen in my house including kids. I'm living with my parents. It is a four- bedroom house. All paying rent $ 400–500 per week all together for that house, because it is $ 50 each. Plus the power cards.
Aboriginal Community Member

For many people the proposed building program was seen as a missed employment and training opportunity for Aboriginal people in the design, construction, and maintenance of housing and relevant health hardware

Rather than having people flying in and flying out to build houses while you've got all these white fellas going in, building a house, and then shooting off. You've got the community, you know 50, or 60 or 100 Aboriginals sitting down watching them build a house.
Non-Aboriginal Doctor

Some people had ambitious long-term vision on ways in which the community could be involved.

'... learn how to fix houses and the plumbing and how it works... it could have set up maintenance centres where there was proper training, proper apprenticeships and proper pay.'
Aboriginal Health Worker

This speaks to the wider concern expressed by communities and stakeholders that the long-term maintenance of the housing depended on ownership and on the appropriateness of the housing.

'The issue for government is that they were going to invest in housing, make a big investment in housing. Investing in housing is all well and good, but if you build houses that are inappropriate, if you allow contractors to dominate the process of building the houses and delivering the infrastructure, without proper Aboriginal eyes overseeing the process then we go through another historical regression... Building houses is needed but it how you build the inside of that house and the family that lives in that house. It is more about making sure that the house on the inside is a shelter indeed, not a shelter that's a temporary solution to a great social problem.
Aboriginal academic. (Australian Indigenous Doctors' Association et al. 2010)

References

Australian Indigenous Doctors' Association and the Centre for Health Equity Training, Research and Evaluation, University of New South Wales (2010) Health impact assessment of the northern territory emergency response. http://www.aida.org.au/viewpublications.aspx?id=3. Accessed 18 June 2013

Kansas Health Institute (2012) Potential health effects of casino development in southeast Kansas. http://www.healthimpactproject.org/resources/document/KHI_Southeast-Kansas-Casion_Complete_HIA_Report.pdf. Accessed 18 June 2013

North American HIA Practice Standards Working Group (2010) Minimum elements and practice standards for health impact assessment, version 2. http://hiasociety.org/documents/PracticeStandardsforHIAVersion2.pdf. Accessed 18 June 2013

San Francisco Department of Public Health (2011) A health impact assessment of California Assembly Bill 889: the California domestic work employee equality, fairness, and dignity act of 2011. http://www.sfphes.org/component/jdownloads/finish/33/78. Accessed 18 June 2013

State of Alaska HIA Program (2011) Technical guidance for health impact assessment (HIA) in Alaska. Alaska Department of Department of Health and Social Services, Anchorage

UCLA Health Impact Assessment Project (2004) Health impact assessment of Sacramento Safe Routes to School: logic framework. http://www.apho.org.uk/resource/item.aspx?RID=63905. Accessed 18 June 2013

UCLA Health Impact Assessment Project (year not stated) Stage 2:scoping. http://www.ph.ucla.edu/hs/health-impact/training/pdfs/HIAman07_s3_Scoping_txt.pdf. Accessed 18 June 2013

Chapter 10
Recommendations

Abstract This chapter discusses the fourth step of health impact assessment (HIA), development of recommendations for how to modify the project or policy under consideration. Recommendations represent a translation of findings from the assessment into actions that may improve the health of the affected population. The chapter begins with a discussion of several key success factors that may influence the extent to which recommendations are likely to be implemented. These are: recommendations should flow from the results of the assessment; they should be based on public health principles of harm avoidance; they should be evidence based; they should both mitigate harms and enhance health benefits; they should be specific and actionable; and they should be useable by those who must implement them. The text also discusses the various advantages and disadvantages of including decision makers in the development of recommendations, as well as possibilities and room for variation in styling the format of the recommendations section. The chapter concludes with examples of recommendations from four HIAs conducted on a diverse set of projects and policies, selected because they represent strong and effective recommendations demonstrating many of the key success factors described earlier.

Keywords Recommendations · Action · Health management plan · Public health principles · Harm avoidance · Mitigation · Enhancement

Recommendations are specific action items that describe how conditions should be amended in order to minimize the predicted adverse impacts of the proposed project or policy and to maximize potential benefits. The development of recommendations is a critical step of health impact assessment (HIA) because it provides an opportunity to translate the results of the assessment into actions that may improve the health of the affected population.

Developing appropriate recommendations can be tricky, because there is no single approach or standard "template" from which recommendations can be drawn. In order to be effective, recommendations must be individualized both to the proposed project or policy and to the local context. They must also take into account the priority health impacts identified in the assessment phase and the jurisdictional limits of different stakeholders, such as the project developer, the local health department, municipal agencies, etc.

The formulation of recommendations is a process that should involve not only the HIA team but also other key contributors. The steering committee can advise

C. L. Ross et al., *Health Impact Assessment in the United States,* 119
DOI 10.1007/978-1-4614-7303-9_10, © Springer Science+Business Media New York 2014

on how to make the recommendations acceptable to a variety of stakeholder groups and can suggest wording to make the recommendations politically feasible. External experts can provide technical information to make the recommendations line up with best practice and can contribute to solving complex technical problems. It is often highly useful to involve local stakeholders (such as community members or local key informants) to ensure that the recommendations both respond to local concerns and are likely to be acceptable and feasible in the particular community. There is sometimes a role for the decision maker in the formulation of recommendations; this is discussed later in the chapter.

Key Success Factors

There are several key success factors that increase the likelihood of the HIA recommendations being implemented. These are:

1. Recommendations should flow from the results of the assessment

The recommendations should address the health impacts identified or predicted in the assessment stage. In this way, the recommendations respond to a demonstrated need and have a strong rationale. More emphasis should be given to recommendations that address those health concerns identified in the assessment phase as a high priority.

2. Recommendations should be based on public health principles of harm avoidance

A key principle of public health practice is that it is more effective to prevent adverse health consequences than to treat problems after they arise (Public Health Leadership Society 2002). Similarly, the emphasis of recommendations should be on preventing or avoiding harm, rather than managing its consequences. This principle dovetails with the "mitigation hierarchy" used in environmental assessment and planning. The mitigation hierarchy states that the preferred order of addressing potential impacts is:

- To **avoid** the impact altogether
- To **minimize** the impact (through decreasing the duration, severity, extent, etc.)
- To **repair** the adverse consequences of impacts
- To **compensate** people for impacts that cannot be avoided or mitigated

(International Finance Corporation 2012)

3. Recommendations should be evidence based

Where possible, the recommendations should be based on evidence of efficacy—or evidence that the intervention has a proven effect—rather than the practitioner's best guess. For example, if the assessment identifies that pedestrian injury in a residential neighborhood is a risk, then the recommendations should rely on evidence that demonstrates the efficacy of recommended actions (for example, the proven impact of crosswalks or curb bulb-outs on pedestrian injuries). If the evidence base is not consulted, then the recommendations may be ineffective at avoiding or reducing harm and may divert resources from other, potentially more effective actions that could have been taken instead.

Evidence can be found in published literature from health or other disciplines, and a thorough literature search should be conducted focusing on meta-analyses or systematic reviews. It should be noted, however, that literature-based evidence is not available in all situations; unique attributes of the specific populations affected, the location, or the nature of the proposal under review may mean there is little published research to support the development of recommendations. In this case, evidence or information on the potential efficacy of proposed recommendations may need to come from other sources, such as subject area experts, local residents, or other key informants.

4. Recommendations should both mitigate harms and enhance health benefits

It is important to develop recommendations to avoid or minimize potential harmful impacts of the proposed project or policy. It is just as important for the HIA to make recommendations taking advantage of the opportunity to enhance health or generate health co-benefits from the project or policy.

5. Recommendations should be specific and actionable

To be maximally effective, recommendations should be specific about what is to be done and who is responsible. This may require including details about:

- The action that should be taken (e.g., *require pre-employment vaccinations for tetanus/diphtheria, measles, mumps, and rubella (MMR), hepatitis A, and hepatitis B*).
- The rationale for why it should be done (e.g., *these vaccinations have been strongly recommended by infection control specialists for workers living in a communal situation*).
- When and how often the action should be taken (e.g., *traffic incident reports should be reviewed every 3 months, starting with the onset of construction activities*).
- Who is responsible: the organization and if possible the specific personnel position (e.g., *the implementation of this recommendation is the responsibility of the Occupational Health & Safety team from Company X*).
- How the proposed action aligns with other planned commitments (e.g., *this recommendation aligns with Company X's current Emergency Response protocols for the project*).

6. Recommendations should be useable by those who must implement them

Not all HIA recommendations will be implemented by the same organization. Some recommendations may be appropriate for a project developer, while other recommendations may be more appropriately carried out by a local or regional health department, by a municipal agency or as a partnership. This may be the case even within a single HIA or in addressing a single issue. For example, in order to reduce the risk of pedestrian injury, action may be required by a project developer (relating to traffic routing and company driver behavior); by the municipal department in charge of roads (relating to traffic signaling or road infrastructure improvements); and by the local health department (relating to injury surveillance).

The organizations that will take up the recommendations have specific mandates, limits on their jurisdiction, and organizational practices. Recommendations are most likely to be taken up if they are framed in a way that works with these organizations' operational practices. For the government, this may mean crafting the recommendation using language that will easily fit into a particular legislative framework or that can be adopted as a statute, ordinance, regulation, or zoning requirement (Committee on Health Impact Assessment, National Research Council 2011). For a private organization, it may mean framing a recommendation in a way that fits with its template for business operations.

Involving Decision Makers

As noted at the start of the chapter, some HIAs have involved the decision makers—the people who will implement the recommendations—in the recommendation development process. Depending on the project/policy being examined, the decision maker could represent private industry or could comprise a municipality or other governmental authority. As with many other aspects of HIA, there are both advantages and disadvantages to involving the decision maker in the development of recommendations. Table 10.1 lists a number of these benefits and drawbacks. The greatest potential advantages arise out of the opportunity to put local stakeholders or community residents in direct contact with the decision maker. Not only does this enable the decision maker to hear concerns and suggestions first hand from community residents, but it can also sometimes result in decision makers publicly making commitments on the spot. The greatest potential drawbacks are that some stakeholders may be reticent to voice their opinions in the presence of certain decision makers; and that the HIA recommendations can appear to have been biased by external pressure. Both these drawbacks can be avoided—for example, by providing community stakeholders with additional private opportunities for input and by providing a detailed description of the HIA's methodology.

Format of Recommendations

As long as the content of the recommendations is clear, the format of the recommendation can be customized to suit the style of the HIA. Most HIA recommendations are embedded within the HIA itself, presented either as part of a specific health issue area (e.g., housing, infectious disease transmission, etc.) or as a separate chapter comprising recommendations that pertain to all health areas.

Table 10.1 Advantages and disadvantages of involving the decision maker in the development of recommendations

Advantages	Disadvantages
Recommendations are more likely to be realistic and feasible	Some stakeholders (in particular community residents) may be reticent to speak in the presence of a decision maker and this may stifle open discussion
May stimulate direct discussion between decision maker and residents/ key stakeholders	Potential for pressure on HIA practitioner to attenuate or eliminate some recommendations
Decision maker may become more invested in the recommendation or the commitment to mitigate health problems	Potential for the HIA recommendations to appear as biased or "bought," even if they are not
May provide an opportunity to secure commitments to action during the process	
May lead to specific and thorough information being included as part of the recommendation, as working with the decision maker enables HIA practitioners to better identify specifics around how to implement recommendations	
Development of recommendations may be better informed about mitigation activities that the decision maker is already planning. May result in recommendations that are better harmonized with those from other assessments or from other planned activities	

Some HIAs—particularly those conducted for industrial or resource development project proposals—result in the development of what is termed a "Health Action Plan." The Health Action Plan is a stand-alone document describing in detail what actions must be taken in order for the project to minimize health risks and meet regulatory requirements. For example, for projects funded by international lenders such as the International Finance Corporation, the development of a Health Action Plan is mandatory and the project proponent's compliance with the Health Action Plan is required for project funding to be issued. This requirement addresses one of the potential drawbacks of recommendations in HIA—the fact that they can be ignored. The external requirement for a Health Action Plan gives the HIA recommendations "teeth." Even when the development of a Health Action Plan is not a requirement, it can be advantageous for the HIA to include something similar, as it enhances the uptake and application of recommendations.

Finally, it should be noted that not all projects/policies assessed in an HIA are appropriate for the development of specific actionable recommendations. This is particularly true of HIAs conducted from within government on high-level or early-stage policy. Policy development is, obviously, a highly political process, in which the HIA may not have jurisdiction to suggest specific recommendations for change. In these cases, the HIA may be limited to (a) providing a declaration of whether to support or not support the policy from a health perspective or (b) recommending one of a number of limited policy alternatives.

Case studies

The following case studies provide excerpts from recommendations taken from four published HIAs conducted on a diverse set of projects and policies. These examples have been chosen because they represent strong and effective recommendations demonstrating many of the key success factors described above.

Title:	Oregon Farm to School Policy HIA	Case Study
Author:	Upstream Public Health	
Year:	2011	
Location:	Oregon	

Project/Policy Assessed by the HIA Oregon's 2011 Farm-to-School and School Garden legislation planned to reimburse schools for purchasing Oregon-produced, Oregon-processed, Oregon-packed, and Oregon-packaged foods and to provide grants to support school gardens, agriculture, and nutrition education.

Strengths of this Recommendation: The recommendation below is written in an easy-to-read style that is accessible to a non-health professional audience. It clearly describes the rationale behind the recommendation and how it links with health outcomes. It also articulates the specific actions that should be taken to amend the policy under consideration in order to meet health goals.

> We recommend amending HB 2800 to specify that while grants are open to all schools, Agriculture and Garden education grants will be preferentially given to schools serving: (1) a low-income student population, defined where 40% are eligible for free or reduced meals, or, (2) a racially diverse student population, defined as 20% or more non-white, or (3) rural or urban areas with limited food access, defined as 12% or more of residents are low-income and live more than 10 miles from a grocery store. We developed this policy amendment to ensure Oregon's most needy youth, including those in food insecure households, members of ethnic and racial groups bearing a disproportionate burden of obesity, and those living in areas of the state with limited garden programs are prioritized for receiving educational grants in HB 2800.

(Upstream Public Health 2011)

Title:	Rapid Health Impact Assessment of the Proposed Farmers Field Development	Case Study
Author:	Human Impact Partners with support from the Los Angeles Community Action Network, the Legal Aid Foundation of Los Angeles and Physicians for Social Responsibility Los Angeles, in conjunction with a panel of impacted residents	
Year:	2012	
Location:	Los Angeles, California	

Project/Policy Assessed by the HIA Anschutz Entertainment Group (AEG) proposed to build a new development project called Farmers Field in the South Park area of Los Angeles. The project would include the development of a new stadium and associated facilities and would require the demolition of several existing structures.

Sample Recommendation The recommendations were developed jointly by the HIA team and a panel of impacted residents and thus strongly reflected residents' concerns about gentrification, affordability, displacement, unemployment, and safety. The HIA stated that recommendations were intended to "mitigate the negative health impacts outlined [listed in the HIA report], without leading to additional adverse impacts. The panel and HIA Team believe that these recommendations are specific, actionable, able to be monitored, enforceable, technically and economically feasible and known to be effective." The recommendations also provided novel information that would not have been part of the proposed development project if the HIA had not been conducted. A sample of recommendations included the following:

> Because jobs and employment will be impacted by the Farmers Field development project:
> * AEG shall develop a local hiring agreement for jobs created as part of the Farmers Field development project. Local low-income residents should be hired into 30–35% of construction jobs, and 40–50% of permanent jobs (including both full and part-time permanent jobs). These percentages of locally hired employees shall remain a requirement as long as the stadium remains in operation. Priority for local hiring shall be given to the following residents:
>   - Low-income residents from zip codes in closest proximity to the proposed stadium development;
>   - Low-income residents from local zip codes with the highest rates of unemployment;
>   - Those residents, particularly low-income residents, who are directly displaced from their homes as a result of the proposed stadium development.
> In addition, qualifications for jobs created by the proposed stadium project shall relate directly to the job duties and responsibilities, and not include unrelated measures that tend to disqualify local residents (e.g., credit checks, arrest records). Hiring practices shall follow the strongest regulatory language that applies. Further, the local hiring agreement shall include a strong monitoring and enforcement plan that is implemented with funding from AEG, and involves local residents and stakeholders.
> * Jobs created by the Farmers Field development shall pay a living wage as determined by the strongest regulatory language, whether it be federal, state, or local (City of Los Angeles). In addition to paying a living wage, all permanent jobs (including part-time and full-time permanent jobs) created by the Farmers Field development shall provide full health benefits to employees.
> * AEG shall fund a program focused on training and hiring for jobs that are created as a result of the Farmers Field development. The program shall focus on populations facing the most serious barriers to employment including, but not limited to:
>   - Day laborers (particularly those workers from the Downtown Day Labor Center)
>   - Formerly incarcerated populations re-entering the workforce
>   - Single parents/heads of households
>   - Homeless residents AEG shall work with IDEPSCA (Instituto de Educacion Popular del Sur de California), LA CAN (Los Angeles Community Action Network), A New Way of Life and other similar organizations to develop this focused training/hiring program.

• Farmers Field development shall include a designated space and coordinated times for local micro-businesses, artisans, and social service organizations to vend their goods and provide direct service and outreach to the community, both on game days and non-game days. Areas available to vendors shall include space within the stadium complex, the parking area, and the green space created around the stadium. This space shall be provided at a low cost or free of cost to the above-mentioned entities. The space provided shall be at least as big as the current Gilbert Lindsey Park on the project site. Conditions for vendors and services to operate in this designated space shall be established in a way such that they do not limit local businesses and services from operating. In addition, AEG shall provide funding to develop a green business incubator to help 20–30 low-income, underrepresented local entrepreneurs from zip codes surrounding the proposed stadium, in helping to start local businesses.

(Human Impact Partners et al. 2012)

Title:	Draft Wishbone Hill Mine Draft Health Impact Assessment	Case Study
Author:	NewFields Companies	
Year:	2012	
Location:	Alaska	

Project/Policy Assessed by the HIA The contentious Wishbone Hill Mine is a proposed coal mine located near Sutton, in southern Alaska, in an area with extensive coal deposits and a history of coal mining.

Sample Recommendation The recommendation below, which focuses on mitigating the potential for traffic-related injury, provides specific information on actions that should be taken by the project proponent. These include further study, development of company protocols and policies, equipment modification, and the development of audit and monitoring programs.

Accidents and Injuries
The focus of this section is on Project-related road traffic related injuries, accidents, and transportation related releases of potentially hazardous materials outside the fence. In general, road travel and risk of transport accident events on Alaska roads is high, particularly during the winter.
General parameters of concern are as follows:
1. **Volume of large heavy-haul truck traffic introduced by the project**
2. **Proximity to local schools and school transport vehicles**
3. **The road and weather conditions (iv) Emergency response plans and protocols**
There are a large variety of potential accident scenarios and conditions that could occur with collateral impacts involving local communities, environmental effects, and/or infrastructure damage.
Mitigation Recommendations
• Conduct a transport safety study and risk analysis for the major road routes so that traffic volumes and road conditions are well understood. An emphasis on locations where Project transport logistics may intersect local populations is critical (i.e., schools, school bus pick-up locations, etc.).
• Develop and present a formal journey management process to key stakeholders.

- Develop and implement medical emergency response plans and drills for off-site accident, injuries, or hazardous materials release events. Coordinate and review emergency response plans with established local, state, and federal emergency response services.
- Require verification of driver safety training for all Project transportation contractors on an annual basis.
- Require installation of vehicle speed/location monitoring devices on offsite heavy-haul transport vehicles. Monitor results and implement corrective actions, as needed.
- Develop, implement, and conduct regularly scheduled drills regarding transportation related spill response plans. Include specific plan for community related activities (i.e., medical monitoring) for specific contaminant spills.
- Provide education programs to workers regarding the prevention of work and Project roadway related accidents.
- Consistently audit contractor vehicular maintenance programs and periodically assess vehicular activity data.
- Require all transportation contractors to implement random alcohol testing of all drivers. Audit records regularly.

(NewFields Companies 2012)

Title:	Health Impact Assessment on Policies Reducing Vehicle Miles Traveled in Oregon Metropolitan Areas	Case Study
Author:	Upstream Public Health & Oregon Health and Sciences University	
Year:	2009	
Location:	Oregon	

Project/Policy Assessed by the HIA This HIA analyzed the health impacts—including changes to air quality, physical activity, and car accident rates—that would be expected if car use were limited to meet state greenhouse gas emission reduction goals.

Sample Recommendation This HIA clearly and convincingly lays out the evidence behind the development of its recommendations. In addition, attention is paid to the ramifications of the recommendation itself on vulnerable subpopulations. This is particularly important because—as the HIA points out—the recommendation that is intended to result in the greatest health improvement across the broad population may have a detrimental effect on the poor that needs, itself, to be mitigated.

> Increasing the costs of individual driving is one proposed method of reducing VMT [vehicle miles travelled] in Oregon. While increasing the costs of driving may be necessary to maintain the existing transportation structures, the literature is not supportive that such changes reduce driving and benefit health. While congestion pricing has positive effects on traffic congestion, it has not been shown to alter the amount people drive, but rather encourages different departure times and routes. The gas tax has been shown to reduce deaths due to collisions and air pollution, although two studies have indicated a VMT tax has greater welfare benefits. The only policies that will be beneficial for health will be policies that induce mode shift away from individual vehicles. Studies examining the effect of employer parking fees indicated employees would shift from individual driving to public transit.
>
> Thus, the policy that would have the most positive benefits for the health of Oregonians is having businesses in metropolitan areas charge a fee for employee parking. However,

if some businesses do not have good public transit service, it may be necessary to develop a plan for increasing transit service to that area or provide exceptions. If a tax is necessary, such as a gas or VMT tax, it is important to ensure that the portion of income that is spent by low income people in the state on transportation does not rise by providing tax refunds or different pricing schemes for different income levels. Since these populations already face health disparities, the added cost of such taxes would further decrease their health by making it harder for them to pay for healthy housing, food and for medical care.

(Upstream Public Health et al. 2009)

References

Committee on Health Impact Assessment, National Research Council (2011) Improving health in the United States: the role of health impact assessment. The National Academies Press, Washington, DC

Human Impact Partners (2012) Rapid health impact assessment of the proposed Farmers Field development. http://www.humanimpact.org/component/jdownloads/finish/8/176/0. Accessed 18 June 2013

International Finance Corporation (2012) Overview of performance standards on environmental and social sustainability, effective Jan 1 2012. International Finance Corporation, Washington, DC

NewFields Companies (2012). Draft Wishbone Hill Mine health impact assessment. Alaska Department of Health and Social Services, Anchorage. http://www.epi.alaska.gov/hia/Wishbone-HillDraftHIA.pdf. Accessed 18 June 2013

Public Health Leadership Society (2002) Principles of the ethical practice of public health, version 2.2. American Public Health Association. http://www.apha.org/NR/rdonlyres/1CED3CEA-287E-4185-9CBD-BD405FC60856/0/ethicsbrochure.pdf. Accessed 18 June 2013

Upstream Public Health (2011) Oregon farm to school policy HIA. http://www.healthimpactproject.org/resources/document/Upstream-HIA-Oregon-Farm-to-School-policy.pdf. Accessed 18 June 2013

Upstream Public Health & Oregon Health and Sciences University (2009) Health impact assessment on policies reducing vehicle miles traveled in Oregon metropolitan areas. http://www.upstreampublichealth.org/sites/default/files/HIA%20VMT%20Reduction.pdf. Accessed 18 June 2013

Chapter 11
Reporting and Dissemination

Abstract This chapter discusses the reporting and dissemination components of health impact assessment (HIA). The chapter first outlines the need to tailor information for different audiences and identifies pros and cons of different report formats including a formal report, executive summary, community report, briefing report, and inclusion in an environmental impact assessment. The chapter then discusses approaches to disseminating the results and reviews guiding principles for effective HIA reporting and dissemination. The "who, what, how, and when" of HIA dissemination is determined by an array of factors including regulatory requirements, the audience, the purpose for sharing the HIA results, and local protocols, modes, and language. These sections are summarized in nine guiding principles for HIA reporting and dissemination. Three case studies conclude the chapter by highlighting aspects of reporting and dissemination that have proven important in real-world applications. The first examines a professional communications strategy. The second looks at the mixed results of new technology. The third and final case study looks at reporting as an iterative, rather than a static, process.

Keywords Reporting · Dissemination · Communication · Formal report · Executive summary · Community report · Briefing report · Clarity · Iterative process

Once a health impact assessment (HIA) is complete, its results are transmitted, most often in the form of a written report, to a variety of different audiences. Recipients include the decision makers who will be supporting the policy, program, or project; stakeholders and special interest groups who may be impacted by the project; individuals who participated in conducting the HIA; and others such as the media, the HIA practitioner's home organization, local or regional public health authorities, etc. Reporting can be tricky; these groups often have different expectations about the degree of detail that should be included in the narrative, the ways in which the information is packaged, the amount of time made available to review it, the venues through which the findings are disseminated, and cultural or organizational protocols around the sequence and timing of dissemination.

HIAs have been documented in a variety of report formats and are beginning to take the shape of more graphic formats as necessitated by the audience or for more effective communication. Whatever the final form, the HIA's results must be

C. L. Ross et al., *Health Impact Assessment in the United States,* 129
DOI 10.1007/978-1-4614-7303-9_11, © Springer Science+Business Media New York 2014

presented in a transparent and unbiased manner. The information needs to clearly build from one section to the next in a logical fashion, with relevant support materials including figures, charts, and appendices. It also needs to present the full set of concerns and evidence addressing the specified questions. Note that the results of an HIA can be used by various groups for advocacy purposes; however, the HIA report should not itself be an advocacy document that highlights certain results while burying others.

Written Reports

Typically, HIAs result in the production of one or more types of written report. These may take one of several forms:

- **Formal report:** A formal HIA report documents the assessment's methodology and findings. These reports are often 25–150 pages in length and are intended to comprehensively detail all relevant aspects of the HIA such that it can withstand scrutiny (see Box 11.1).
  - Pro: The formal report allows for complete reporting and transparent documentation of the HIA's process and results.
  - Con: The formal report's lengthiness and detailed format may be inappropriate for a general audience.

Box 11.1   Typical table of contents for a formal HIA report

Executive Summary
Introduction

> The introduction should include a definition of health and also the rationale for conducting the HIA.

Description of Project/Policy Being Assessed
Community Profile/Baseline
Policy Context

> The policy context should describe health-related legislation, policy, and regulations affecting how the project/policy must be implemented (e.g., relevant noise or waste ordinances).

HIA Methodology

> Among other elements, the HIA methodology should describe the definition and purpose of HIA, the HIA project team, the analysis methods used, and the manner in which stakeholders were engaged.

Scope of Health Issues to be Assessed

This section should describe the results of scoping, including which health issues will be included in the assessment and which health issues were considered, but discarded.

Assessment Results/Impacts

The assessment results can be organized in many different ways: around project/ policy components, around determinants of health, or around health outcomes. However, the reporting of the assessment should include a description of impact pathways (such as a logic framework), a description of the predicted changes to health and health determinants and a characterization of the probable extent of effects.

Recommendations for Mitigation and Enhancement
Conclusions/Summary of Key Findings
References

- **Executive summary:** An executive summary of the HIA (2–10 pages) is often included at the beginning of a formal report or can act as a stand-alone document. It succinctly describes the HIA for readers who do not have the time or interest to read the entire formal report. It often follows the same structure as that report and includes a summary of the methodology, scoping results, assessment results, recommendations, and conclusions.
  - Pro: The executive summary provides readers with an abbreviated version of the HIA, with emphasis placed on results, impacts, and recommendations.
  - Cons: The executive summary may be too brief for the audience to fully comprehend the HIA or to be convinced of the significance of its findings. The executive summary is also often formulated from the writer's point of view, rather than framing the issues around questions that are important to stakeholders.
- **Community report:** Community reports are intended to present results to a particular stakeholder group, usually residents of the affected community. Community reports often make a particular attempt to avoid jargon and technical language and to present the HIA's findings in a way that is relevant to the specified stakeholder group.
  - Pro: The community report's language, length, and layout are customized for a lay audience and the content focuses on the areas of greatest relevance to the community.
  - Con: The community report is unlikely to meet the needs of all "community" audiences, meaning multiple versions may be required.
- **Briefing report:** A briefing report provides a two- to four-page summary of the HIA in a visually appealing format. It is intended to stimulate the reader's interest to find out more through one of the longer formats or as otherwise directed. The briefing report quickly moves the reader from the background of the general

topic and its relevance in the specific HIA concern and context to a summary of the predicted health impacts and key recommendations.

- Pro: The briefing report is useful for motivating the audience to action.
- Con: The briefing report is an incomplete document and requires additional review of other materials in order to offer the reader a thorough understanding of the HIA's implications.

- **Environmental impact assessment:** HIAs conducted as part of an environmental impact assessment (EIA)/environmental impact statement (EIS) are generally included as subchapters within that EIA (see Chap. 3 for more information on EIAs, social impact assessments (SIAs), and other impact assessments). The format and approach of the HIA are usually highly constrained by the overall EIA's approach and by the regulatory or legal requirements of what the EIA needs to do or provide. EIA reports are generally voluminous, often thousands of pages long.
  - Pro: The HIA becomes part of the public record and decision-making process and as part of the EIA it may become legally enforceable.
  - Con: The HIA can get "lost" in the large amount of material present in a typical EIA; the HIA might not be able to organize itself in a way that is most meaningful either to the involved audiences or to the way in which the health "story" is told.

Dissemination

HIA reporting requires a clear plan for communicating the findings and recommendations to the various stakeholders. Regulatory requirements, the audience, the purpose for sharing the HIA results, and local protocols will determine the "who, what, how, and when" of HIA dissemination:

- *Regulatory requirements:* There may be requirements for how the HIA results must be submitted if they are to be considered as part of an official regulatory decision-making process.
- *Audience:* Recipients of the HIA's findings may include decision makers who have control over the policy, program, or project; stakeholder and special interest groups who may be impacted; individuals who participated in the HIA; and others such as the media, the HIA practitioner's home organization, and local or regional public health authorities.
- *Purpose:* Dissemination of results requires consideration of the primary objectives in doing so. It can be useful if these objectives are spelled out as specific, measureable, achievable, results-centered, and time-bound—*S.M.A.R.T.* (CDC 2008).
- *Local protocols:* Thought should be put into which decision-makers or stakeholders need to receive the first report, and how public the delivery should be.
- *Modes:* Practitioners can use a variety of methods to disseminate the findings. The standard approach is to distribute the various report formats as hard copies and electronic versions, to hold a press conference, and/or to make public

presentations of the results before a variety of audiences. Additional approaches that may broaden the reports' impact include sending summary letters and fact sheets on the HIA or specific health topic to decision-makers deliberating on the project.

- *Language:* Translating the reports into relevant languages (aside from English) is another dimension of effectively disseminating results. Translation is especially important when working in or with a community that has many non-English speakers or low levels of literacy. To address general literacy concerns, findings could be translated into pictures, thereby enabling the audience, regardless of literacy level, to read, evaluate, and interpret the results for themselves. Some cultures prefer to receive information orally rather than in written form; this should also be considered.

Guiding Principles for HIA Reporting and Dissemination

In order to make written reports as effective and communicative as possible, there are several general principles to remember:

1. Use simple, clear language, and avoid technical jargon wherever possible.
2. Present the most important information first; it cannot be assumed that the reader will get through the entire document.[1]
3. Connect the HIA findings to the interests of the audience.
4. Write into the HIA's recommendations clear action steps.
5. Emphasize the significance of the health benefits embodied in the recommendations.
6. Encourage the client, media, and stakeholders to share the results with their own networks by making the various report products available to them for distribution.
7. Involve stakeholders in co-presenting findings.
8. Translate reports into other languages as appropriate.
9. Use visual aids as another way to translate results and to quickly and effectively communicate health implications.

---

[1] One example of a format used to put important information first is the 1:3:25 structure developed by the Canadian Health Services Research Foundation (CHSRF 2001). The term "1:3:25" refers to the number of pages in each section of the report—one page that presents bulleted main messages of the report, followed by a 3-page executive summary and a 25-page technical report. The one-pager is key. It is not a summary of all the methods or findings; rather, it is the lessons decision-makers should take away from the research. As the CHSRF states: "This is your chance, based on your research, to tell decision-makers what implications your work has for theirs." In the case of an HIA, these are likely to be the recommendations, as they comprise the most valuable take-away information for decision-makers about the HIA (Harris et al. 2007).

Case Studies

Title:	HIA of the California Healthy Families, Healthy Workplace Act	
Author:	Human Impact Partners	
Year:	2008	
Location:	California	

A professional communications strategy Human Impact Partners, a nonprofit agency based in Oakland, California, notes that a key factor in successful HIA reporting is having a well-thought-out communications strategy. "Having the report itself only gets you so far. In order to really make a difference with HIAs you need a larger communications plan with the partners that have worked on the HIA." An effective communications strategy involves strong stakeholder engagement; a strategically framed key message; and materials and channels appropriate to the various audiences you are trying to reach. Conversely, breakdowns in the communications strategy, either due to lacking a good communications plan or to unengaged partners, limits an HIA's potential reach and impact.

Human Impact Partners learned this key lesson in July 2008 when they completed an HIA on the *California Healthy Families, Healthy Workplace Act,* a piece of legislation that would guarantee workers in California access to paid sick days. Presently in the USA, about 40% of workers do not have paid sick days; these workers are predominantly low-income employees, with many working within the food and restaurant industries. A key finding coming of this HIA was that allowing sick workers on the job could potentially lead to the spread of communicable diseases via the food preparation and distribution chain. In that way, Human Impact Partners explains, "It isn't just about workers, it affects all of us. Paid sick days, and allowing sick workers to have paid time off if they are ill, would benefit all of California."

To get their message out, Human Impact Partners turned to communications professionals. With the help of communication experts, Human Impact Partners developed a glossy four-pager and sent out a press release on their HIA findings and key message to media channels. The results were positive. Spanish-language television, National Public Radio (NPR), a number of local newspapers (*San Francisco Chronicle, Orange County Register*), and online magazines and blogs all picked up the story. The relevance of the health perspective was recognized in what was formerly seen as just a "jobs issue." This case example illustrates the significant impact an HIA can make when practitioners employ communications professionals to help them with their messaging. The unique approach of this communications strategy proved very effective in conveying the HIA's findings to the right people within the right framing (Human Impact Partners 2008).

Title:	HIA of a gold mine	
Author:	Environmental Resources Management	Case Study
Year:	2012	
Location:	Southwest USA	

The mixed results of new technology: Environmental Resources Management (ERM), a global provider of environmental, health, risk, and social consulting services, learned that the type of technology that you use in communicating your HIA's results to stakeholders can affect the success of reporting. While new technologies can be a powerful way to deliver information and spur discussion around HIA, they need to be carefully thought out and thoroughly planned to ensure stakeholder participation. As not all groups are likely to be equal adopters of new information technologies, the success of these approaches could be compromised as a result.

ERM learned this important lesson in January 2012 while conducting an HIA on a gold mine project in the Southwest USA. ERM produced a preliminary HIA report outlining some of the chief impacts and early recommendations from key stakeholders. To gather additional input, the firm then shared these findings with the gold mining company (internal project stakeholders) and external community stakeholders (businesses, health facilities, utilities, city officials, etc.) at two separate points in time. As a first round of meetings, ERM held face-to-face workshops with the external community stakeholders (which included a public health and safety subgroup). Unfortunately, and rather unpredictably, a massive storm occurred during the workshop. Because of this weather emergency, the public health and safety subgroup was unable to attend. For the second round of meetings, in order to accommodate budget limitations, ERM thus held a WebEx presentation to present their preliminary findings to the internal project stakeholders and to provide another opportunity for the public health and safety subgroup to weigh in. (WebEx is a communications technology similar to teleconferencing that allows participants in different locations to use their web browsers to view a live video and oral presentation.)

The success of the WebEx meeting was mixed. Of project personnel from the company, who were experienced in this mode of communication and able to gather into one conference room, attendance was high and the meeting was productive. For the public health and safety subgroup (approximately five individuals), the outcome was not as successful: Attendance was zero. "We did not identify the reasons for the lack of attendance—potentially technical issues or schedule conflicts or lack of reminders," describes ERM. In retrospect, noted ERM, a number of measures should have been taken in order to enhance attendance for the WebEx meeting, such as checking to make sure that the public health and safety subgroup had the capabilities for WebEx participation; confirming the participation of individuals prior to the meeting; sending out a reminder of the meeting 1 day in advance; and holding the meeting at a time that would not conflict with participants' work commitments. ERM notes, however, that the public health and safety stakeholders were less likely than other stakeholders to have the necessary flexibility in their work schedules. As a third attempt to inform the public health and safety stakeholders and to provide an opportunity for their input on the preliminary findings, ERM e-mailed them the draft report and a contact to send their comments to. This case illustrates that successful HIA reporting is inclusive reporting; new technology requires some special considerations.

Title:	Oregon Farm to School Policy HIA
Author:	Upstream Public Health
Year:	2011
Location:	Oregon

Case Study

Reporting as an iterative process: One key to successful HIA reporting may be in adopting a fresh approach. "I don't think about reporting at the end of an HIA," says an HIA practitioner from Upstream Public Health, a nonprofit organization researching and identifying innovative ways to improve the public's health in Oregon. "I think about HIA reporting at every stage I am at."

Upstream vigorously applied this iterative philosophy of reporting at every stage of the HIA in 2011, when they conducted an assessment on Oregon's *Farm to School and School Garden Policy*. The *Farm to School and School Garden Policy* would guarantee that schools could purchase Oregon-produced, -processed, -packed, and -packaged foods inexpensively. The policy would also provide funds to support agriculture and nutrition education, as well as school gardens for students.

While the HIA was being conducted, Upstream undertook several activities to "ground-truth" the results and recommendations that were coming out of the process. Upstream held a public forum to gain feedback on the draft HIA. "We asked the public to tell us: you saw what we figured out, you saw why, now what do you think? Are we missing something completely? Is there somewhere else to go?" Upstream also worked with policy- and decision-makers during the recommendations phase. "The type of recommendations at the state or federal level might be very general and have to be revised a couple of times to try to get the best possible health benefit for specific communities. You have to draft and redraft."

These kinds of interactive reporting activities helped participants and the public understand why Upstream was doing the HIA and how they reached the conclusions that they did, so when the final report emerged, "it wasn't coming out of nowhere" (Upstream Public Health 2011).

References

CDC Division for Heart Disease and Stroke Prevention (2008) State program evaluation guides: writing SMART objectives. Department of Health and Human Services, Centers for Disease Control and Prevention. Atlanta

CHSRF (2001) Communication notes: reader-friendly writing 1:3:25. Canadian Health Services Research Foundation. Ottawa

Harris P, Harris-Roxas B, Harris E, Kemp L (2007) Health impact assessment: a practical guide. Centre for health equity training research and evaluation, University of New South Wales. Sydney

Human Impact Partners (2008) A health impact assessment of the California Healthy Families, Healthy Workplaces Act of 2008. http://www.humanimpact.org/doc-lib/finish/5/72. Accessed 18 June 2013

Upstream Public Health (2011) Oregon farm to school policy HIA. http://www.healthimpactproject.org/resources/document/Upstream-HIA-Oregon-Farm-to-School-policy.pdf. Accessed 18 June 2013

Chapter 12
Evaluation

Abstract This chapter provides an overview of health impact assessment (HIA) evaluation. While not all HIAs include an evaluation component, this practice helps advance the evidence base on the value of HIA, provides guidance for improvement in the conduct of future HIAs, and demonstrates accountability of the HIA practitioners to funders and stakeholders. The chapter describes the purpose, methods, and results of the evaluation step in HIA. Formative and summative HIA evaluations are described, which differ based on when feedback is given to the HIA preparer and their team. The three primary HIA evaluation types are also discussed: process evaluations (evaluating how the HIA was conducted), impact evaluations (evaluating the immediate impact of HIA on decision makers), and outcome evaluations (evaluating long-term impact on health outcomes). The chapter then offers a detailed outline of HIA evaluation research questions and potentially useful data sources. The chapter concludes with two HIA case studies that highlight the format and results of evaluations.

Keywords Evaluation · Resource constraints · Summative evaluation · Formative evaluation · Process evaluation · Impact evaluation · Outcome evaluation · SMART

Evaluation is the primary method for determining if a policy, program, or project has been effective in achieving its stated aims and objectives. Evaluations help an organization or agency to determine the value and effectiveness of its activities and aid in the identification of improvements and changes. In the context of health impact assessment (HIA), evaluation comprises a review of the HIA process; the impact that the HIA had on different audiences, such as decision makers, other stakeholders, and the organization that commissioned the HIA; and the effect on health outcomes.

The use of evaluation in HIA has been widely advocated as a part of good practice (Kemm 2012; Harris-Roxas and Harris 2013). Evaluation can demonstrate the value of HIA to the planning process by showing what the HIA achieved (Quigley and Taylor 2003). This ties in closely to the need for accountability and justifying the use of resources in an HIA (Ali 2009). Also self-reflection and learning inherent in evaluation has the potential to improve HIA practice, not just for the practitioners or organization that conducted the HIA but also among the wider HIA community if the evaluation results are disseminated.

C. L. Ross et al., *Health Impact Assessment in the United States,*
DOI 10.1007/978-1-4614-7303-9_12, © Springer Science+Business Media New York 2014

However, in practice, evaluation has rarely been conducted and few published examples of HIA evaluations are in the public domain either in the USA or internationally. As noted by Taylor et al. (2003) "there is currently no review-level evidence available to demonstrate if and how the HIA approach informs the decision-making process and, in particular, if it improves health and reduces health inequalities." Without an evidence base of evaluations, it becomes difficult to determine the effectiveness of HIA (Quigley and Taylor 2004; Harris-Roxas and Harris 2013).

Evaluation in HIA remains sparsely developed for a number of reasons. Primary among these is resource constraints. Many organizations struggle to amass the necessary resources (in terms of both financial and personnel) that are required to conduct an HIA and are reluctant to commit the further resources needed for evaluation. Other hurdles to conducting HIA evaluations include:

- Limited skills in evaluation
- Confusion between research, monitoring, and evaluation
- Limited funding and valuation from funders to conduct HIA evaluations
- The time-limited nature of the HIA process restricts the time available for evaluation
- Lack of consensus on what to evaluate (process, impact, or outcome—see below)

Evaluation Approach

Evaluation is a distinct discipline with its own methods and professionals who specialize in this area. It is possible to commission an external expert to conduct the HIA evaluation. This provides a number of advantages including high evaluation quality and impartiality in presenting findings and recommendations. However, this route can be expensive and may further constrain the number of evaluations completed. It is also possible to have a subset of the HIA team complete the evaluation, even if they are not trained evaluators (Quigley and Taylor 2004). It can also be useful to have other HIA stakeholders involved throughout the evaluation process.

The evaluation process should be guided by an evaluation plan that clearly identifies goals and objectives, the analytical approach, and the overall framework for conducting the evaluation. It is important to establish these parameters as early as possible—even before embarking on the HIA if possible. The plan should include the following information:

- The roles and responsibilities of stakeholders and all team members in the evaluation
- The purpose of the evaluation based on the aims and objectives of the HIA
- The costs, benefits, and resources required to implement the evaluation plan
- The research questions to be answered
- Whether a logic model would be helpful
- The indicators, research methods, and tools to be used to conduct the evaluation
- The identification of required data and how they will be collected

- The timeline for data collection and who will collect them
- The strategy for disseminating the evaluation plan with stakeholders, team members, and decision makers and the ongoing communication strategy

While evaluation is listed as the sixth step in the HIA process, an evaluation does not have to start after the first five steps are completed. It is also possible to initiate an evaluation process that runs concurrently with the earlier steps of the HIA. The timing of feedback from the evaluation describes the critical distinction between summative and formative evaluations. Summative evaluations generally take place at the end of the HIA process and focus on summarizing the program's impact, outcomes, and effectiveness. Formative evaluations are intended to inform the HIA process and to provide ongoing feedback that will maximize the likelihood of the HIA's success in the end. A formative evaluation would emphasize process, needs assessments, implementation, and structure of the program (Ali 2009).

Evaluation follows a structured approach that is in many ways parallel to the steps of the entire HIA, as shown in Fig. 12.1. The approach starts with the a priori identification of objectives and resources, the development of relevant research questions and indicators, the collection of data, the assessment of data, and the reporting and dissemination of the evaluation results.

There are several distinct types of evaluations including process, impact, and outcome. These evaluation types, described below, are applicable to the evaluation of HIAs. Each answers a different set of questions, and which is used depends on the kind of activity being evaluated and the aims and objectives of the evaluation.

Process evaluation, as implied in the name, focuses on the procedural elements of the HIA. Process evaluation assesses the effectiveness of how the HIA was designed and undertaken, including preparation, research, reporting, participation, and follow-up. Process evaluations focus on lessons that can assist future HIA processes and are intended to instruct HIA practitioners and stakeholders as to why an HIA is successful or not (Taylor 2003). Process evaluations take the shortest amount of time and require the fewest resources to complete.

Impact evaluation assesses the impact of the HIA on decision makers and other stakeholders. Impact evaluation assesses the extent to which the aims and objectives of the HIA were achieved and the extent to which the HIA recommendations were accepted and implemented (Taylor 2003). Impact evaluation provides lessons on ways to improve the success of communicating the HIA results and increasing the uptake of HIA recommendations by decision makers and others (Ross et al. 2012; Dannenberg et al. 2006).

Outcome evaluation assesses the accuracy of the HIA predictions about changes in population health that resulted from the project or policy. Outcome evaluation, while perhaps the most interesting, is also the most conceptually difficult and often impossible to achieve for several reasons. The first is that human health is affected by a wide range of factors, and teasing out which factors are responsible for any observed changes (i.e., the process or policy examined by the HIA vs. other environmental or societal influences) can be extremely difficult. The second is that if HIA recommendations are implemented and health detriments are avoided as a result, there may be no health changes to observe in relation to the HIA's original

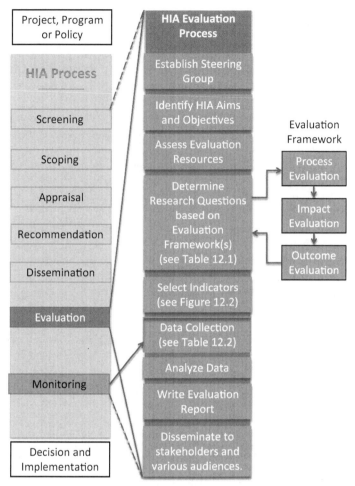

Fig. 12.1 Conceptual model for HIA evaluation. (Adapted from Taylor et al. 2003; Quigley and Taylor 2004)

predictions (Quigley and Taylor 2004). For these reasons, as well as the length of time and amount of health data required, outcome evaluations are rarely attempted.

Table 12.1 lists a number of research questions that can be used for process and impact evaluations.

Well-written research questions identify a distinct dimension of the HIA process, impact, or outcome, and do so in a way that the quality of the HIA process, impact, or outcome can be credibly assessed. Research questions should be specific, measurable, attainable, relevant, and time bound (SMART), as mentioned in Chap. 11 (CDC 2008).

Specific—when was the population served or impacted
Measureable—quantifiable or qualitative
Attainable—narrowed appropriately
Relevant—tied to program aims and objectives
Time bound—specify the time frame for measurement

Table 12.1 Suggested research questions for process and impact evaluations. (Taylor et al. 2003)
Suggested questions for evaluation

Process evaluation can provide lessons about why and how the HIA worked, including:	Impact evaluation can consider whether, and how well, the HIA worked, including:
• How was the HIA undertaken—including details of time, place, geographic area/population group affected by the proposal, what the proposal sought to achieve, and the methods used?	• How and when were the recommendations accepted and implemented by the decision makers—and what factors contributed to this?
• What resources (financial, human, time) were used, and what was the associated opportunity cost?	• What are the likely reasons why recommendations were rejected?
• What evidence was used, and how did it inform the development of recommendations?	• Were the aims and objectives of the HIA met?
• How were health inequalities assessed?	• What other impacts were associated with the HIA? For example, improved partnership working, or raising the profile of local health needs and putting health on partner agencies' agendas, or organizational development and new ways of working within and across the organizations involved
• How were recommendations formulated and prioritized (what factors influenced this decision-making process)?	
• How were the decision makers involved and engaged in the process, what were their expectations, and were they fulfilled with the limited resources available?	
• How and when were the recommendations delivered to the relevant decision makers?	
• What did those involved in the HIA think about the process used?	

Indicators and Data Collection

Data are one of the most important dimensions of HIA evaluation, and evaluation usually relies primarily on qualitative sources, with the addition of some quantitative data. A set of indicators are identified that parallel the focus of the evaluation type selected. Process evaluation indicators comprise process-related items such as whether stakeholders were identified and involved at key stages of the HIA process; whether meeting minutes or notes were circulated; and whether sufficient personnel and other resources were available. Impact evaluation indicators consist of items such as whether partnerships were effective throughout the HIA process; if health issues became more prominent on the local agenda; or if decision makers considered recommendations from the HIA. Outcome evaluation indicators focus more closely on population health datapoints and indicators related to the social determinants of health. Figure 12.2 suggests a number of indicators that could be used for process, impact, outcome evaluations.

A variety of data sources can be used to draw out data related to the chosen indicators. Some of the data would have been generated during the course of the HIA (for example, contact logs or meeting minutes) while other information needs to be gathered through interviews or focus groups with the HIA team, the organization that commissioned the HIA, the decision makers who received the results, or other stakeholders. Table 12.2 presents a list of qualitative and quantitative data sources that can be used at this stage.

Process indicators
• Identifying key stakeholders and involving them at key stages throughout the process.
• The setting up of a reference or steering group to carry out/oversee the work.
• Time spent by individuals on specific stages of the process.
• Minutes of all meetings circulated to stakeholders.
• Evidence of identification of best available evidence and how it was collated.
• Involvement of community in the process; who, how often, and community perceptions of being involved.
• Staff available for the HIA; experience, training required, turnover.
• Assessment of timescales being met; if not, why not?
• Recommendations delivered to decision makers in appropriate format at the appropriate time

Impact indicators
• Evidence of effective partnership working.
• Community development, e.g. local representatives developed, community organizations supported, empowerment of local people, skills and confidence developed.
• Health issues more prominent on local agenda.
• Improved knowledge of the causes of ill health (social model of health) by non-health participants.
• Decision makers considered recommendations from HIA.
• Recommendations (which ones) adopted by decision makers and changes made in the proposal.
• Changes in proposal were implemented (may require longer term monitoring).

Outcome indicators
Health, social, educational, and employment improvements in the local populations, such as:
• Improvements in quality of life, sense of wellbeing, sense of security.
• Increased advice and support services, welfare provisions, childcare services, daycare and take up.
• Provision of and involvement in education and training.
• Improved housing quality, access to affordable housing, accessible housing for people with disability.
• Improved satisfaction with healthcare services, access to a range of services and appropriate use.
• Reduced levels of accidents, crime, stress, truancy and social exclusion.
• Reduced levels of asthma, depression, falls, drug and alcohol misuse, smoking and admissions to hospital.
• Improvements in physical activity, nutrition, social activity and sexual health.
• Reduced disparity between different sections of the population for outcome indicators—reducing inequalities.

Fig. 12.2   HIA evaluation indicators. (Quigley and Taylor 2004)

Table 12.2 Data sources for HIA evaluation. (Adapted from Quigley and Taylor 2004)

Qualitative data	Quantitative data
Monitoring data from the HIA	Monitoring data from the HIA
Individual interviews	Questionnaires and surveys
Focus groups	Secondary data
Reports, meetings minutes, handouts, and plans	Meeting attendance sheets
Diaries/log books	
Participant observation	
Photos/videos	
Questionnaires and surveys	
Case studies	
Media (newspaper articles, blogs, etc.)	

As with all other steps in the HIA process, data gathering for the purposes of evaluation must be done in an ethical manner that ensures confidentiality of participants' responses and makes clear how information will be collected, stored, used, and published (Quigley and Taylor 2004).

Evaluation Reporting

The results of the evaluation should be presented in a report that clearly describes the methods used for the evaluation, the results that were found, and any recommendations that are made by the evaluation team as a result. The report can be highly detailed and formal or it can be informative yet brief. The purpose remains the same: to provide evidence of effectiveness (or the lack thereof) of the HIA and to provide feedback that will guide the conduct of future HIAs. No matter what format or method is used, the evaluation report should be transparent and unbiased.

Finally, the dissemination of the evaluation results is an important aspect to consider at the start of the evaluation process. There are many audiences that may be interested in the results, for different reasons. These include people who contributed information to the evaluation, the HIA funders, people and groups who are stakeholders in the policy/project or in the HIA process, the HIA team as well as HIA practitioners in general.

Lessons Learned in HIA Evaluation

Although evaluation may seem like an onerous or complex task, it should be remembered that the intention is to improve HIA practice and promote the use of effective HIA. As such, even a small-scale evaluation using only minimal resources and time can be more helpful than nothing at all.

Some high-level lessons to remember about evaluation, adapted from Taylor et al. (2003), are as follows:

- Evaluation can provide information to improve HIA practice.
- It can help establish support for HIA by showing that it has improved decision making and that better quality decisions have resulted.
- It can help establish accountability by tracking how recommendations were received and acted on by decision makers, funders, stakeholders, and community representatives.
- Consideration of the evaluation process should start at the beginning of the HIA in order to ensure that it is completed.
- A separate evaluation budget may need to be established in order to secure sufficient resources.
- Utilizing the perspectives of different stakeholders can enrich the evaluation but may also pose challenges especially in communicating conclusions.

Case Studies

Title:	Evaluation of Health Impact Assessment: Clark County Bicycle and Pedestrian Master Plan	Case Study
Author:	Clark County Public Health	
Year:	2011	
Location:	Washington	

In May of 2010, Clark County Public Health (CCPH) issued a rapid HIA on the Clark County Bicycle and Pedestrian Master Plan. The evaluation looked at the role of the HIA in the development and adoption of the Clark County Bicycle and Pedestrian Master Plan, which was adopted in November 2010. As described in the evaluation report:

> To understand the way information from the HIA was used in the decision making process, CCPH staff conducted a series of interviews with those involved in the planning and decision-making process. Drawing from a list of 23 county staff, committee members, and elected officials, CCPH staff interviewed seven committee members and all three county commissioners about their experience with engaging health issues during their decision making process. County commissioners made the final adoption decision, but committee members formed the plan in its early stages and were responsible for the fundamental elements and final proposals.

The evaluation report presented key themes from the interviews, several of which are reproduced below.

Health information was useful and influenced the plan.
Several informants mentioned that while health information was useful, the HIA may not be the only way to get it across. Maps were mentioned as a particularly useful way to visualize disparities.

The HIA broadened perspectives and increased understanding of the consequences of policy decisions.
An overwhelming message from the interviews is that having health data available helped to broaden the perspective of those involved and prompted them to consider the impacts of their decisions from many angles.

The HIA reframed the scope of the plan.
Some informants commented that the HIA helped change the focus of the plan from one that dealt mostly with recreational cycling for current users to one that emphasizes active transportation for future users.

The HIA served as a communication tool and rationale for the plan.
Decision makers were able to use information from the HIA to communicate about the plan with each other and with the public. Health information was sometimes used to promote the plan, sometimes as a rationale, and on a few occasions was cited in defense of the plan.

The HIA exposed equity issues that were not brought up elsewhere.
Informants reported that in the absence of the HIA, equity would not have otherwise been considered, at least not to the same extent as it was. Some suggested that equity concerns would not have been incorporated into the prioritization criteria if there had been no HIA.

Public health was seen as highly credible, and stakeholders' view of public health changed as a result of the process.
There were several stories of committee members realizing what public health can contribute to a planning process, and the information provided by public health was seen as high quality and trustworthy.

The evaluation report also documented the extent to which the recommendations of the HIA were incorporated into the final Master Plan. Each recommendation in the HIA was analyzed to determine the extent to which it had been adopted: not adopted, partially adopted, or fully adopted. An example of this evaluation follows:

Recommendation 1: Include low-speed roadway designs as bicycle and pedestrian projects.
Finding: Partially adopted

The plan addresses this recommendation through policy 6.2, "Include low-speed roadway designs as bicycle and pedestrian projects". While the verbatim integration of the HIA recommendation as a policy is certainly a positive affirmation of the recommendation, the proposed projects do not include traffic calming, bicycle boulevards, shared lane markings, narrow roadways, or any other features that would be indicative of low-speed roadway designs. (Clark County Public Health 2011)

Title:	**Choice Neighborhood Initiative Albany, Georgia: Rapid to Intermediate Health Impact Assessment**	Case Study
	Second Street Redevelopment Macon, Georgia: Rapid to Intermediate Health Impact Assessment	
Author:	Center for Quality Growth and Regional Development	
Year:	2013	
Location:	Georgia	

In July 2012, the Center for Quality Growth and Regional Development (CQGRD) completed rapid-to-intermediate HIAs for two redevelopment projects in the cities of Albany and Macon, Georgia. The evaluation assessed the effectiveness of the tasks undertaken in the HIA process and the impact of the two HIAs on decision making. As described in the evaluation report:

> The focus of this process evaluation is to review the tasks that were undertaken with regards to the completion of the HIAs, and to determine if those objectives included met. The evaluation also assesses the impact of the HIA recommendations once the documents were delivered to decision makers. The report examines the process of presenting HIA recommendations to decision makers, reaction to the HIA, impact of HIA on Plans, and related aspects of the HIA process.

The evaluation report assessed the HIAs based on six questions developed through a literature review and a review of the aims and objectives of the HIAs. The questions included:

1. How was the HIA undertaken with regard to time, place, and population?
2. What resources were used and what was the cost?
3. How were recommendations formulated and prioritized?
4. How and when were the recommendations delivered to decision makers?
5. Did the HIA provide useful information to the policy-making process?
6. Did the HIA lead to changes to the design of the project or policy?

The HIA conducted on the redevelopment of McIntosh Homes (Albany) evaluated the impact of the redevelopment project on local residents, students, and businesses. The HIA presented analysis and recommendations aimed at reducing the risk and occurrence of diabetes, asthma, traffic-related injuries, low socioeconomic status, low educational attainment, high crime rates, and decreased mental health due to neighborhood change. In the evaluation, each recommendation in the HIA was analyzed to determine the extent to which it had been implemented. An example of this evaluation follows:

> Reduce High Crime Rates in Neighborhood
> *Recommendation 1:* Regular maintenance of neighborhood conditions to avoid symbols of neglect and abandonment.
> *Finding:* Fulfilled.
> The Albany Housing Authority (AHA) received a score of 90 % on the Real Estate Assessment Center's physical inspection for the target area, and the AHA received an overall Public Housing Assessment System (PHAS) Score of 94 with a rating of "high performer".
> *Recommendation 2:* Incorporate urban design elements to reduce crime (lighting, neighborhood maintenance, etc.).
> *Finding:* Partially fulfilled.
> The Public Safety working group is applying for a Byrne Criminal Justice Innovation (BCJI) grant to address crime prevention in the target area. The plan will incorporate crime prevention by environmental design principles.

The HIA conducted in Macon assessed the health impacts of a project intended to incorporate multimodal transportation, green space, and economic development into the downtown corridor. The project had a large number of potentially affected populations: neighborhood residents, community organizations, churches and faith-based organizations, government agencies, student and teachers, health-care providers, and local businesses. The HIA's recommendations aimed to minimize potential adverse consequences in the areas of diabetes and heart disease, asthma, crime and safety, poor female health literacy and birth outcomes, and economic development. As in the Albany example, the evaluation tracked the HIA recommendations to evaluate the extent to which each had been adopted or implemented:

Improve Conditions of Vulnerable Populations.
Recommendation 1: Provide employment opportunities that are well matched to skills.
Finding: Partially fulfilled.
Recommendation 2: Consider alternative industrial uses for vacant/unused industrial infrastructure.
Finding: Not fulfilled.
Recommendation 3: Provide equitable transportation access.
Finding: Partially fulfilled.
The HIA recommended provided employment opportunities that are well matched to the skills of local residents; the Second Street project's conceptual plan seeks investment to "create jobs," but it does not address the specific types of jobs or the skills match. Moreover, the HIA recommended provided equitable transportation access. The Second Street plan does not specifically address neighborhood equity, though its complete streets concept may provide viable non-auto transportation modes. The Second Street plan did not include the HIA recommendation to consider alternative industrial uses for vacant/unused industrial infrastructure. (Ross et al. 2013)

References

Ali S, O'Callaghan V, Middleton JD et al (2009) The challenges of evaluating a health impact assessment. Crit Public Health 19(2):171–180

CDC Division for Heart Disease and Stroke Prevention (2008) State program evaluation guides: writing SMART objectives. Department of Health and Human Services. Centers for Disease Control and Prevention, Atlanta

Clark County Public Health (2011) Evaluation of health impact assessment: clark county bicycle and pedestrian master plan. http://bikeportland.org/wp-content/uploads/2011/12/HIA_BPplan-copy.pdf. Accessed 14 July 2013

Dannenberg AL, Bhatia R, Cole BL et al (2006) Growing the field of health impact assessment in the United States: an agenda for research and practice. Am J Public Health 96(2):262–270

Harris- Roxas B, Harris E (2013) The impact and effectiveness of health impact assessment: a conceptual framework. Environ Impact Asses 42:51–59

Kemm J (2012) Evaluation and quality assurance of health impact assessment. In: Kemm J (ed) Health impact assessment: past achievement, current understanding and future progress. University Press, Oxford

Quigley RJ, Taylor L (2003) Evaluation as a key part of health impact assessment: the English experience. B World Health Organ 81(6):415–419

Quigley RJ, Taylor LC (2004) Evaluating health impact assessment. Pub Health 118:544–552

Ross C, Elliott ML, Rushing MM et al (2012) Health impact assessment of the Atlanta Regional Plan 2040. Center for quality growth and regional development. Georgia Institute of Technology, Atlanta

Ross C, Elliott M, Smith S, Botchwey N et al (2013) Albany and Macon, GA health impact assessment evaluation report. Center for Quality Growth and Regional development. Georgia Institute of Technology, Atlanta

Taylor L, Gowman N, Quigley R (2003) Evaluating health impact assessment. Health Development Agency

Chapter 13
Monitoring

Abstract This chapter describes the health impact assessment (HIA) monitoring process as practiced in the USA. The chapter begins with a discussion of monitoring as one of the least developed of all HIA stages, often confused with evaluation. Monitoring assesses how effectively the project, policy, or program is achieving goals as predicted by the HIA and may help with early mitigation of negative health outcomes. The chapter then highlights what can be monitored noting four key steps. Indicators and data needs are discussed next, referencing the value of development of such indicators for health monitoring. A sample monitoring plan template is included to guide the reader through implementation on their own HIA. The chapter concludes with a discussion of challenges to successful monitoring.

Keywords Monitoring · Implementation · Mutual learning · Indicators · Monitoring plan · Institutional change

The purpose of monitoring is to track the health impact assessment (HIA) and its effect over time. The monitoring process can be envisioned as a system of checks and balances to ensure accountability in the implementation of the HIA's recommendations and to gauge compliance with regulations. Most important of all, monitoring provides a preview of both adverse and beneficial health consequences that may occur as the proposed project or policy is put in place.

Monitoring is one of the least well developed of all the phases of HIA practice. HIA reports often conclude by recommending monitoring as a critical next step through surveillance and other data collection systems that continuously provide information regarding changes in health and social indicators. HIA proponents seek empirical evidence of HIA's efficacy to ensure a solid foundation from which to advocate its continued application. As such, the formalization of monitoring techniques becomes even more critical in the US context (Dannenberg et al. 2006). Good monitoring techniques will aid in the development of consistent strategies that make completed HIAs comparable to one another.

The discussion of HIA monitoring and evaluation in peer-reviewed literature is mostly descriptive and tends to focus on identifying impacts of HIA on decision-making processes (Bhatia et al. 2011; Slotterback et al. 2011). "Mutual learning" is very important in the monitoring literature and refers to stakeholder participation and the degree to which the HIA influenced the perception of increased importance of health issues in planning. In addition, it is important to understand

C. L. Ross et al., *Health Impact Assessment in the United States,* 151
DOI 10.1007/978-1-4614-7303-9_13, © Springer Science+Business Media New York 2014

how stakeholders in the community, as well as those conducting the HIA or contributing their expertise, learn from each other and how that affects decision-making. In addition to affecting decision-making, the monitoring process must measure the extent to which the HIA integrates itself into comprehensive planning and whether it leads to the creation of other community-based health initiatives. A primary challenge is the need to create or establish a rigorous monitoring framework with available indicators and reliable data.

What Can Be Monitored

The primary objectives of the monitoring process are to catalog how recommendations from the HIA have been integrated into project or policy implementation and to assess the resulting health impacts following implementation. Monitoring the implementation of HIA recommendations and the resulting health impacts is particularly significant when the HIA predicts adverse outcomes whose nature, magnitude, and timing are unknown. Monitoring can help assess how effectively the project, policy, or program is achieving goals as predicted by the HIA (Cave and Curtis 2001) and may help with early mitigation of negative health outcomes.

Actions include:

- Establishing standardized and easily accessible data collection systems to monitor changes in health status that result from project implementation and creating feedback mechanisms to clarify causal linkages between project and outcomes
- Providing stakeholders with evidence to make adaptations to mitigate harmful health impacts and maximize positive health outcomes
- Documenting whether the HIA recommendations that were implemented achieved their intended health-related objectives

Indicators and Data Needs

Monitoring involves the collection of several types of qualitative and quantitative data. To identify how health outcomes and determinants change over time as a result of project or policy implementation, a set of indicators must be identified that can be standardized and easily accessed over time, as discussed below.

Development of Indicators for Health Monitoring

Indicators to be used for health monitoring serve as measurable outcomes of the evolving health conditions and experiences of the affected populations. Some indicators that can be included in this phase are health outcomes, health behaviors, and health determinants. In addition to providing time-trend information on health issues, these types of indicators can also function to systematically monitor urban environmental changes; provide early warning of economic, social, and environmental damage; provide data for target setting and performance reviews; and serve as aids for public information and communication. Indicators are most useful if they can be accessed at different points in time to be able to demonstrate trends in how conditions are changing or remaining the same. As such, indicators should be chosen that are periodically updated, use the same definition and methodology over time, are reliable and valid, and to the extent possible, are tied to those changes that will be caused by the project/policy (as opposed to changes for other general social conditions).

Indicators for monitoring are selected through both top-down and bottom-up approaches. Top-down frameworks are usually defined by researchers and experts and are derived from global- or national-level indicator frameworks. Bottom-up approaches may come from the community. However, a central tenet of the HIA process is health equity, which makes a strong case for bottom-up approaches to indicator development (Harris-Roxas et al. 2012).

To date, the most well-developed existing instruments for monitoring take the form of checklists. A good example is contained in the Health Impact Assessment Toolkit developed by Health Impact Partners, shown in Table 13.1. Another well-developed checklist is the Sustainable Communities Index (SCI) developed by the San Francisco Department of Public Health. The SCI provides an exhaustive list of indicators derived from specific goals and objectives that measure healthy community development in San Francisco. These indicators can be used for HIA itself but the website also identifies monitoring indicators to evaluate the impact and measure the progress of community plans.

It is important to develop the monitoring process independently rather than as an accessory to the evaluation process. Monitoring can be envisioned as a long-term process that extends well beyond the scope of the HIA evaluation and can serve as a surveillance system in a constantly changing environment. Data collection systems that are set up as part of the monitoring process can fill important research gaps and aid other HIAs conducted in the same area, as well as provide important health indicators for other development processes. Monitoring can become an important tool in evaluation and in reaching larger goals of community sustainability.

Challenges to Successful Monitoring

Undertaking an HIA may prompt the need to collect local public health statistics. Ongoing monitoring of these statistics, as well as other procedural elements, may also be required. The resources to continue monitoring HIA outcomes over time may become an issue when projects extend far into the future.

Existing cases of monitoring continue to be sporadic and are often inextricable from the evaluation process. Collecting health statistics may be difficult if such

Table 13.1 Sample monitoring plan template and questions from Human Impact Partners HIA toolkit. (Adapted from Bhatia et al. 2011)

Monitoring plan elements	Indicators
Background: • State the plan, project, or policy evaluated by the HIA • Describe the key elements of the plan, project, or policy that were analyzed by the HIA • List process and outcome recommendations made to decision-makers. If prioritized, list in that order • List decision-makers (e.g., agencies and elected officials) involved in deciding on the plan, project, or policy • Identify 2–3 goals for the monitoring process • Identify resources to conduct, complete, and report monitoring activities, including data collection • Define roles for individuals or organizations Identify criteria or triggers for action	Not applicable
Decision outcome: • What was the outcome of the decision related to the plan, project, or policy under review? • Were recommendations implemented after the decision? • Overall, did the final plan, project, or policy decision change in a way that was consistent with the recommendations of the HIA?	Create tracking chart to note on a quarterly basis: • Whether decision was made • Which recommendations were incorporated into the plan, project, or policy • Whether each accepted recommendation was implemented as agreed to
Decision process: • To what extent did stakeholders use HIA findings? • To what extent did decision-makers use HIA findings? • Did the HIA inform a discussion of the trade-offs involved with a project/policy? • Were discussions of connections between the decision and health evident in the media, statements by public officials or stakeholders, public testimony, public documents, or policy statements? • Did the HIA help to build consensus and buy-in for policy decisions and their implementation? • Did the HIA lead to interest from previously uninvolved groups? • Did the HIA encourage public health agencies to participate in new roles in policy and planning efforts? • Have requests for the study of health impacts on additional projects, plans, or policies in the same jurisdiction been followed? • Are there new efforts to institutionalize HIA or other forms of health analysis of public policy? • Did the HIA lead to greater institutional support for consideration of health in formal decision-making processes?	Create tracking chart that can note on a bimonthly basis: • Media • Testimony • Letters • Communications materials • Referencing of health evidence in public documents

Table 13.1 (continued)

Monitoring plan elements	Indicators
Health determinants: • What specific health determinants will be assessed (e.g., air quality, noise, affordable housing, traffic calming, communicable disease—ideally, these are the health determinants related to the recommendations)?	Create tracking chart that can note on a annual basis: • Whether any change in the determinant has been observed • Direction of change

information is not accessible and the tendency to incorrectly link monitoring to evaluation may present a challenge for this step. As discussed earlier, it is important to understand the differences between monitoring and evaluation and to separate the two steps.

In summary, the essential task of the monitoring process is an ongoing assessment of HIA.

References

Bhatia R, Gilhuly K, Harris C et al (2011) A health impact assessment toolkit: a handbook to conducting HIA, 3rd edn. Human Impact Partners, Oakland. http://www.humanimpact.org/doc-lib/finish/11/81. Accessed 18 June 2013

Cave B, Curtis S (2001) Health impact assessment for regeneration projects: principles, vol 3. East London & The City Health Action Zone, London

Dannenberg AL, Bhatia R, Cole BL et al (2006) Growing the field of health impact assessment in the United States: an agenda for research and practice. Am J Public Health 96(2):262–270

Harris-Roxas B, Viliani F, Harris P et al (2012) Health impact assessment: the state of the art. Impact Assess Proj Apprais 30(1):43–52

Slotterback CS, Forsyth A, Krizek KJ et al (2011) Testing three health impact assessment tools in planning: a process evaluation. Envi Impact Asses 312:144–153

Chapter 14
Engaging Stakeholders and Vulnerable Populations in HIA

Abstract This chapter provides instruction on effective ways to engage stake-holders and vulnerable populations in health impact assessment (HIA), as a vital and integral component of HIA practice. The chapter begins with an introduction to community engagement, participation, and inclusion. It describes who might comprise HIA stakeholders and emphasizes that the purpose of engaging stake-holders is both to improve the quality of HIA itself and to help the HIA remain in conformance with the underlying value of democracy. Too often, engagement is not conducted with sufficient rigor and omits the input of the most vulnerable pop-ulations subject to the potential impact. The chapter provides guidance on how to identify and engage stakeholders in ways that are tailored to their specific context. It also provides an inventory of stakeholder engagement processes in a sample of HIAs completed in the USA. The chapter ends with a framework practitioners can follow to identify and engage all stakeholders in a process that is inclusive and effective.

Keywords Vulnerable populations · Stakeholders · Community engagement · Stakeholder · Engagement · Engagement process · Engagement methods · Engagement framework

As described in earlier sections of this book, health impact assessment (HIA) evalu-ates the potential implications of a proposed policy, project, or plan for the health of a given community. HIA practitioners strive to engage affected stakeholders through meetings, surveys, focus groups, and other forms of outreach so that the particular health needs of the affected community as well as the impact of the pro-posal on health outcomes can be accurately identified.

Community engagement has a long history with Sherry Arnstein's seminal paper, "A Ladder of Citizen Participation" (1969) as a noteworthy contribution. Speaking to planners, Arnstein frames effective community engagement as a bal-ance of power, and thus a challenge to guide the planning process while allow-ing its outcome to be driven by the community, climbing ever higher on the "lad-der" of participation as this ideal is approached. This is a difficult balance to meet, as citizen participation can become a token element of the planning process, in

C. L. Ross et al., *Health Impact Assessment in the United States,*
DOI 10.1007/978-1-4614-7303-9_14, © Springer Science+Business Media New York 2014

which an essentially uninvolved community takes part in an "empty ritual" that is dominated by the planner and other officials. Arnstein directs planners to engage the community more fully by moving up the ladder of citizen participation, culminating at its highest rungs with the planner ceding control to the community, taking direction and heeding the desires of the public to create a citizen-owned outcome, or even turning complete control of the project and funds over to community groups.

Quick and Feldman draw a distinction between "participation" and "inclusion" in community engagement (2011). Participation occurs when planners seek community input on the content of a particular project, plan, or program; true inclusion requires ongoing community "coproduction" of solutions to public policy issues. In this framework, a community may participate without being included; to be included, the community, as in Arnstein's ladder, will feel ownership over the outcome of the planning process. Processes that seek participation only may exacerbate existing tensions between the community and public officials, while inclusive processes will mediate these tensions. These two dimensions of community engagement do not work at cross-purposes; however, planners should seek high levels of both participation and inclusion for their constituents.

Nora Roberts (2004) identifies the 20th century as a time of both increasing interconnectedness and decentralization, leading to an expansion of direct citizen participation. The benefits of direct participation range from strengthened group identity to a more educated citizenry and the legitimation of government actions. However, along with expanded participation comes a set of challenges. Among other dilemmas, in a complex society, direct participation struggles to incorporate all groups seeking representation. Additionally, it remains to be seen whether groups that have been "systematically excluded" from democratic processes will find a place in direct participation. Identification of stakeholders and vulnerable populations and standardizing the process of engagement in HIA rely on understanding power, inclusion, and direct citizen participation in general.

Who Are Stakeholders?

The *Guidance and Best Practices for Stakeholder Participation in Health Impact Assessments* identifies stakeholders as "individuals or organizations who stand to gain or lose from a decision or process" (Stakeholder Participation Working Group 2012). This includes individuals or organizations who:

- May be affected by the proposed project or policy
- Have an interest in the health impacts of the policy or project under consideration
- Because of their position, have an active or passive influence on the decision-making and implementation process of the proposed project or policy or
- Have an economic or other vested interest in the outcome of the decision

In practice, as described in the guidance document, stakeholders often fall into one of the following categories:

- Community-based organizations
- Residents
- Service providers
- Elected officials at the municipal, regional, or state/provincial or federal levels
- Small businesses
- Industry, developers, and big business
- Public agencies
- Statewide or national advocacy organizations
- Academic, learning, and research institutions

The Purpose of Engaging Stakeholders

There are a number of justifications for involving stakeholders in an HIA process. A basic reason is that the involvement of stakeholders helps the HIA remain in conformance with the underlying value of democracy, which emphasizes the right of people to participate in the formulation of decisions that affect their lives (North American HIA Practice Standards Working Group 2010). In addition, the engagement of stakeholders improves the quality of the HIA.

The *Guidance and Best Practices for Stakeholder Participation in Health Impact Assessments* describes the importance of stakeholder engagement in terms of improving HIA process, quality, accuracy, and validity:

In the HIA process, engaged and active stakeholders can:

- *Increase the accuracy and value of the HIA by providing multiple perspectives.*

Working with stakeholders brings varying perspectives to the HIA and is integral to identifying the health impacts that are of greatest importance to the population identified in the HIA. Through the participation process, the knowledge, experience and values of diverse stakeholders can become part of the evidence base.

- *Incorporate information not readily available with other forms of evidence.*

Stakeholders can share anecdotal information, histories and stories that provide a more well-rounded understanding of existing community conditions and potential health impacts. Stakeholders can also help refine research questions, support context-specific analysis of research findings, and help develop more feasible recommendations.

- *Increase the efficacy of the HIA to impact the policy decision by fostering active support for the HIA recommendations.*

Participation in the HIA process can provide stakeholders an opportunity to shape the analysis and provide meaningful input. Stakeholders can account for community concerns and visions, political realities, and reach diverse audiences for input and support. Since the recommendations stemming from the HIA analysis may also have the most impact on communities and other stakeholders, it is imperative they help shape them. (Stakeholder Participation Working Group 2012)

Table 14.1 Stakeholder engagement at each step of the Health Impact Assessment process. (Adapted from Tamburrini et al. 2011; Veazie et al. 2005)

Stage	What practitioners should do
Screening	Utilize stakeholder concerns to determine health effects
	Identify and notify stakeholders of decision to conduct an HIA
Scoping	Use input from multiple perspectives to inform pathways
	Use multiple avenues to solicit input (from stakeholders, affected communities, decision-makers)
	Ensure a mechanism to incorporate new feedback from stakeholders in the scope
Assessment	Use local knowledge as part of the evidence base
Recommendations	Use expert guidance to ensure recommendations reflect effective practices
Reporting and Communication	Summarize primary findings and recommendations to allow for stakeholder understanding, evaluation, and response
	Document stakeholder participation throughout the process in the full report
	Make an inclusive accounting of stakeholder values as part of determining recommendations
	Allow for and formally respond to critical review
	Make the report publicly accessible
Evaluation	HIA evaluation must be useful to all stakeholders
	Engage stakeholders in interpreting evaluation findings
Monitoring	Plan should address reporting outcomes to decision-makers
	Monitoring methods and results should be made available to the public

The approach to and the utility of stakeholder engagement change somewhat at each step of the HIA process. Table 14.1 lists how HIA practitioners can use stakeholder engagement to inform the HIA at each step of the stakeholder process.

Engaging Vulnerable Populations

Within an HIA, vulnerable populations are those that are likely to disproportionately bear adverse health effects, especially among groups already suffering health disparities. In many cases, vulnerability can be predicated on a variety of attributes, such as biological factors (e.g., age), social constructs (e.g., gender, ethnicity), material conditions (e.g., income or employment status), or exposure to adverse environments (e.g., populations located in specific geographic areas). However, vulnerability is not necessarily limited to these groups, and the HIA practitioner must consider whether there are other populations that will be particularly vulnerable. Any population that is "at elevated risk of suffering harm as the result of one or more" factors can be considered vulnerable to some extent (Kochtitzky 2011).

Vulnerability can be either exacerbated or ameliorated by the choices made in planning and policy-making. For that reason, the involvement of vulnerable populations in decision-making is particularly important. However, conditions associated with vulnerability status may prevent individuals from participating in the HIA process, by presenting social, economic, or physical barriers to access. In particular, those individuals and groups who lack access to information have limited mobility, face physical or linguistic barriers, or are socially isolated may choose not to participate, fear they cannot participate, be unable to participate if they wanted to, or may not even be aware of the opportunity to do so. In this environment, vulnerable populations may require more accommodations than other populations in participating in HIA processes and are more likely to be discouraged or excluded by the engagement process.

For example, Kwiatkowski (2011) identifies cultural barriers to effective community engagement with Canadian indigenous communities. He argues that the cultural or health norms of the affected population must be taken into account when designing the engagement process. These indigenous beliefs may differ from dominant Western attitudes, and thus efforts by practitioners or researchers to engage the population will prove to be futile if these differences are not understood, acknowledged, and respected. This challenge applies not only to indigenous populations but also to immigrant groups and religious minorities who may have differing cultural beliefs.

How to Engage Stakeholders

There is no single best way to involve stakeholders in HIA; rather, the methods for involvement should be tailored to the specific context. Contextual elements that are important to consider include available time of stakeholders, language and literacy constraints, cultural nuances, community centers for meetings, etc. Methods that can be used include creation of community steering or advisory groups, copartnership with key stakeholders, consensus-based decision-making, interviews, surveys, questionnaires, fishbowls, comment forms, project website, articles, newsletters, workshops, tours, design charrettes, focus groups, and study sessions (Stakeholder Participation Working Group 2012).

It is important to note that HIAs typically involve both individuals (e.g., local residents) who represent their own personal perspective and also organizations that represent the multiplicity of public interests.

Although engaging stakeholders is a good practice backed up by a strong rationale for the benefits of doing so, in practice there are substantial challenges that may be faced including lack of sufficient financial resources or an insufficient timeline. In some populations or cultures, it can take a longer period of time to develop a relationship of trust. Stakeholders may themselves be uninterested in participating because of either burnout or mistrust. An integrated assessment needs to align with stakeholder engagement among all disciplines and be wary of the demands on residents so that their active interest and participation can be maintained. It is also important to ensure that expectations of stakeholders as a result of their participation are accurate; it can be detrimental to engage people in a process where they provide input into what they think is decision-making, if the HIA actually has no ability to influence the decision.

Kearney (2004) notes that citizen participation in HIA has the potential to be "tokenistic," and that effective community engagement can be a difficult achievement. Practitioners are often unable to meet the needs of the community to allow for effective engagement by holding meetings at times that are feasible for the majority of the community. In addition, stakeholders are often prepared for the worst possible outcome of community engagement efforts (Kearney 2004).

Box 14.1 presents the results of an inventory of completed HIAs that cataloged the stakeholder processes that were used in each. As shown in the box, a diversity of approaches was used and the success of engagement processes was mixed.

Box 14.1   An inventory of stakeholder engagement processes in completed HIAs

A sample of completed HIAs was evaluated in order to understand the current state of community engagement methodology and the engagement of vulnerable populations in HIA. Seventeen HIAs were evaluated. To maximize comparability and the likelihood that the HIA would have engaged the local community, the HIAs were restricted to those that addressed a built environment issue, had a local-level agency as the decision-making authority, and provided a complete report documenting their methodology. Each HIA was inventoried to identify the types of engagement processes used, the extent, and influence of community engagement on the HIA outcome and engagement of vulnerable populations.

Fourteen of the 17 inventoried HIAs included some form of community engagement, while the remaining three did not include any community engagement.

As shown in Table 14.2, the forms of community engagement used included public meetings, advisory committees, surveys, focus groups, interviews, Photovoice, conference calls, rapid community HIAs, neighborhood tours, community walkability/bikeability assessments, and community mapping exercises. In particular, selective methods such as advisory committees and stakeholder interviews, as well as semi-selective methods such as focus groups, were frequently used. Among open methods of engagement, surveys and community meetings were conducted most frequently. Many HIAs combined more than one method of engagement, such as having an advisory committee involved throughout the process, while a survey was conducted and incorporated during the assessment phase. Six HIAs combined selective and open engagement methods, while four relied on open methods only, and three used only selective methods.

The extent to which community engagement influenced the process or outcomes of the HIA varied. In general, advisory committees had the greatest influence on the HIA process, as advisory committees often had input in the scoping phase of the project, allowing these committees to help determine the issues at the forefront of the HIA. In several cases, advisory committees remained involved throughout the process, giving participants the opportunity to influence the HIA from beginning to end, including shaping both the scope and the recommendations. However, advisory committees were in some cases composed of subject experts in public health and HIA practice, rather than community stakeholders who are directly representative of the local population.

Among the HIAs reviewed, engagement of vulnerable populations was not substantial. Three HIAs of the 17 did not identify vulnerable populations. The remaining 14 HIAs all identified one or more potentially affected populations who could be classified as vulnerable and 11 reported some form of engagement with members of these populations. Five of the 11 targeted outreached towards all vulnerable populations affected, while four sought to engage some but not all of the populations that had been identified as vulnerable. The remaining two HIAs engaged members of vulnerable populations only incidentally, in that participation of members of these groups was allowed and reported but not targeted.

The most frequent way in which members of vulnerable populations were engaged was through the use of tools or processes in a minority language (most commonly Spanish). This was done in four HIAs. In addition, representatives of vulnerable populations participated on two advisory committees and four HIAs conducted focus groups, interviews, or community meetings specifically for members of an affected vulnerable population.

Building a Framework for Effective Stakeholder Engagement

In order to successfully engage stakeholder groups, practitioners need to explicitly incorporate targeted engagement processes in the HIA methods. To help practitioners begin to think about this process, a framework for effective engagement is proposed below. In this framework, the engagement of vulnerable populations is not separate from general community engagement, but rather is integrated into the process.

1. Look at prior HIAs for insights
   Completed HIAs are a valuable resource for how to conduct a community engagement process by helping to identify affected populations as well as the means and value of reaching out to those groups.

Table 14.2 Summary of HIA stakeholder engagement processes

Engagement methods used	Public meetings, advisory committees, surveys, focus groups, interviews, Photovoice, conference calls, rapid community HIAs, neighborhood tours, community walkability/bikeability assessments, and community mapping exercises
Number of people reached	0–264
Community influence in HIA outcome	From high (input incorporated early and often) to none (no engagement process): High (3) Moderate/high (7) Low/moderate (4) None/low (3)
Degree of selective to open engagement	From selective (advisory committees) to open (surveys, public meetings): Mixed/semi-selective (8) Open (5) Selective (1) No engagement (3)
Vulnerable populations identified	Black, Asian, Hispanic, elderly, children, low income, other
Outreach to vulnerable populations	From extensive (significant successful effort made) to none (no effort made): Extensive outreach/mostly successful (3) Some outreach/partially successful (7) No outreach to vulnerable populations (4) No engagement (3)
Methods for engaging vulnerable populations	Advisory committee representation, non-English language assistance

- Identify stakeholder groups and vulnerable populations. Completed HIAs conducted on similar projects or for similar geographic areas can provide insights into groups that may be affected by the proposal under review.
- Evaluate available engagement methods. HIAs that affect similar populations may suggest methods of engagement that may be effective in reaching out to those groups. While selective engagement methods can ensure the representation of vulnerable populations, vulnerable groups are not necessarily homogeneous. Input from a small number of group members may not capture a representative view of the population as a whole. On the other hand, open methods of engagement have the potential to include a wide array of viewpoints, but are not always successful in garnering responses. For example, in the Derby redevelopment HIA (Tri-County Health Department 2007), only 13 individuals participated in the Photovoice project, of whom only 7 were area residents (6 other individuals were staff from the agency conducting the HIA). In the Aerotropolis HIA (Ross et al. 2011), a Spanish-language survey was made available, but no responses were gathered.
- Assess potential benefits of engagement processes. Previously completed HIAs may also provide examples of instances in which extensive engagement adds significant value to the outcome.

2. Identify partners to act as bridges to the community and select modes of outreach
that will connect with the community
Once stakeholders have been identified and an engagement process chosen, practitioners must find a way to draw individuals and communities into the engagement process. When practitioners do not already have a strong relationship with
the community, partners in local organizations can provide a bridge that allows
the HIA team to connect with the community. Once groups to target for outreach
are known, organizations, which may include faith-based organizations, social
service providers, or advocacy groups, can help evaluate possible methods and
strategies for overcoming barriers to engagement.
3. Document and quantify outreach—methods and results
A common problem noted in the HIA inventory in Box 14.1 is that community
engagement was not always described in the HIA report, making it difficult to
determine the true extent of the engagement process. Lack of documentation also
limits the value of the HIA as a learning tool for other practitioners. During and
after the HIA process, practitioners should record engagement efforts that were
used and the resulting level of participation.
4. Evaluate outreach—methods and results
Practitioners should also take time to evaluate the stakeholder engagement process as well as its outcomes. In doing so, practitioners will inform their own
work and may provide suggested improvements for future HIAs.
5. Reinforce new relationships to build on and use in the future
Following the completion of an HIA, practitioners should reinforce the new relationships formed with partner organizations and within the community. Doing so
will help practitioners gain support within the community for their recommendations, encourage community members to remain engaged in issues that can affect
their health, and encourage partners and community members to contribute to
practitioners' future projects. Practitioners can do this by sharing results of the
HIA with the community and keeping the community involved in ongoing monitoring and evaluation efforts.

An active and thorough community engagement process is an essential element of
achieving the goals of HIA, including educating the public about a proposal and its
potential health impacts; gathering all relevant information about the circumstances
and health concerns of community residents; and generating support for the HIA's
recommendations to shape the health outcomes of the proposal. Legitimate inclusion of vulnerable populations throughout this process is an integral aspect of HIA
practice itself. This chapter has provided both an examination of issues surrounding
these questions of vulnerability and an actionable framework that practitioners can
use in their own engagement processes.

References

Arnstein S (1969) A ladder of citizen participation. Jam Am I Planners 35(4):216–224
Kearney M (2004) Walking the walk? Community participation in HIA: a qualitative interview
study. Environ Impact Asses 24(2):217–229

Kochtitzky C (2011) Vulnerable populations and the built environment. In: Dannenberg AL, Frumkin H, Jackson RJ (eds) Making healthy places. Island Press, Washington

Kwiatkowski RE (2011) Indigenous comity-based participatory research and health impact assessment: A Canadian example. Environ Impact Asses 31(4):445–450

North American HIA Practice Standards Working Group (2010) Minimum elements and practice standards for health impact assessment, version 2. http://hiasociety.org/documents/PracticeStandardsforHIAVersion2.pdf. Accessed 18 June 2013

Quick KS, Feldman MS (2011) Distinguishing participation and inclusion. J Plan Educ Res 31(3):272–290.

Roberts N (2004) Public deliberation in an age of direct citizen participation. The Am Rev Public Adm 34(4):315–353

Ross C, Elliott M, Marcus Rushing M et al (2011) Aerotropolis Atlanta brownfield redevelopment. Center for quality growth and regional development. Georgia Institute of Technology, Atlanta. http://www.cqgrd.gatech.edu/research/aerotropolis-atlanta-brownfield-redevelopment-health-impact-assessment. Accessed 18 June 2013

Stakeholder Participation Working Group of the 2010 HIA of the Americas Workshop (2012) Best practices for stakeholder participation in health impact assessment. http://hiasociety.org/documents/guide-for-stakeholder-participation.pdf. Accessed 18 June 2013

Tamburrini A, Gilhuly K, Harris-Roxas B (2011) Enhancing benefits in health impact assessment through stakeholder consultation. Impact Assessment and Project Appraisal 29(3):195–204

Tri-County Health Department (2007) Health impact assessment, Derby redevelopment, historic commerce city, Colorado. http://www.healthimpactproject.org/resources/document/derby-redevelopment.pdf. Accessed 18 June 2013

Veazie MA, Galloway JM et al (2005) Taking the initiative: implementing the American Heart Association guide for improving cardiovascular health at the community level: healthy people 2010 heart disease and stroke partnership community guideline implementation and best practices workgroup. Circulation 112:2538–2554.

Part IV
HIA Today and Tomorrow

Chapter 15
HIA and Emerging Technologies

Abstract This chapter discusses emerging technologies and how these new opportunities for participation, data collection, analysis, and dissemination influence health impact assessment today and how they may be integrated into future practice. Technologies are discussed in two broad categories: those technologies used for engagement and communication and those used for information gathering and analysis. Engagement and communication technologies discussed include social media, cell phones, webinars/conferences, and podcasting. Technologies discussed for information gathering and analysis include online surveys, dataset access, manipulation and visualization, and geographic information systems and other mapping technologies. The chapter ends with a case study that highlights how online multimedia tools have been used to enhance communication with stakeholders.

Keywords Social media · Cell phones · Podcasting · Online surveys · Webinars · Data set access · Geographic information systems (GIS) and other mapping technologies · Case studies

The technological changes that have swept through society in the past few decades cannot be ignored when it comes to health impact assessment (HIA) and other processes related to community engagement. While it is crucial to be sensitive to the existence of a "digital divide" dictating who has access to which new technologies, it is also of key importance to understand how these new developments are changing approaches to both data collection and analysis and to public participation.

Overall, there is much opportunity in using new technologies. For example, geographic information systems (GIS) provide us with a slew of powerful analytical methods that simply were not possible in earlier years. The dissemination of information to the public through the strategic use of cellular- and web-based technologies might be vastly less expensive and has a greater reach than using more traditional techniques. There are many reasons to embrace and, even more importantly, to understand these new directions.

C. L. Ross et al., *Health Impact Assessment in the United States*,
DOI 10.1007/978-1-4614-7303-9_15, © Springer Science+Business Media New York 2014

Technologies for Engagement and Communication

Social Media

Major changes in the way we use the Internet have led to a shift away from static websites and toward various social media—interactive and fluid networks that place users at the center of their own online experience, not only consuming information but also generating and relaying it. The specifics of which networks are popular and how each works are in constant flux, but the wider cultural and civic phenomenon of social media seems to have found strong staying power. The arrival, for many people, of web applications for cell phones has resulted in an even greater presence of these Internet-based social media in day-to-day life.

Because social networks have become so inescapable, their incorporation into community engagement processes now represents not merely a site of opportunity but, rather, a near necessity. For example, it is now widely accepted that if an organization or initiative wants to appear proactive about outreach, it is necessary that it maintains a presence on the major social networks of the day, at a minimum. The rapid rate of response that this new mode of interaction requires can be both a blessing and a curse; on the one hand, the rise of social media has frequently been cited as a vector of social change, supposedly playing a part in events such as the Arab Spring movement in the Middle East. On the other hand, the amount of attention that is required to manage even low-level social media campaigns can be a drain on time and resources. Nonetheless, if approached thoughtfully, social media can provide a great opportunity, within the context of HIA or other engagement-intensive processes, to penetrate segments of the public (particularly youth) that are otherwise often difficult to access or involve. Social media activity can be successful at reminding the public that a process continues to be ongoing, as well as at cultivating low-stakes relationships with individual members of the public.

Cell Phones

Cellular technology offers a number of opportunities for HIA practitioners and other professionals working on projects in health and the built environment.

While telephone surveying has long been relied upon as a method for accessing a diverse and semi-random sample, its value and validity have been fast declining as the prevalence of landlines dwindles among many population groups. Blumberg and Luke (2007), for example, found that particularly high proportions of young adults and low-income individuals lived in households lacking landlines, which has the potential to introduce significant bias into research using landline-based survey or communication methods. Fortunately, cell phone-based surveying has recently become feasible, opening up telephone surveying to a wider and hopefully more representative demographic swath.

Looking at the issue with a scope broader than surveying alone, the increasing prevalence of cell phone technology has major implications for human communication both in the USA and in other countries. Practitioners in both the public health and community development fields have already begun using cell phones in parts of the world where data collection has often been difficult; for example, Mitchell et al. (2011) found potential in using cell phones as a tool for HIV information dissemination in Uganda and Mittal et al. (2012) describe the "Bribecaster" mobile application, designed to help cell phone users report corruption in India and other countries. It is important, nonetheless, to be attuned to the fact that in spite of increased prevalence, consumer technologies like cell phones often still represent a significant "digital divide" between those who possess them and those who do not.

Webinars and Conferencing

Webinars and other emerging technologies for conferencing offer promising new ways for professionals and/or stakeholders to collaborate and share information remotely without being limited to audio alone, as with telephones.

A webinar (carrying within its name the educational concept of "seminar") is essentially an online conference allowing multiple people to view the same presentation and usually interact in some way. Webinars can vary significantly, but most often take the form of a slide show similar to a Microsoft PowerPoint presentation, over which the presenter or presenters use a microphone to deliver their talk. An assortment of possibilities exist for integrating interactive participation on the part of those following along; these include, for example, concurrent group chat functionality and the ability to join the conversation via audio or video.

Webinars fill a new middle ground between being physically present for an information session and absorbing material completely on one's own. Increasingly, institutional incentives encourage participation in this emerging interactive presentation method; for instance, members of the American Institute of Certified Planners can earn their required Certification Maintenance (CM) credits by opting to sit in on a variety of free webinar sessions. As the HIA field expands, webinars offer significant potential as a tool to help unite geographically dispersed professionals into a cohesive profession.

Podcasting

Podcasts are an emerging medium consisting of audio episodes usually downloaded to an MP3 player or other mobile electronic device. Podcasts often resemble traditional radio shows in form, yet are generally listened to asynchronously rather than at a specific airing time. HIA practitioners might find potential in podcasting by episodically releasing information on an assessment as part of the reporting and dissemination phase.

Technologies for Information Gathering and Analysis

Online Surveys

Traditional survey techniques, although tried and true, suffer from a number of logistical difficulties that make their use cumbersome or expensive. Most of these difficulties stem from the need for training and paying interviewers to contact respondents individually, to agree on a time to conduct the survey, to administer the survey in person or over the telephone, and to upload the paper or electronic results into a database. As a result, surveys can take many weeks or months to complete and may cost tens of thousands of dollars to ensure an adequate sample size.

Web-based online surveys offer a way to avoid some of this time and expense while also increasing convenience for many respondents. Potential respondents are provided with a hyperlink or a website address where the survey can be accessed. A survey can be open, allowing anyone to take it and to upload his or her response, or a survey may be tied to a unique identifier number that is only usable by a particular respondent.

Online surveys share many features with conventional computer-assisted telephone interview (CATI) or computer-assisted personal interview (CAPI) surveys, such as the use of multiple question types, "skip logic" where the questions that are asked depend on the user's response to previous questions, randomization of question order, etc. In terms of data compilation and analysis, online survey systems range from fairly basic to extremely complex, with some providing the option of exporting results into SPSS or other statistical analysis programs. In general, the simpler tools are available at little or no cost while additional sensitivity and power are more expensive. Almost all online survey platforms or hosts have interfaces that allow new users to quickly and easily design their web surveys without requiring knowledge of programming or HTML.

The use of web-based surveys may introduce bias into the research process if respondents do not constitute a representative sample of the population. Not all people have equal access to a computer or the Internet, or are equally comfortable with providing information in an online survey. Whether this potential bias is important or not for a particular HIA will depend on the intended objectives and whether representativeness of the entire population is important.

Dataset Access, Manipulation, and Visualization

In recent years, a number of platforms have appeared online that increase the ease with which public data can be accessed and analyzed. Some act as basic data repositories; that is, they collect, store, and share a large number of datasets that may be relevant to users. Other platforms are more sophisticated and enable easy data analysis or visualization; these generally allow a user to choose a dataset, then to choose the information within the dataset that he or she aims to visualize, and finally to proceed to an analysis without the time investment or foundation of statistical knowledge required to use standard data analysis platforms such as SAS. Many sites have taken a collaborative approach in which users can not only access datasets and analyses, but also contribute additional information.

These public data repositories and tools provide a number of advantages to the HIA practitioner. Data can be more easily accessed and manipulated and the free availability of these tools, in general, enables greater amounts of data to be incorporated into projects with limited budgets for time and materials. In addition, more obscure data that may not be available on federal data websites can be easily accessed and may facilitate a widening of the scope of information that can be used in these reports.

The number and focus of these data-sharing platforms are changing rapidly and any list is likely to be outdated quickly. However, several sites that are particularly relevant for data that may be useful for HIA are outlined in Box 15.1.

Box 15.1   Public Data Access and Analysis Platforms Useful for HIA

The "Google Public Data Explorer" (http://www.google.com/publicdata) is intended to make large datasets easy to explore, visualize, and communicate. Users without extensive statistical knowledge are able to manipulate the way they view and compare data and public data are readily available. Data available are fairly extensive and diverse and are expanding on a daily basis.

"Amazon Public Data Sets" (http://aws.amazon.com/publicdatasets/) is an archive of publicly available large datasets created by developers, researchers, universities, and businesses. Datasets range from historical census information to genome mapping projects. Users have free access to all available data.

"Gapminder" (http://www.gapminder.org/) provides a way to easily visualize complex information. The tool was originally created as a way of showing disparity between different populations and still has a data focus that is relevant for many public health issues.

"CDC Wonder" (http://wonder.cdc.gov/) provides access to a number of high-quality US public health datasets that can be queried online or downloaded for offline use. The intention is to make the information resources of the Centers for Disease Control and Prevention (CDC) available to public health professionals and the public at large.

"The Data Hub" (http://datahub.io/) is a community-run catalog of useful sets of data on the Internet. While it provides mainly links to data sources rather than providing any data manipulation or visualization tools, the user-generated content is updated frequently and growing rapidly and the data are open license, meaning that anyone is free to use or repurpose it.

GIS and Other Mapping Technologies

The rise of new geographic-based innovations poses, perhaps, the most exciting opportunity for HIA practitioners. Even in the relatively few years since GIS technology began to enter the mainstream of practice, it has become a seemingly indispensable tool through which community designers can better understand and communicate the way information relates to spatial contexts. Even if GIS plays a less ubiquitous role within the public health field, it still holds wide importance and applicability there, as well as in a plethora of other professions ranging from criminal justice to business.

ArcGIS has emerged as the primary platform used to conduct GIS analysis. While ArcGIS is expensive and has a fairly steep learning curve, putting it out of reach for many organizations, it also has considerable power as a tool. However, other, more user-friendly ways to interact with maps have arisen. Chief among these is Google Maps, an application that ties seamlessly into other products such as Street View, an interface for viewing the panoramic photo associated with a specific location. Google's launch of the Google Maps API, a service allowing easy integration of its maps into various website uses, only increased the service's popularity. Other projects make it even simpler for average users to tap into the potential of geographic tools; one called IssueMap (http://www.issuemap.org), for example, promises to turn spreadsheet-formatted data into a map automatically. It is certain that the amount of cartographic power now in the hands of the average person is unprecedented and because of HIA's intimate relationship to place and space, this will continue to have important implications.

Case Studies

Few HIAs have been conducted to date that harness the potential power of the emerging technologies described above. The use of data access and manipulation tools for generating data for baseline and assessment is common; GIS has also been successfully used in a number of HIAs (see, for example, the Atlanta BeltLine HIA in Chap. 5), and social media is becoming an increasingly common way for HIA practitioners to communicate among themselves (see, for example, the HIA Twitter feed listed in Appendix 2). However, examples of how HIAs have exploited emerging technologies to improve stakeholder engagement are still scarce.

Title:	Health Assessment on the Impact of the Bernalillo County Pedestrian and Bicyclist Safety Action Plan: Accessibility and Safety on Mountain View's Second Street	Case Study
Author:	Bernalillo County Place Matters Team	
Year:	2012	
Location:	New Mexico	

The Bernalillo County HIA provides an example of how online multimedia tools can be employed to effectively communicate with stakeholders (Bernalillo County Place Matters Team 2012). In addition to producing a formal HIA report, an interactive website (http://www.bcplacematters.com/2ndstreet/index.htm#ad-im) was designed to help disseminate the results of the HIA. The site effectively uses a combination of attractive graphics, maps, photos, and embedded video presenting the experiences and views of local residents. While the website is "static" in the sense that users cannot input content, its format is designed to have a broad appeal and to communicate information other than just through written narrative.

In conclusion, two things are certain: New technologies will continue to emerge and evolve, and harnessing their potential through a thorough understanding of their implications will benefit professionals working in community design, public health, and other fields. HIA's status as a relatively new practice puts practitioners in an ideal position to successfully capitalize on emerging technologies and to make sure that doing so becomes a key and integrated part of what it means to conduct HIA moving forward.

References

Bernalillo County Place Matters Team (2012) Health assessment on the impact of the Bernalillo County pedestrian and bicyclist safety action plan. http://bernalillo.nockergeek.net/#ad-image-0. Accessed 18 June 2012

Blumberg SJ, Luke JV (2007) Coverage bias in traditional telephone surveys of low-income and young adults. Public Opin Quart 71(5):734–749

Mitchell KJ, Bull S, Kiwanuka J, Ybarra M (2011) Cell phone usage among adolescents in Uganda: acceptability for relaying health information. Health Educ Res 26(5):770–781

Mittal M, Wu W, Rubin S et al (2012) Bribecaster: documenting bribes through community participation. Association for Computing Machinery (ACM). http://hdl.handle.net/1721.1/72949. Accessed 15 May 2013

Chapter 16
Organizational Capacity for HIA

Abstract This chapter discusses organizational capacity as a necessary factor for the successful completion and implementation of health impact assessment (HIA). Organizational capacity refers to the capabilities, knowledge, and resources that an organization needs in order to capably undertake an HIA. The chapter presents three broad categories of organizational capacity: institutional support, knowledge and resources, and outside context/climate. Institutional support is described as the structures and motivations within the organization conducting the HIA. Knowledge and resources comprise the capacity to undertake the HIA using resources from within or external to the organization. Outside context/climate refers to the need for conditions outside the sponsoring organization that are amenable to accepting and implementing the results of the HIA. The chapter concludes with a presentation of ten strategies that can help organizations reach capacity based on an evaluation of HIA successes and failures across two decades from jurisdictions around the world.

Keywords Political support · Institutional support · Champions · Sustainable funding · Alliances · External climate · Knowledge and resources

Organizational capacity refers to the capabilities, knowledge, and resources that an organization needs in order to successfully undertake a health impact assessment (HIA). Without sufficient organizational capacity, the chances are greatly reduced of delivering an effective HIA with recommendations that are implemented. In this chapter, we consider three factors that an organization will need to assess before embarking on an HIA:

- "Institutional support" from within the organization itself
- Access to sufficient "knowledge and resources" to conduct the HIA
- A political or decision-making "climate or context" amenable to receiving and implementing the results of the HIA

The way in which these three factors are operationalized will vary depending on the type of organization conducting the HIA, as well as on the scale of the policy/project being assessed. The climate necessary for a successful HIA as part of state or federal government policy-making, for example, is very different from that required for the success of an HIA undertaken by a community organization or nongovernmental organization (NGO). The success factors and strategies discussed below are

C. L. Ross et al., *Health Impact Assessment in the United States,*   177
DOI 10.1007/978-1-4614-7303-9_16, © Springer Science+Business Media New York 2014

written as broad considerations that can be customized by the practitioner to the specific contexts of different organizations and individual HIAs.

Institutional Support

Institutional support is the first of the three critical components for the successful completion of an HIA. In this context, institutional support refers to structural factors and motivation levels within the organization conducting the assessment. It is very important to have an organizational mandate to conduct the HIA; this mandate will better enable the organization to secure resources and institutional backing. Such backing is key for support in conducting the HIA, promoting the results, and maintaining the motivation to finish the process in the face of other pressures confronted by the organization.

The level of support needed to conduct the HIA depends on the size and nature of the organization sponsoring or undertaking it. A small NGO, for example, may need simply an agreement to dedicate the time and resources required and a plan for how to effectively disseminate results. An HIA undertaken, however, within a large political jurisdiction (at the state level, for example) may require a much more complex and sensitive set of agreements.

No matter how large or small the organization is, a primary consideration is maintaining the political support of senior management. HIA can raise sensitive issues and the commitment of senior management within the organization is critical, if the HIA practitioner is to be supported and results are to be implemented.

The Canadian province of British Columbia provides a fascinating example of how the lack of organizational support can lead to failure. The use of HIA for government policy, programs, and legislation in British Columbia was first recommended by a Royal Commission in 1991. By 1993, HIA had begun to come into use for decision-making at the Cabinet level. During this period, a range of excellent implementation tools and guidance documents were developed within the province and as a result of the work done in British Columbia at that time, Canada developed a reputation as a leader in HIA.

However, as Banken (2001) describes: "In 1995, the momentum for HIA seemed irreversible. In 1999, HIA was no longer an active issue in British Columbia's health system." This shocking reversal and the ultimate failure to institutionalize HIA in British Columbia was due to a number of factors. A new provincial government was voted in, and with it came a change in governmental priorities and a lack of support for the use of HIA. The new government also favored an administrative approach to health rather than one based on concern over the determinants of health. The Province lost key personnel who had acted as champions for HIA. The HIA implementation process was "watered down" and, finally, practitioners failed to demonstrate the benefits of HIA before the window of opportunity closed. Ultimately, it was the crumbling of institutional support that reversed British Columbia's initial leadership in the institutionalization of HIA as a core component of public policy.

Knowledge and Resources

Knowledge and resources describes the capacity to undertake an HIA using resources within or external to the organization. Conducting an HIA requires a diverse set of skills: the management and organization of information; skill at writing; skill at working with decision-makers; familiarity with public policy or industry decision-making processes; familiarity with the policy or program to be assessed; content expertise in the health subject or focus of the HIA; and, not insignificantly, experience with how to conduct an HIA. Very often, these skills are not found in a single individual and a team is required in order to be able to execute and carry out the work required to conduct a successful HIA.

The minimum that an organization needs is:

- Sufficient personnel time to dedicate to conducting the HIA. The amount of person-time required will not be the same for all HIAs. A rapid or desktop HIA may be carried out primarily by one or two people over a period of 2–6 weeks. A comprehensive HIA, on the other hand, may involve three to five HIA practitioners who work on the project for several months (or, occasionally, years).
- The individuals conducting the HIA need to have sufficient training. If this capacity does not already exist in-house, a training course may be necessary.
- The individuals conducting the HIA should have, in addition to training, sufficient and relevant HIA tools and techniques at their disposal. As discussed in Chaps. 7–10, there are myriad ways to approach different HIA components such as screening, developing a community profile, assessing specific health impacts, and developing recommendations. Amassing these tools and techniques does not typically require large amounts of money, but it does require time to identify and develop familiarity with those tools that will be most appropriate for a particular HIA.
- In some cases, outside expertise may be required, which may increase monetary costs. Sometimes support is needed regarding how to conduct the HIA itself— mentoring, for example, or hiring an external consultant to lead the assessment. External experts may also be needed to advise on specific health content areas, as a single organization or HIA practitioner may not have expertise in disciplines as diverse as, for example, traffic safety, toxicology, social determinants of health and health equity, cardiovascular mortality, indigenous health issues, and land-use planning.
- Finally, many elements of the HIA will require an allocation of monetary resources, such as running focus groups, disseminating findings, or conducting surveys. The organization needs to have sufficient financial resources to cover these costs.
- In addition to the practitioners conducting the HIA, it is often advisable to set up a steering committee of topical advisors (see Chap. 8 "Scoping"). This advisory group should apply their specific expertise to commenting on the questions, methods, and content of the HIA, thereby guiding the organization to produce sound results and recommendations.

External Context and Climate

Finally, the context or climate outside the sponsoring organization needs to be amenable to accepting and implementing the results of the HIA. This may involve a
range of stakeholders. Most importantly, there are the decision-makers—those people who ultimately decide whether and/or how to implement the policy or program
that the HIA has reviewed. This group has to be willing to listen to the results of
the assessment and to adopt the results and recommendations into their decision-
making process. In addition, other stakeholder groups, such as community groups,
NGOs, industry, municipal or regional government, or others, should be interested
in disseminating and promoting the results. Without the buy-in and readiness to
participate of both decision-makers and other stakeholders, the HIA will likely fall
on deaf ears and result in no change or implementation. Conducting an early assessment of the climate in which the HIA will take place may help organizations avoid
devoting resources to assessment projects that are unlikely to lead to change.

Organizations need to develop these relationships as part of the HIA process.
It is critical to bring stakeholder groups, including the ultimate decision-makers,
onboard early in the HIA process so that they are able to understand the value and
relevance of the HIA process for them. This also can help identify the way in which
results should be prepared and presented in order to best facilitate their acceptance
and integration by decision-making entities (see Chap. 11). This does not, however,
mean changing the results in accordance with what stakeholders want to hear, but
it does mean presenting the results in a way that is meaningful to the relevant audience, that uses language they can understand, and that is formatted in a way that
they can use.

It is important to form alliances with other organizations. In the context of government, this may often mean cross-sectoral support, which can be a significant
factor in the success of an HIA (Lee et al. 2013).

As shown in Fig. 16.1, the likelihood of success for the HIA is maximized when
all three of these areas—institutional support, knowledge and resources, and a fa-
vorable external climate—are available.

Strategies for Maximizing Likely Success of the HIA

Political jurisdictions around the world have been incorporating HIA into government policy-making process for over two decades; these include the provinces of
British Columbia and Quebec in Canada; the state of South Australia; the countries
of New Zealand, Wales, and the Netherlands; and others. An evaluation of successes and failures in these jurisdictions has identified a number of strategies that were
critical to their successful implementation of HIA (d'Amour et al. 2009; Gagnon
et al. 2008; Signal et al. 2006). These strategies are relevant to each of the three factors discussed above (institutional support; knowledge and resources; and outside
context/climate). Although they have been drawn from, and speak specifically to,

Fig. 16.1 Maximizing the
likely success of the HIA

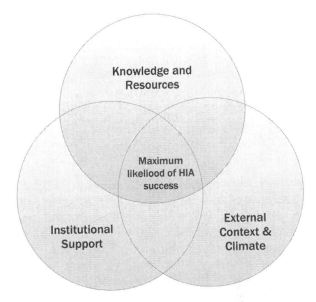

HIAs developed within a government policy development context, the strategies provide lessons for other types of organizations as well.

1. A dedicated HIA team with sustainable funding

The establishment of an "HIA unit" has been essential to the success of implementing "health in all policies" frameworks internationally. New Zealand, Quebec, South Australia, and the Netherlands, among others, have all funded "HIA support units" that provide advice, support, and expertise to government agencies.

2. Sector-specific HIA leads or "champions"

There is a need for an interdepartmental network of individuals who are able to undertake or facilitate an HIA. Appointing an HIA lead or "champion" for each government agency creates an administrative structure that assists in the uptake and use of HIA in policy development. A "network of champions" can also help promote awareness of HIA within the government and contribute to the sustainability of an HIA program by providing continuity of knowledge.

3. Confidence to undertake the HIA process:
- An understanding of the wider determinants of health
- Training for individuals and organizations in the purpose of HIA
- Access to public health and HIA technical expertise

Case studies demonstrate that a lack of understanding or confidence was a significant barrier for agencies in undertaking HIA as part of policy development. Conversely, case studies have also clearly shown that an increase in understanding on the part of agency staff (including familiarity with the determinants of health and how policies affect health) results in a corresponding increase in HIA interest and use.

4. Positive experience with HIA

An obvious but nonetheless important predictor of commitment to the HIA approach is an agency having had a positive experience with HIA in the past. If "early adopters" can demonstrate this positive experience (via improved partnerships, more effective policies, enhanced decision-making, etc.), their enthusiasm will support communication efforts regarding the value of HIA and its rationale for all government agencies.

5. A phased approach to implementation that begins by demonstrating value and experience in HIA

Successful implementation is generally built on a phased, multi-strategy approach. Time and resources are required to build capacity, to promote awareness, and to develop evidence of success supporting HIA within government. The demonstrated value of policy-based HIA, and the development of political will for it within government, is also necessary before proceeding with broad institutionalization of HIA. Case studies from Quebec, New Zealand, and South Australia have demonstrated success rooted in phased approaches to implementation that began with capacity building within the government and among other stakeholders.

6. Structured periods of "pilot testing" the HIA approach

The inclusion of a structured period for pilot testing the HIA approach has been identified as a critical factor. Pilot studies enable the adaptation and refinement of models in accordance with the needs of government stakeholders. Pilot tests also build experience with using policy-based HIA, provide evidence of success, and initiate conversation about the value that HIA brings to public policy development.

7. An organizational framework based on cross-governmental leadership

An organizational framework defining roles and responsibilities for government stakeholders helps ensure that any plans for implementation are executed and that momentum is not lost. Internationally, a cross-ministry committee or structure has been almost universally used to manage implementation activities related to the institutionalization of policy-based HIA.

8. Political support and support from senior management

A key barrier to the application of HIA in policy development is the lack of political support or support from senior management. The will to undertake policy-based HIA must come from beyond the health sector and needs instead to originate at a high government level. Support from senior management in various government agencies is critical to the success of implementing policy-based HIA.

9. Expertise provided by the public health sector

The important role of the health sector in providing expertise and in initiating policy-based HIA within government has been clearly identified in international and national case studies. The public health sector can provide expertise in gathering and appropriately interpreting health-related data for use in the assessment. In addition, support from the public health sector provides a strong rationale for engaging in HIA.

10. Statutory requirement for HIA

Case studies have shown that without a legislated requirement for HIA, implementation is not likely to be sustained over time. This has been observed in jurisdictions that have successfully institutionalized HIA, including the UK, Quebec, Australia, and New Zealand. As described earlier in this chapter, British Columbia provides a counterexample; there, policy-based HIA was well under development, but was not yet embedded in legislation when a change of government led to the loss of political support for the process. Despite its early traction, the application of HIA to public policy in British Columbia was essentially abandoned for the following decade.

References

Banken R (2001) Strategies for institutionalizing HIA. WHO European Centre for Health Policy, Brussels

d'Amour R, St. Pierre L, Ross MC (2009) Discussion workshop on health impact assessment at the level of provincial governments. National Collaborating Centre for Health Public Policy, Montreal

Gagnon F, Turgeon J, Dallaire C (2008) Health impact assessment in Quebec: when the law becomes a lever for action. National Collaborating Centre for Health Public Policy, Montreal

Lee JH, Röbbel N, Dora C (2013) Cross-country analysis of the institutionalization of health impact assessment, social determinants of health discussion paper series 8 (policy & practice). World Health Organization, Geneva

Signal L, Langford B, Quigley R et al (2006) Strengthening health, wellbeing and equity: embedding policy-level HIA in New Zealand. Social Policy J N Z 29:17–31

Chapter 17
A Look Forward

Abstract This chapter examines the overall potential of health impact assessment (HIA) to improve health status of Americans. The primary opportunities and challenges to increasing the effective utilization of HIA are explored through a review of the primary questions that have been asked about the impact and contribution of HIA. The chapter then focuses on the capacity of HIA to contribute to continuous improvement in the health status of people and communities and on expanding the inclusion of HIA in the decision-making cycle. A primary conclusion is that HIA will need to rely on partnerships and expanding the network of professionals and health-care providers outside the health profession trained to conduct HIAs. Strategies for integrating HIA, other public health activities, and policy initiatives are discussed along with an assessment of the potential to utilize the output of other health assessments as inputs into HIA.

Keywords Challenges · Partnerships · Integrating HIA · Fostering change · Health risk assessment · Public-health agencies · Social impact assessment · Health professionals

As discussed in the early chapters of this book, health impact assessment (HIA) is a relatively young discipline compared with other longer-established assessment types, most notably environmental impact assessment (EIA). At this time, standard methods and best practices have been developed for HIA, and context-specific analysis tools and evidence sources continue to expand. The use of HIA also continues to increase. Between 1999 and 2009, 54 HIAs were completed in the USA; however, in the following 4 years, almost 200 more HIAs were completed or documented as underway.

Although there is currently no legal mandate for HIA to be undertaken in the USA, the potential for HIA to be used to address health concerns is strong. Arizona State University, Sandra Day O'Connor College of Law, conducted a study of HIA use in non-health sectors. The study team examined policies and legal requirements in 20 states, ten localities, and five tribal nations. They identified environment and energy, transportation, agriculture, and waste disposal and recycling as non-health areas having the most concentration of health concerns. They also identified an extensive number of laws that require consideration of health effects in the decisions in non-health sectors (Hodge et al. 2011).

C. L. Ross et al., *Health Impact Assessment in the United States,*
DOI 10.1007/978-1-4614-7303-9_17, © Springer Science+Business Media New York 2014

While the focus on health in non-health sectors, identified above, points to both strengths and opportunities for HIA to be used to improve the health of the US population, a number of questions remain about its efficacy, appropriate use, and its potential to improve the overall status of health and health-care delivery in the USA. Among the questions that have been raised about HIA are:

- What difference has HIA made in the USA?
- What is the value of HIA?
- What needs to be done to increase understanding and acceptance of HIA among decision-makers, HIA practitioners, and the lay public?
- How should HIA be financed to allow it to be thoroughly integrated in decision-making and planning, and a sustainable and readily used tool?
- What is the most-effective strategy for training departments of planning, public health, health-care professionals, and others to conduct HIAs?
- How do we continue to develop and identify the knowledge and skills critical to the growth and use of HIA?
- How do we expand the network of professionals and health-care providers to engage with other stakeholders and professions outside the health profession trained to conduct HIAs?

As suggested by these questions, a number of challenges must be met if HIA is to be fully integrated and accepted as a tool to improve health status in the USA. A primary concern is the amount of resources, financial and human, required to conduct HIA. How is it possible to promote and expand HIA practice given the current framework for acquiring and managing the resources that are required? While the national mandate to undertake HIA may be the most compelling and comprehensive, it is also within the jurisdiction and authority of states, agencies, and the private sector to promulgate and support the use of HIA.

HIA: Fostering Change

Strategies for integrating HIA, other public health activities, and policy initiatives into related areas are important to expanding HIA practice and fostering change. The ability to utilize the output of other health assessments as inputs into the HIA process is a strategy worthy of consideration; however, it requires even greater integration with allied professions and disciplines. The opportunity presented by the integration of HIA into environmental requirements articulated in the National Environmental Policy Act (NEPA) has received widespread attention and is discussed extensively in Chap. 3. However, there are other opportunities for integration, directly from the public health world and from the growing impact assessment world.

The Mobilizing for Action through Planning and Partnerships (MAPP), Community Health Assessment and Group Evaluation (CHANGE), and Protocol for Assessing Community Excellence in Environmental Health (PACE EH) are all common public health tools to assess and monitor community health (see Box 17.1).

These tools may be used to identify and incorporate intervention strategies and practices into planning and public health processes.

Box 17.1   Definitions of MAPP, CHANGE, and PACE-EH tools

The Mobilizing for Action through Planning and Partnerships (MAPP) tool is defined by the National Association of City and County Health Officials (NACCHO) as "a community-driven strategic planning process for improving community health. Facilitated by public health leaders, this framework helps communities apply strategic thinking to prioritize public health issues and identify resources to address them. MAPP is not an agency-focused assessment process; rather, it is an interactive process that can improve the efficiency, effectiveness, and ultimately the performance of local public health systems." (NACCHO 2013)

The Community Health Assessment and Group Evaluation (CHANGE) tool is described by the Centers for Disease Control (CDC) as follows: "The CHANGE tool helps community teams (such as coalitions) develop their community action plan. This tool walks community team members through the assessment process and helps define and prioritize possible areas of improvement. Having this information as a guide, community team members can create sustainable, community-based improvements that address the root causes of chronic diseases and related risk factors. It can be used annually to assess current policy, systems, and environmental change strategies and offer new priorities for future efforts." (CDC 2013a)

The Protocol for Assessing Community Excellence in Environmental Health (PACE EH) is described by The Centers for Disease Control (CDC), the National Center for Environmental Health (NCEH), and the National Association for County and City Health Officials (NACCHO) as a methodology that "guides communities and local health officials in conducting community-based environmental health assessments. PACE EH draws on community collaboration and environmental justice principles to involve the public and other stakeholders in: (1) Identifying local environmental health issues, (2) Setting priorities for action, (3) Targeting populations most at risk, and (4) Addressing identified issues." (CDC 2013b)

The MAPP, CHANGE, and PACE EH tools are used extensively in public health and address the root causes of disease. However, they focus on existing conditions within the community. HIA, on the other hand, is a tool intended to predict changes that could potentially happen within a community when a new policy/program/ project is introduced, given current conditions. Thus, it presents an alternative and complementary way of safeguarding community health.

From the impact assessment world, social impact assessment (SIA) comprises another opportunity for integration. One goal of SIA is to drive improvements that increase the value of programs to the people they serve. SIA "helps organizations to plan better, implement more effectively, and successfully bring initiatives to scale. SIA facilitates accountability, supports stakeholder communication, and helps guide the allocation of scarce resources" (Zappala and Lyons 2009). Linking HIA and SIA has the potential both to promulgate the use of HIA and to enhance the ability of organizations accomplish their objectives. The Atlanta BeltLine Redevelopment Project (described in Chap. 5) is one example where HIA was used to increase the physical activity and green space available to stakeholders during the renovation of Atlanta's urban core. In this case, HIA was used to support social objectives; in other cases, SIA may be defined such that human health comprises one component of the socioeconomic environment. It is important to bear in mind that the use of HIA and SIA may be of equal importance to the organization, and that HIA may sometimes need to assume a secondary role.

Health risk assessment (HRA) represents another assessment approach primed for a closer interaction with HIA. HRAs, as described in Chap. 3, estimate the risk of adverse health effects caused by exposure to specific chemicals or hazards. They usually follow a defined methodology outlined by the Environmental Protection Agency (US EPA 2012) and commonly focus only on biophysical risks from exposure to hazardous substances. While this focus is not sufficient to address the broad range of potential effects on human health, consideration of the potential for contaminant exposure remains a critical pillar of safeguarding public health in the context of development.

The circumstances in which HIA is applied need to be considered carefully and in conjunction with identifying how to maximize the potential for HIA to make a unique contribution. One school of thought suggests that the best approach to maximize the use and acceptability of HIA is to undertake the greatest possible number of HIAs. However, another valid approach may be to target more carefully those opportunities that are best suited to demonstrating the contribution of HIA and creating the greatest value. What are the big opportunities and issues that are likely to emerge on the public agenda, as well as those to be addressed by the private sector, where HIA could be applied and demonstrate its value? How can HIA practitioners and proponents prepare to make contributions to these efforts through positioning HIA to be a major part of the decision-making process as the result of its larger integration in the debates? The value of these two approaches needs to be given greater consideration by current practitioners and proponents of HIA. Perhaps, more consideration of this issue can be established as a high priority in the immediate future to both evaluate and consider criteria, implementation, and resource requirements of different approaches to increasing HIA acceptability and practice.

Public health agencies are well situated to provide leadership in HIA initiatives. Their ability to incorporate HIA on a routine basis presents a prime opportunity to institutionalize HIA. Currently, few public health departments are providing this leadership; however, most public health departments are staffed by professionals who have the skills and expertise to commission, undertake, and/or review HIAs, and public health agencies have an optimal position and mandate to monitor, safeguard, and improve public health. A fuller integration of HIA into the programs and practices of public health departments—in the same way that MAPP, CHANGE, and PACE EH have been integrated—is an excellent way to increase the use of HIA in an appropriate venue. In addition, public health agencies often interact with other health professionals and this provides excellent points of contact for these agencies to expand the number of professionals familiar with HIA and its potential to contribute to positive health outcomes. Involvement is also possible and desirable at the state level. Legislation permitting an expanded role for state health agencies in HIA has been proposed in several states including Massachusetts, California, Maryland, Minnesota, and West Virginia (Committee on Health Impact Assessment, National Research Council 2011).

Finally, it is important to recognize that demand for HIA depends on a broad-based recognition that the decisions and actions of different sectors have strong implications for the health of individuals and communities. This message is not new and has been promoted extensively by a wide range of public and private organizations and agencies, within the USA and internationally. However, results are mixed and there has been no widespread, well-organized effort to educate those who are most affected by new policies, strategies, or projects. Any effort to increase the uptake of HIA should therefore also consider the need for capacity-building in this regard. Greater understanding of HIA is important, but more critical is recognition of the fact that projects and policies outside of the health sector have an enormous impact on health.

A look to the future might foresee the inclusion of health considerations in the majority of decisions surrounding policies, programs, and projects, thereby ensuring healthier communities and people—and with HIA taking a strong but not solitary role.

References

Centers for Disease Control (2013a). CHANGE tool—healthy communities program. http://www.cdc.gov/healthycommunitiesprogram/tools/change.htm. Accessed 3 July 2013
Centers for Disease Control (2013b). EHS—CEHA—PACE EH development. http://www.cdc.gov/nceh/ehs/CEHA/PACE_EH.htm. Accessed 3 July 2013
Committee on Health Impact Assessment, National Research Council (2011) Improving health in the United States: the role of health impact assessment. The National Academies Press, Washington, DC
Hodge JG, Fuse Brown EC, Scanlon M, Corbett A (2011) Legal review concerning the use of health impact assessments in non-health sectors. Health Impact Project, Arizona State University Sandra Day O'Connor College of Law, Pew Health Group and Robert Wood Johnson Foundation
National Association of County and City Health Officials (2013) Mobilizing for action through planning and partnerships (MAPP). http://www.naccho.org/topics/infrastructure/mapp/. Accessed 3 July 2013
U.S. Environmental Protection Agency (2012) Human health risk assessment. http://epa.gov/riskassessment/health-risk.htm. Accessed 1 July 2013
Zappala G, Lyons M (2009) Recent approaches to measuring social impact in the third sector: an overview, CSI background paper no. 5. The Center for Social Impact. http://www.csi.edu.au/site/Knowledge_Centre/Asset.aspx?assetid=b20aada17ffad8f7

Appendices

Appendix 1: HIA Reporting Checklist

The checklist below presents a summary of the information that should be included in an HIA report in order to ensure comprehensiveness and transparency, and to give the reader sufficient information to be able to evaluate both the health impact assessment (HIA) itself and the project or policy proposal that is being assessed.

The reporting checklist was adapted from a review package for HIA reports developed by Mette Fredsgaard, Ben Cave, and Alan Bond.[1]

Organization

- Information should be logically arranged in sections or chapters and the whereabouts of important data should be described in a table of contents or index.
- There should be a lay summary (executive summary) of the main findings and conclusions of the study. Technical terms, lists of data, and detailed explanations of scientific methods should be avoided in this summary.
- All evidence and data sources should be clearly referenced.

Project Context

Description of project

- The aims and objectives of the project should be stated and the final operational characteristics of the project should be described. Possible alternatives that are being considered should also be described and it should be noted if no alternatives are being assessed.
- The estimated duration of the construction phase, operational phase, and where appropriate, decommissioning phase should be given.
- The relationship of the project with other proposals should be stated.

---

[1] Fredsgaard MW, Cave B, Bond A (2009) A review package for health impact assessment reports of development projects. Ben Cave Associates Ltd.

C. L. Ross et al., *Health Impact Assessment in the United States,*
DOI 10.1007/978-1-4614-7303-9, © Springer Science+Business Media New York 2014

Site description and policy framework

- The report should describe the physical characteristics of the project site and the surrounding area. The physical characteristics may include the location, design, size, and an outline of the area of land taken during the construction and operation phase. Presentation or reference to diagrams, plans, or maps will be beneficial for this purpose. Graphical material should be easy to understand without having any knowledge about planning and design.
- The report should describe the way in which the project site and the surrounding area are currently used.
- The report should describe the policy context and state whether the project accords with significant policies that protect and promote wellbeing and public health and reduce health inequalities. The policies may be local, regional, national, or international policies or they may be sector specific.

Community profile

- The potentially affected communities should be identified, along with the main ways in which the project may affect these communities.
- A public health profile should be created for the potentially affected communities. The profile should establish an information base from which requirements for health protection, health improvement, and health services can be assessed.
- The profile should identify vulnerable population groups. The profile should describe, where possible, inequalities in health between population groups and should include the wider determinants of health.
- The information in the profile should be specific about the timescale, the geographic location, and the population group being described and links should be made with the proposed project.

Methods

Governance

- The governance process for the HIA should be described. (e.g., Was the HIA guided and scrutinized by a steering group? What was the membership of the steering group? Which organization has final ownership of/accountability for the report and its findings? Was the commissioner's relationship to the HIA process including the development of findings and reporting of the HIA made explicit?).
- The terms of reference for the HIA should be available to the reader and the geographical, temporal, and population scope of the HIA should be made explicit.
- Any constraints in preparing the HIA should be explained. This might include limitations of method or availability of evidence, for example, time, resources, accessibility of data, nonavailability/involvement of key informants and stakeholders. It might also describe any limitations in the scope of the HIA.

Stakeholder Engagement

- The report should identify relevant stakeholder groups, including organizations responsible for protecting and promoting health and wellbeing that should be involved in the HIA.
- The report should describe the engagement strategy for the HIA.

Identification and prediction of health impacts

- The report should describe the screening and scoping stages of the HIA and the methods used in these stages.
- A description of how the *quantitative* evidence was gathered and analyzed (where appropriate) should be given and its relevance to the HIA justified.
- A description of how the *qualitative* evidence was gathered and analyzed (where appropriate) should be given and its relevance to the HIA justified.

Assessment

Description of health effects

- The potential health effects of the project, both beneficial and adverse, should be identified and presented in a systematic way. (Does the identification of impacts consider short-term, long-term (and are these timescales defined?), direct and indirect impacts on health and wellbeing? Does the identification of health impacts distinguish between the construction phase, the operational phase and where relevant the decommissioning phase?)
- The identification of potential health impacts should consider the wider determinants of health such as socio-economic, physical and mental health factors.
- The causal pathway leading to health effects should be outlined along with an explanation of the underpinning evidence.

Risk assessment

- The nature of the potential health effects should be detailed. (e.g. Does the assessment consider the severity of impact/exposure (intensity, reversibility, and impact on vulnerable population groups), the impact magnitude (number of people affected and duration of impact/exposure), and the importance (political and ethical)? Have the health impacts of each alternative been assessed? Sometimes the health impacts are ranked and prioritized before making recommendations, if so, have the criteria for prioritizing and ranking health impacts been given?)
- The findings of the assessment should be accompanied by a statement of the level of certainty or uncertainty attached to the predictions of health effects.
- The report should identify and justify the use of any standards and thresholds used to assess the significance of health impacts.

Analysis of distribution of effects

- The affected populations should be explicitly identified.
- Inequalities in the distribution of predicted health impacts should be investigated and the effects of these inequalities should be stated.

Recommendations

- There should be a list of recommendations to facilitate the management of health effects and the enhancement of beneficial health effects. Some HIAs include recommendations as a management plan and list the roles and responsibilities of stakeholders and provide a timetable for action. Do the recommendations link with the findings of other relevant studies for example, environmental impact assessment (EIA)?

- The level of commitment of the project proponent to the recommendations and mitigation methods should be stated.
- There should be a plan for monitoring future health effects by relevant indicators and a suggested process for evaluation.

Reporting

Discussion of results

- The report should describe how the engagement undertaken has influenced the HIA, in terms of results, conclusions, or approach taken.
- The report should state the effect on the health and wellbeing of the population of the option and any alternatives that have been considered.
- The report should justify any conclusions reached, particularly where some evidence has been afforded greater weight than others.

Appendix 2: Resources for HIA

HIA Associations

- *SOPHIA (Society of Practitioners of Health Impact Assessment)* http://www.hia-society.org
  SOPHIA is an organization serving the needs of HIA practitioners in North America and worldwide and is currently the only professional association for HIA practitioners. The mandate of SOPHIA includes promoting high-quality HIA practice and supporting both new and established HIA practitioners through providing online resources and opportunities such as peer review and mentoring.
- *International Association of Impact Assessment (IAIA) Health Section* http://www.iaia.org/
  IAIA is a forum for advancing innovation, development, and communication of best practice in impact assessment. The international membership promotes development of local and global capacity for the application of environmental, social, health, and other forms of assessment in which sound science and full public participation provide a foundation for equitable and sustainable development.

Planning and Public Health Associations

- *American Planning Association (APA)—Planning and Community Health Research Center* http://www.planning.org/nationalcenters/health/index.htm
  APA is an association for professional planners and students to access resources, news, outreach, education, and networking opportunities related to urban planning. APA's Planning and Community Health Research Center offers resources related to planning healthy places with the understanding that the design of our communities is inextricably tied to health.

- *American Public Health Association (APHA)* http://www.apha.org/
  APHA is a national association of public health professionals working to improve the public's health and to achieve equity in health status for all. APHA provides public health leadership and resources, education, meetings and conferences, as well as information for policy and practice.

Online HIA Community

- *HIA Blog* http://healthimpactassessment.blogspot.com
- *HIA twitter* @hiablog
- *HIANET email discussion group* (to subscribe, follow instructions at https://www.jiscmail.ac.uk/cgi-bin/webadmin?A0=HIANET)

Repositories of Completed HIAs, Guidelines and Toolkits

- *The Health Impact Project (HIP)* http://www.healthimpactproject.org/
  HIP, a collaboration of the Robert Wood Johnson Foundation and The Pew Charitable Trusts, is s a national initiative designed to promote the use of HIA as a decision making tool for policymakers. In addition to offering a library of completed HIAs, their website also includes training materials, PowerPoint presentations, policy briefs and reports, toolkits and guides, literature, and data sources.
- *SOPHIA (Society of Practitioners of Health Impact Assessment)* http://www.hia-society.org
  SOPHIA houses a number of high-quality HIA tools and resources, including showcase examples of excellent HIA reports. The SOPHIA website is also a useful resource for information about HIA training courses, conferences, funding opportunities, and practitioners.
- *UCLA HIA Clearinghouse Learning and Information Center (HIA-CLIC)* http://www.hiaguide.org/
  HIA-CLIC acts as a clearing house for completed HIA reports from the US, and collated background information on the evidence base for health effects in specific sectors such as agriculture, housing, and others.
- *HIA Gateway* http://www.hiagateway.com
  The HIA Gateway, based in the UK provides access to resources and information on HIA for those new to HIA, practitioners of HIA, and those wishing to commission HIAs or other impact assessment process. It houses the largest number of HIAs completed internationally.
- *Health Impact Assessment: Information & Insight for Policy Decisions* http://www.ph.ucla.edu/hs/health-impact/
  The HIA project is a joint endeavor of the Washington, D.C. based Partnership for Prevention and researchers at the UCLA School of Public Health. The resource provides a methodology section, reports and publications, training and relevant links.

- *San Francisco Bay Health Impact Assessment Collaborative* http://www.hiacollaborative.org
  The San Francisco Bay Area HIA Collaborative is a group of academic, government, and non-profit HIA practitioners who have joined together to be more effective in conducting HIA, engaging stakeholders in partnerships, providing training, and helping to develop policy. The website offers a library of helpful tools to conduct HIAs, partnerships, case studies, and policy.
- *Healthy Places: Health Impact Assessment* http://www.cdc.gov/healthyplaces/hia.htm
  This resource, offered by the Centers for Disease Control, recommends HIA as a planning resource for implementing the Healthy People 2020 Objectives. The resource provides fact sheets, general information and clearing houses, online courses and university education opportunities, methodology, tools and evidence for practice, connections to EIA, public policy development, and research for practitioners.
- *Design for Health* http://designforhealth.net/hia/
  This website offers guidance on HIAs targeted to planners. They discuss HIA tools, resources, and general background about HIA, examples of completed HIAs and offer summaries of the peer reviewed literature on a number of topics specifying where evidence is strong, weak, and areas needing more research.
- *HIA Connect* http://www.hiaconnect.edu.au/
  HIA Connect was developed as part of the New South Wales HIA project to support people undertaking HIAs. The site is maintained by the Centre for Health Equity Training, Research and Evaluation (CHETRE), part of the UNSW Research Centre for Primary Health Care and Equity at the University of New South Wales in Sydney, Australia. HIA connect provides resources and information about health impact assessment including a library of reports, evidence, research, and news.
- *IMPACT* http://www.liv.ac.uk/ihia/IMPACT_HIA_Reports.htm
  IMPACT is based in the Division of Public Health, a WHO Collaborating Centre, at the University of Liverpool. The Unit was established in 2000 and provides HIA research, consultancy, and HIA training and capacity building. The website also provides a library of completed HIA reports.
- *World Health Organization (WHO)* http://www.who.int/hia/en/
  WHO is the directing and coordinating authority for health within the United Nations system and is responsible for providing leadership on global health matters. The site provides basic info about HIA as well as tools and methods, examples across sectors, networks, and examples of HIA in policy and decision making.
- *National Collaborating Centre for Healthy Public Policy (Canada).* http://www.ncchpp.ca/docs/HIAGuidesTools2008en.pdf.
  The NCCHPP has put together a very useful guide entitled Health Impact Assessment (HIA): Guides & Tools Inventory.

Other Helpful Resources

- *County Health Rankings* http://www.countyhealthrankings.org/
  This collection of reports available at the county level provides statistics on health outcomes and health determinants to help community leaders and the public see where we live, learn, work, and how play influences, how healthy we are and how long we live.
- *Healthy Development Measurement Tool (HDMT)* http://www.thehdmt.com/
  Started by the San Francisco Department of Public Health, the HDMT is composed of a set of metrics to evaluate the extent to which land use plans, projects, or policies advance human health. The HDMT is broadly organized into six elements that comprise a Healthy City: Environmental Stewardship, Sustainable and Safe Transportation, Public Infrastructure, Social Cohesion, Adequate and Healthy Housing and Healthy Economy.
- *Built Environment and Public Health Curriculum* http://www.bephc.com
  BEPHC.com is designed to provide a critical overview of built environment and public health topics organized into a coherent program of study for a full academic semester, or as individual modules to integrate into specific course topics. Resources provided include guidance on course design, sample syllabi, helpful readings, articles, and websites, organizations, conferences, videos, webinars, and an international listing of planning programs with educational offerings related to public health. It also provides guidance on how to integrate HIAs into teaching or course offerings.
- *InformeDesign* http://www.informedesign.org/
  InformeDesign is an evidence-based design tool that transforms research into an easy-to-read, easy-to-use format for architects, graphic designers, housing specialists, interior designers, landscape architects, and the public. The site is an excellent source of recent data that can help practitioners and policy makers stay up to date on the latest health and place research.
- *NCCOR Catalogue of Surveillance Systems* http://tools.nccor.org/css/
  This web tool provides a catalogue of existing surveillance systems that contain data on diet and physical activity measures. It includes local, state, and national systems that provide data at multiple levels. Users can identify and compare surveillance systems to meet research needs and link to other resources of interest.
- *US Green Building Council's Leadership for Energy and Environmental Design, Neighborhood Development (LEED, ND)* http://www.usgbc.org/DisplayPage. aspx?CMSPageID=148
  LEED ND, collaboration between USGBC, Congress for the New Urbanism, and the Natural Resources Defense Council, is a neighborhood development rating system that integrates the principles of smart growth, urbanism, and green building into the first national system for neighborhood design. In addition to the rating system, the website offers programs and guides, project profiles, case studies, presentations, and additional resources.

Appendix 3: Sample Assessment Sections

The three sample assessment sections that follow pertain to the case studies discussed in Chap. 7: Assessment.

Sample Assessment Section 1:

The following excerpt is taken from the Kansas Health Institute's report *Potential Health Effects of Casino Development in Southeast Kansas* (2012).

The excerpt presents the HIA's summary of health effects associated with potential employment at the casinos.

Casino Employment

Employment and Health

Overall, people who have better access to jobs enjoy better health and have slower declines in health status over time. The presence of a casino in Cherokee or Crawford counties could increase local employment levels. Tangible (e.g., health insurance, income) and intangible benefits (e.g., sense of meaning) of employment may have positive impacts on health.

- **Health insurance.** Having insurance increases access to health services, which in turn affects a person's health and well-being.[44] Regular and reliable access to health services also can prevent disease and disability, detect and treat health conditions, increase quality of life, reduce the likelihood of premature death and increase life expectancy.[45]

- **Income.** People with higher incomes are more likely to have longer life expectancies[46] and healthier body mass index (BMI).[47]

The extent of positive health effects associated with casino employment depends largely on multiple features of the physical (e.g., exposure to secondhand smoke), psychological (e.g., shift work) and social (e.g., economic adequacy) job environment. The following impacts that could result in negative outcomes have been associated with casino employment:

- **Shift work.** Shift and late-night work in casinos can interrupt sleep schedules and lead to insomnia.[48] As a result, shift workers experience an increased risk of morbidity and mortality.[49]

- **Secondhand smoke exposure.** Exposure to secondhand smoke occurs in casinos that don't ban smoking on their premises; such exposure has significant health consequences for non-smokers, such as lung cancer and increased risk of heart disease.[50] Indoor smoking bans that apply to casinos lead to improved air quality and decreased exposure to secondhand smoke, and lower rates of hospitalization for heart attacks.[51]

- **Risk behaviors.** Evidence indicates that casino employees have higher rates of pathological gambling, smoking, alcohol problems and depression than the general adult population.[52]

- **Public assistance.** Casino employment may provide new employees with opportunities to improve their income. However, there can be potential unintended consequences of increased earnings, such as loss of eligibility for public benefits (e.g., child care subsidies, health care coverage, food stamps and others).[53]

Figure 11. Potential Health Impacts of Casino Employment

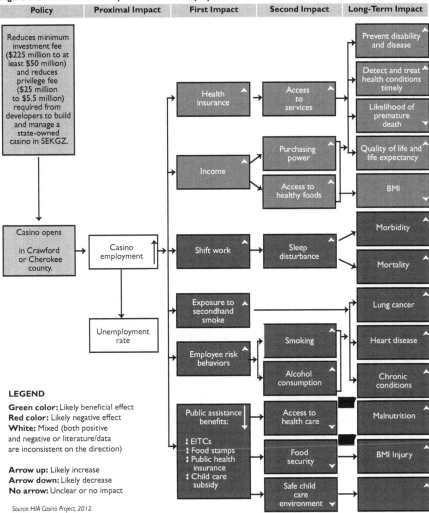

| Policy | Proximal Impact | First Impact | Second Impact | Long-Term Impact |

LEGEND

Green color: Likely beneficial effect
Red color: Likely negative effect
White: Mixed (both positive and negative or literature/data are inconsistent on the direction)

Arrow up: Likely increase
Arrow down: Likely decrease
No arrow: Unclear or no impact

Source: HIA Casino Project, 2012.

As a result, employees can work and earn more income, but not enough to make up for the loss of these benefits. This can further affect their ability to buy needed nutritious foods and health insurance, thus negatively affecting health.[54]

What We Learned From the Community

Low socioeconomic status (SES) and its myriad of impacts on the health of the region seemed to be the overarching theme from the community respondents. Some mentioned poverty and low SES specifically, while others merely alluded to it in citing the poor overall health of Southeast Kansas residents, tied in part to low SES. Regardless of the weight that individual respondents gave to the impact of low SES and poverty, depressed economic conditions and their health impacts ran as a common theme among a vast majority of respondents. Here are some of their statements related to health, poverty and gambling:

"POVERTY HAS TAKEN ITS TOLL ON SOUTHEAST KANSAS — I'M NOT SURE IT'S REVERSIBLE."

- "It would focus more on the income of people and what impact gaming has on discretionary income."

- "Using money that should be used for essentials to gamble."

- "Income levels [are a key factor in the health of a community.]"

- "The culture, social norms and income of an area [affect the health of the community]."

- "The financial condition of the family unit [affects the health of the community]."

- "The transfer of money from the family unit to the gaming industry undermines the well-being of the family unit."

- "Yes — we have to consider that [health data] pretty universally because of the socioeconomic status of our kids. So many things affect their health; we just have to keep that in mind."

- "There is enough to eat — you don't have three families living together."

- "Poverty has taken its toll on Southeast Kansas — I'm not sure it's reversible."

Much like the common theme of poverty and its multitude of impacts on health, the issue of a casino and jobs emerged as the "yin" to poverty's "yang" in the community. As the respondents noted, jobs and the economy are important to any community:

- "Employment potential for some folks — really hard to find a job in this area."

- "Jobs [are a key factor in the health of a community]."

- "It [the casino] would be great for the economy, but not for the health of the residents of

"EMPLOYMENT POTENTIAL FOR SOME FOLKS — REALLY HARD TO FIND A JOB IN THIS AREA."

Southeast Kansas."

- *"Jobs, more money in the community."*

- *"Economic stability."*

- *"It [the casino] would provide additional employment and things in the area, and a lot of times if people are involved, they have access to health care and income to use it."*

- *"Miami, Oklahoma, may be a good model to study because they have seen so many collateral businesses come out of bringing in a casino. It really has made their town boom."*

- *"There was an expectation on environment or — you do want to see — the fact that you are in the poorest region of the state and the reality of poverty in the county. The last time we had the racetrack here, a majority of the employees were uninsured. Will those employees be insured? ... You can't know that."*

- *"I suppose positive in the sense there might be a little more business support of the community with the casino."*

- *"Economically, it would help big time for our community."*

Several community members also identified smoking as a priority health concern in the region. One member said that the state "smoking ban needs to spread to casinos to mitigate the negative impact of smoking in casinos."

What We Learned From the Literature

Jobs and Unemployment

Often a casino is brought into a community to spur economic development. Baxandall's study on the effects of casinos across 26 states found that population levels in casino counties grew around 5 percent faster than non-casino counties.[55] These same counties saw an employment rate increase of 1.1 percent, although there was no significant difference in unemployment rates. This suggests that rises in employment were offset by the increase in population, meaning that there were more jobs dispersed among more people.[56] Wenz did not find a statistically significant increase in quality of life in casino counties.[57] The *Gambling Impact and Behavior Study* found that per capita income stays the same while unemployment rates decline.[58] This suggests that there are new jobs, but they are not necessarily better jobs. Long's look into rural casinos of Colorado and South Dakota found that jobs did increase in the area, but it was unclear how many local residents were employed by the casino.

Shift Work

Employment at a casino often results in late shift hours and interrupted sleep schedules, which can lead to insomnia.[59] Shift workers have an increased risk of morbidity and mortality.[60] Insufficient sleep is also related to a decrease in quality of life[61] and chronic conditions that are associated with insufficient sleep, such as diabetes, cardiovascular disease, obesity and depression.[62] Atlantis created a randomized control study of shift workers, and the researchers found that exercise interventions can significantly improve sleep quality.[63] Shift work or late-hour work impacts employees and their families. Strazdins found that nonstandard work schedules were associated with children's emotional and behavioral difficulties, which may have been due to more hostile and ineffective parenting, parental depression and poorer family functioning.[64,65] Marriages can also be affected by nonstandard work schedules; men with children who are married less than five years and work nights are six times more likely to become separated or divorced from their partner, while women who are married more than five years and work nights and have children are three times more likely to become separated or divorced.[66] When a married couple work nights but have no children, these effects are not seen.[67]

Exposure to Secondhand Smoke

Exposure to secondhand smoke is another concern for casino employees. If smoking is allowed in casinos, as is the law in Kansas, the casino employees are exposed to unhealthy levels of environmental tobacco smoke, which includes carcinogens.[68] These unhealthy levels of exposure can lead to lung cancer and heart disease.[69] Often people will suggest using air conditioning to "wipe away" the smoke from the area, but heating, ventilation and air-conditioning systems can actually distribute the smoke throughout a building.[70] Even conventional air cleaning systems will not properly clean the air: The system can remove the large particles, but the smaller particles or gases from the tobacco smoke will remain.[71] The surgeon general's report on secondhand smoke concluded that the only way to properly protect employees is to have a smoke-free workplace.[72]

Employee Risk Behaviors

Secondhand smoke is not the only way that casino employees can be harmed by tobacco products. Shaffer found that 39.3 percent of casino employees are regular smokers, a rate that is significantly higher than that of smokers in the general population (29.2 percent).[73] Working in a casino also may decrease the likelihood of quitting smoking. Chan found that employees at casinos that allow smoking thought that it was harder to quit smoking when exposed to secondhand smoke at work.[74] Employees also thought that if they were in a smoke-free workplace, they may be more likely to try to quit.[75] Shaffer found that casino employees have higher rates of pathological gambling as compared to the general population, but their problem gambling rates are lower than the average American.[76] The same study found that alcohol problems, depression and smoking are more common among casino employees.[77]

Hing's review of the literature found that new employees may be more at risk for gambling problems but will learn to adapt to the constant gambling presence with time.[78] This study also found that alcohol consumption was high among casino employees, who drank as a way to relax after work.[79] The use of alcohol can increase risky gambling behavior, so drinking can potentially increase gambling among the casino employees.[80] Gambling can also be used as a way to de-stress after work, which can lead to habitual gambling.[81] Options to decrease staff gambling addiction include offering workshops on how to handle job stress, creating a supportive environment for non-gamblers, witnessing the negative effects of gambling addiction among casino patrons and seeing the losses incurred by gambling.[82]

Public Assistance/Public Assistance Benefits

The seminal example of Atlantic City has been studied to determine the impacts of a casino on public assistance, and it found that public assistance cases in the area dropped, partly due to the casino hiring public assistance recipients.[83] A survey of casino employees from 104 land-based, riverboat or tribally owned casinos found that 8.5 percent said their job at the casino allowed them to no longer receive public assistance payments and 9 percent said their casino-based job helped get them off food stamps.[84] Interestingly, being a public assistance recipient is a risk factor for problem and pathological gambling, according to a study done in Sweden.[85,86]

What We Learned From Data

Ford County & Boot Hill Casino Example

Employment at the Boot Hill Casino

According to casino officials, the Boot Hill Casino in Ford County currently employs about 300 workers (280 full-time equivalent workers) (Figure 12, page 36). All of those employees live in Kansas, and fewer than 20 relocated to Ford County to work at the casino. All full-time employees are eligible for health insurance coverage through the casino.

Overall Employment Levels

Since construction on the first phase of the casino began in 2009, overall employment in Ford County has been about 2.5 percent to 3.5 percent higher than it was in 2008, as shown in Figure 13. This equals about 480 more employed individuals each year (2009, 2010 and 2011) since construction began. Some of these additional jobs may end once construction of the casino's second phase is complete or may be unrelated to the development of the casino, so the HIA includes an estimate of the number of jobs using casino job creation multipliers reported in a south-central Kansas casino study.

Job multipliers indicate how many indirect jobs (i.e. jobs outside the casino) might be created as a result of the increased economic activity with the casino. Although different areas typically have different multipliers, the south-central Kansas casino multipliers were applied to the estimated number of full-time Boot Hill employees (280). Based on those calculations, an estimated 335 to 375 direct and indirect jobs related to the casino have been created in Ford County. The opening of a hotel next to the casino this year may generate additional casino-related employment.

Unemployment Rate

Despite increased employment levels in Ford County, the unemployment rate there

Figure 12. Profile of Boot Hill Casino in Dodge City, Ford County (2010).
BOOT HILL CASINO

Casino Format	Land-based (state-owned)
Casino Employees	303
Casino Employee Wages	N/A*
Gross Casino Gaming Revenue	$37.79 million
Gaming Tax Revenue	$9.48 million
How Taxes Spent	State debt reduction, infrastructure improvements, property tax relief, problem gambling treatment
Legalization Date	2007
First Casino Opening Date	2009
State Gaming Tax Rate	22% state tax, 3% local government tax and 2% tax to fund problem gambling treatment
Mode of Legalization	Legislative action, local option vote
Visitor Volume	Data not available

2010 marked the first full year of operations at the country's only state-owned resort casino, and employment, gaming and tax revenue increased as the market in Kansas continued to mature.

*The AGA was unable to obtain employee wage data for Kansas.
Source: American Gaming Association (AGA). *State of the States: The AGA Survey of Casino Entertainment,* (2011 edition).

has grown from a low point of 3 percent in 2008 to a high point of 4 percent in 2011. Over the same time period (2001–2011), unemployment rates for the state and for Crawford and Cherokee counties have risen sharply, as seen in Figure 14. However, the sharp increase in unemployment seen in the statewide rate in 2009 isn't evident in Ford County. That could be a result of jobs created as part of casino construction (started in early 2009) and the subsequent opening of the Boot Hill Casino in December 2009.

Figure 13. Ford County Total Employment

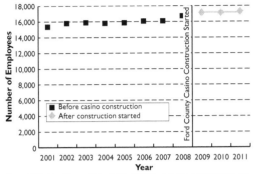

Source: KHI Analysis of Bureau of Labor Statistics (BLS), Quarterly Census of Employment and Wages Data, 2001–2011.

Figure 14. Statewide and Local Unemployment Rates

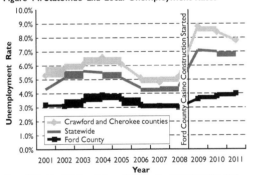

Source: KHI Analysis of BLS, Quarterly Census of Employment and Wages Data, 2001–2011.

Health Disparities and Vulnerable Populations

Social or economic circumstances may make some population groups more vulnerable to the casino impacts. For the purpose of the HIA casino employment proximal impact (Table 8, page 39), vulnerable population groups include casino workers and/or individuals who are:

- Low-income
- Elderly
- Young adults (students)
- Shift workers, especially with children
- Individuals with substance use disorders
- Individuals who have mental illnesses
- Individuals who are uninsured

Health Implications for SEKGZ

Based on literature review and labor market data for Ford County (which has no nearby casinos) and the Northeast Kansas Gaming Zone, the addition of a SEKGZ casino is likely to increase local employment by 300 to 350 jobs. Furthermore, overall local employment levels can be expected to rise once casino construction begins. Literature review shows that building a casino in SEKGZ would not likely result in a lower local unemployment rate because rises in employment are usually offset by an increase in population, meaning that there are more jobs dispersed among more people. In addition, the literature review shows that the impact of a casino on the local unemployment rate depends on the extent that newly hired employees relocate or commute from elsewhere, other changes in the local labor market or population, and how other economic conditions affect the local labor market.

In general, stakeholders noted that a casino could bring economic benefits, including "a little more business support of the community" and "jobs and money in the community." However, stakeholders were somewhat divided in their views about a casino's potential health impacts. Some stakeholders thought a casino would improve access to health care and result in health benefits associated with increased income. Other stakeholders raised concerns about the negative impacts of a casino on the financial stability of families if people spend their money on gambling rather than essentials. Stakeholders also noted a number of factors that are likely to influence the degree to which a SEKGZ casino actually improves the health of residents; for example, whether a casino provides health insurance for its employees and their families.

Based on findings from the literature review, data analysis and stakeholder opinion, new casino jobs may increase income for residents of Cherokee and Crawford counties as well as offer insurance to full-time employees. Increased income and access to health insurance may improve access to health care services and healthy foods, thus improving the health (e.g., reducing mortality and morbidity, increasing quality of life and life expectancy, reducing BMI) of SEKGZ casino employees and their families. As noted earlier, employment, insurance and income have strong, positive links to health. In order to achieve these positive health impacts, it is important to address potential negative effects of casino employment, such as shift work and exposure to secondhand smoke, which can lead to increased risk of morbidity and mortality, lung cancer and heart disease (Table 9).

Table 8. Potential Health Impacts of Casino Employment on Vulnerable Populations

Proximal Impact	Examined Health Factors	Examined Health Outcomes	Vulnerable Populations
Casino Employment	Income and health insurance, shift work and sleep disturbance, secondhand smoke exposure, risk behaviors, public assistance.	**Positive:** Lower rates of disability and disease, timely detection and treatment of health conditions, decreased likelihood of premature death, improved quality of life, increased life expectancy, lower BMI. **Negative:** Increased risk of morbidity and mortality, lung cancer, heart disease, chronic conditions, malnutrition, BMI and injury.	Low-income casino workers and their families; uninsured casino workers; casino shift workers, especially those with children; elderly; students; casino workers (e.g., young adults, individuals with mental illnesses, individuals with substance use disorders).

Source: Kansas HIA Project, 2012.

Table 9. Summary Health Impacts of a Casino Presence in SEKGZ: Casino Employment

Health Factor or Outcome	Expected Change Based on Literature	Observed Changes in Kansas (Based on Data)	Stakeholder Projections	Expected Health Impact	Magnitude of Impact	Likelihood of Impact	Distribution	Quality of Evidence
				Based Primarily on Evidence From Literature				
Casino employment	Increase	Increase	Increase	Mixed	Low	Likely	Casino workers and their families	****
Unemployment rate	No change	No change	Decrease	No effect	None	None	No change	***
Health insurance	Increase	N/A	Mixed	Positive	Low	Likely	Casino full-time workers and their families	****
Income	Increase	N/A	Mixed	Positive	Low	Likely	Casino workers and their families	****
Shift work and sleep disturbance	Increase	N/A	N/A	Negative	Low	Likely	Casino workers and their families	**
Secondhand smoke exposure	Increase	N/A	Increase	Negative	Medium	Likely	Casino workers and patrons	****
Employee risk behaviors	Increase	N/A	Increase	Negative	Low	Possible	Casino workers	***
Public assistance benefits	Decrease	N/A	Mixed	Negative	Low	Possible	Public assistance recipients who become casino workers	**

Note: See legend, page 40.
Source: Kansas HIA Project, 2012.

Legend for Table 9

Expected Change Based on Literature	• No change — The literature achieves consensus that this indicator will likely remain unchanged. • Mixed — The literature lacks consensus about this indicator's potential impact. • Increase — The literature achieves consensus that this indicator will likely increase. • Decrease — The literature achieves consensus that this indicator will likely decrease. • N/A — There is no available literature on this indicator.
Observed Changes in Kansas (Based on Data)	• No change — Data analysis did not show any large changes. • Mixed — Data analysis from different regions showed opposite changes. • Increase — Data analysis showed this indicator will likely increase. • Decrease — Data analysis showed this indicator will likely decrease. • N/A — Data analysis was not possible or performed for this indicator.
Stakeholder Projections	• No change — Stakeholders did not anticipate any changes. • Mixed — Stakeholders were divided in their opinions. • Increase — Stakeholders anticipated seeing an increase. • Decrease — Stakeholders anticipated seeing a decrease. • N/A — Stakeholders did not express their opinions about this issue.
Expected Health Impact	• Positive — Changes that may improve health. • Negative — Changes that may worsen health. • Mixed — Changes can be positive as well as negative. • Uncertain — Unknown how health will be impacted. • No effect — No identified effect on health. Note: When findings from different sources (data, literature, stakeholder opinion) were not consistent, expected health impact was determined primarily based on findings from the literature because the HIA team determined it was the best available source of information.
Magnitude of Impact	• Low — Affects no or very few people (such as only certain groups of casino workers). • Medium — Affects larger numbers of people (such as casino workers and patrons). • High — Affects many people (such as the city of Pittsburg).
Likelihood of Impact	• Likely — It is likely that impacts will occur as the result of this proposal. • Possible — It is possible that impacts will occur as the result of this proposal. • Unlikely — It is unlikely that impacts will occur as the result of this proposal. • Uncertain — It is uncertain that impacts will occur as the result of this proposal.
Distribution	The population most likely to be affected by changes in the health factor or outcome. Determination was based on literature review, data analysis and expert opinion. • No change — Did not anticipate any changes.
Quality of Evidence	**** More than five strong studies. May also include data analysis and expert opinion. *** Five or more moderate studies. May also include data analysis and expert opinion. ** Five weak studies. May also include data analysis and expert opinion. * Fewer than five studies.

Sample Assessment Section 2:

The following excerpt is taken from the San Francisco Department of Public Health report *A Health Impact Assessment of California Assembly Bill 889: The California Domestic Work Employee Equality, Fairness, and Dignity Act of 2011* (2011).

The excerpt presents the HIA's analysis for the health effects of uninterrupted sleep requirements.

7 HEALTH IMPACTS OF PROPOSED UNINTERRUPTED SLEEP REQUIREMENTS

Passage of the California Domestic Work Employee Equality, Fairness, and Dignity Act of 2011 would require employers to allow their employees eight hours of uninterrupted sleep in adequate sleeping conditions when their employees work 24 hour or longer shifts or live in their employer's home. This chapter analyzes how this proposed legal requirement would effect the health of domestic workers and care-recipients in California utilizing the logic model used for this assessment illustrated in Figure 3.

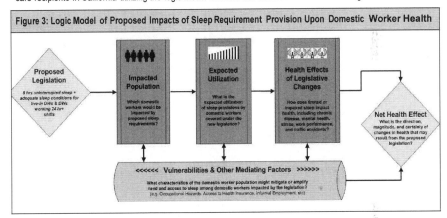

Figure 3: Logic Model of Proposed Impacts of Sleep Requirement Provision Upon Domestic Worker Health

Consistent with the logic model, the analysis answers the following questions:

7.1 What are the known health effects of limited or impaired sleep?

7.2 What is the evidence for insufficient sleep among domestic workers?

7.3 Which domestic workers would be impacted by a change in sleep requirements?

7.4 How would the legislation change hours or quality of sleep of domestic workers?

7.5 How would the legislation impact care-recipients?

7.6 What is the likelihood, certainty, and magnitude of health effects resulting from the legislative changes to sleep requirements?

7.7 What barriers, vulnerabilities, or uncertainty factors could modify the health effects of the law?

Box 4: AB 889 Sleep Provisions

1455. (a) A DW employee who is required to be on duty for 24 consecutive hours or more shall have a minimum of 8 consecutive hours for uninterrupted sleep, except in an emergency. (b) ...may agree in writing to exclude a bona fide regularly scheduled sleeping period... (c) ...not receive 8 consecutive hours... if... employer did not hire a replacement worker for at least 8 consecutive hours in a 24 hour work period. ...
(d) ...employer who violates...shall pay a sum of $50... for each day...violated provision.
1456. (a) A live-in DW employee who is not required to be on duty for 24 consecutive hours or more shall have at least 12 consecutive hours free of duty during each workday of 24 hours, of which a minimum of 8 consecutive hours are for uninterrupted sleep. A live-in DW employee suffered or permitted to work during the 12 consecutive off-duty hours shall be compensated .... (b) No live-in domestic work employee shall be required to work more than five days in any one workweek, without a day off of not less than 24 consecutive hours, except in an emergency. If the live-in domestic work employee is suffered or permitted to work in excess of five workdays in any workweek, the domestic work employee shall be compensated....
(c) ...employer who violates...shall pay a sum of $50...for each day that he or she violated this provision.
1457. Live-in DW employees and DW employees who work 24 hours or more shall have sleeping accommodations that are adequate, decent, and sanitary according to usual customary standards... shall not be required to share a bed.

7.1 What are the known health effects of limited or impaired sleep?

Sleep is essential for health. Scientists generally agree that sleep has multiple physiological functions. Researchers are still working to understand the complex functions of sleep; however, the evidence definitively shows that sleep plays a critical role in the normal function of the body's cardiovascular, respiratory, nervous, endocrine and immune systems. The restorative or "life-sustaining" function of sleep allows for healthy functioning of the endocrine and immune systems. The cognitive function of sleep allows for healthy brain development, and optimal learning and memory throughout life (Frank 2005, Harvard DSM, Walker 2009).

Health requires regular, sufficient sleep in a daily cycle. Circadian rhythms are the body's natural physiological and behavioral cycles. Circadian rhythms regulate body temperature, heart rate, muscle tone, and daily hormone secretion; modulate physical activity and food consumption; and control the sleep-wake cycle. Habitual sleep in keeping with circadian rhythms is associated with lower risk of cardiovascular disease, diabetes, and obesity; higher cognitive function; decreased risk for depression and anxiety; lower rates of injury; and decreased risk for immune impairment (Ulmer 2009, Frank 2006). Physiological processes – such as brain activity, heart rate, blood pressure and respiration – operate differently during sleep compared to wakefulness. These differences are also impacted by the type of sleep – known as non-rapid eye-movement (NREM) sleep and rapid eye-movement (REM) sleep (Colten 2006).

Basal sleep need is the amount of sleep the body needs on a regular basis for optimal performance. Sleep need varies somewhat by individuals; however, public health evidence shows that the optimal nightly average is seven or eight hours (Colten 2006, Lee-Chiong 2006, Pandi-Perumal 2007).

Sleep less than the basal sleep need leads to sleepiness and fatigue. Fatigue refers to a physical state of exhaustion, manifested in symptoms such as lethargy, lack of energy, tiredness, decreased strength and difficulty with concentration. Sleepiness and fatigue lead to functional impairments such as slower reaction time, reduced vigilance and deficits in information processing, which have consequences not just for the individual worker but also for the employer and broader society (U.S. DOT 1998). Dose-response studies have established that there is a relationship between the average number of hours of sleep and health outcomes including risk of hypertension, diabetes, obesity, mental health problems and mortality (Gangwisch 2006, Di Milia 2009, Hall 2008, Ayas 2003(a), Ayas 2003(b), Geiger-Brown 2004).

In a normal sleep-wake cycle, after a period of wakefulness, the body normally signals the need for sleep. However, after 16 to 18 hours of wakefulness, the brain's circadian system no longer opposes the physiological pressure for sleep. Thus, acute sleep deprivation begins when an individual remains awake over 16 hours or into their habitual sleep period. This results in sleepiness, fatigue, memory and attention lapses, and decreased cognitive and motor performance (Ulmer 2009, Colten 2006). Sleep debt is accumulated sleep deprivation.

Recognizing the relationship of sleep and health, minimum sleep and rest standards have been disseminated for certain occupational types. Most commonly, these regulations are promulgated to protect public health and safety and not the health of the worker. Appendix B summarizes sleep standards for several different types of workers in the United States.

The sections below provide a summary of the evidence for the direct and distal effects of sleep upon health as illustrated in Figure 4. We were able to identify systematic reviews or meta-analyses for the following health endpoints: mortality (Cappuccio 2010, Gallicchio 2009), obesity (Patel 2008, Cappuccio 2008), and cardiovascular disease (Cappuccio 2011). For other health endpoints, the protocol for literature review is described in the section on methodology.

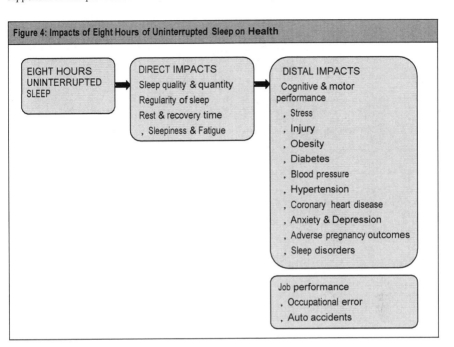

Figure 4: Impacts of Eight Hours of Uninterrupted Sleep on Health

---

Box 5: Health Effects of Shift Work

Research on shift work provides evidence relevant to the potential health impacts of sleep. Shift work is defined as a schedule in which at least fifty percent of the employee's required work occurs between 4pm and 8am (Shen 2006). Rotating shift work is defined as a schedule in which the employee's required work alternates between the day, evening, and night shifts (Kawachi 1995). Individuals working night shifts are more likely to have insufficient or poor quality sleep than those with day time shifts (Akerstedt 2003, Ohanyon 2010).

Cross-sectional studies of shift workers in a variety of industries – manufacturing, long-haul driving, nurses, medical interns, nursing home attendants and other health care workers – provide evidence relevant to the cognitive and motor performance impacts of insufficient sleep. In a study of 405 shift workers, Shen et al. (2005) found a significant correlation between frequency of shift work and fatigue and the extent to which workers reported that fatigue intruded on their everyday life. Workers who engaged in shift work three or more days a week reported the highest levels of fatigue, with common complaints including irritability, difficulty concentrating and a lack of energy for other activities.

Research shows that shift workers are at greater risk for obesity and have higher mean BMI than day workers (Eberly 2010). A cross sectional study of 27,485 workers in Sweden found that women working night shifts have increased risk for metabolic syndrome[27] compared to workers who just work during the day. Women working shifts had a relative risk of 1.71 of testing positive for three metabolic variables, compared to women working normal day hours (Karlsson 2001).

Shift work is associated with significant mental health impacts, especially for women working as caregivers. Geiger-Brown and colleagues (2004) studied 473 female nursing assistants working in nursing homes in the United States to understand how schedule demands impacted workers' mental health. Working two or more double-shifts per month was associated with increased risk for all mental health indicators studied. Double-shift workers were at three times the risk for depression and showed a 75% increased risk for anxiety. Further, odds of depression were four times higher for nursing assistants that had multiple schedule demands: working over 50 hours a week, more than two weekends a month and more than two double shifts a month (Geiger-Brown 2004).

Shift work, and especially night shift work, increases the risk and severity of injuries for health care workers. Horwitz et al. (2004) conducted a cross sectional analysis of workers' compensation claims filed by hospital employees in Oregon from 1990 -1997. The injury rate for day shift workers was 176 per 10,000 compared to 324 for the evening shift and 279 for the night shift. Injuries to workers on the night shift were more severe overall with workers injured on the night shift averaging 46 days off for injury disability compared to 39 days off for evening shift workers and 38 for day shift. (Horwitz 2004)

In a prospective nationwide survey of medical residents, Barger et al. (2005) found that 86.5% of residents working extended shifts in the hospital slept four hours or less during their work shift of 24 hours or more. The survey found that the increased odds for reporting a motor vehicle crash after an extended shift was 2.3 and the increased odds for a near-miss accident was 5.9, compared to residents not working extended shifts. Each additional extended work shift scheduled in a month increased the monthly risk of crash during the commute by 16.2 percent (Barger 2005).

---

[27] Metabolic syndrome refers to a set of metabolic risk factors for coronary heart disease and type 2 diabetes. Metabolic risk factors include abdominal obesity, high triglycerides, low concentrations of HDL cholesterol, elevated blood pressure, and glucose intolerance (AHA 2010).

Box 6: Health Effects of Long Working Hours

The diagram below outlines a framework for studying the undesirable impacts of long working hours. This diagram was created by the National Occupational Research Agenda (NORA) Long Work Hours team to support future research on the health impacts of long work hours. The team, which included experts from industry, labor and government, conducted an extensive literature review and gathered input from attendees at a conference on long work hours to develop the framework illustrated below.

Similar to the findings in the Sleep section below, the Long Work Hours team found that long work hours can impact (1) workers' injuries, illnesses, quality of life and earning capacity; (2) the relationships, income and work burden of family members of the worker and the care-recipient; (3) the worker's productivity, quality of care, and injury costs; and (4) more broadly, the community at-large via likelihood of accidents, work errors and occupational injury and illness costs. The researchers found that long work hours contribute to reduced/disturbed sleep, fatigue, stress, negative mood, discomfort, pain, and neurological, cognitive and physiological dysfunction. These impacts may be mediated by worker vulnerabilities, the characteristics of the job, and various societal and individual level factors. This research framework and agenda could be helpful to shaping the formation of research on domestic workers and the impacts of sleep and rest requirements upon the worker and quality of care.

For more information about the NORA Long Work Hours report and other health effects of work schedules, please visit http://www.cdc.gov/niosh/topics/workschedules/

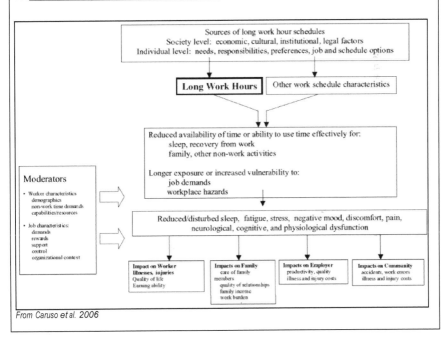

From Caruso et al. 2006

7.2.1   Sleep and Life Expectancy

Large cross-sectional and prospective studies show that people who routinely sleep five or fewer hours a night have a 10 -15% increased risk for all-cause mortality compared to people who sleep seven to eight hours a night (Gallicchio 2009, Kripke 2002, Patel 2004, Tamakoshi 2004, Ferrie 2007). A meta-analysis of 16 studies (27 cohort samples with 1.4 million participants) found that short sleep duration (less than five or seven hours of sleep) increases risk of death by 12% compared to those who slept seven or eight hours a night (Cappuccio 2010). Cappuccio and colleagues found that the causative mechanisms for increased morbidity from short

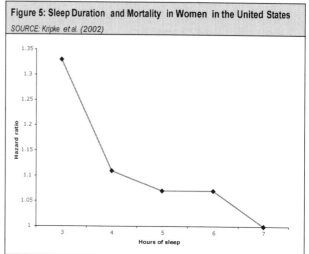

Figure 5: Sleep Duration and Mortality in Women in the United States
SOURCE: Kripke et al. (2002)

sleep duration were metabolic syndrome and stress-related (increased cortisol secretion and inflammation). Sleeping more than eight or nine hours was also associated with increased risk of death, compared to those who slept seven or eight hours per night, however the mechanism was unknown and authors believed that confounding and co-morbidities may have influenced risk. Kripke et al. (2002) found evidence for an exposure-response relationship between average hours of sleep and mortality (See Figure 5). Using the Whitehall II cohort of British civil servants, Ferrie and colleagues (2007) found that decreases in sleep duration over a three- to five- year period were associated with a 110% excess risk of mortality from cardiovascular disease after controlling for relevant risk factors.

7.2.2   Sleep and Chronic Disease

Research shows that insufficient sleep is associated with increased risk for obesity, diabetes, hypertension and coronary heart disease (Isomaa 2001, Lakka 2002, Knutson 2007, Cappuccio 2008, Patel 2008, Gottlieb 2006).

Hypertension
A longitudinal analysis of 4,810 participants in NHANES I (National Health and Nutrition Examination Survey) found that sleep duration of less than five hours per night was associated with a significantly increased risk of hypertension for participants 32-59 years old – twice the risk compared to those who slept eight hours a night (Gangwisch 2006).

Heart Disease
A systematic review and meta-analysis of articles published between 1997 and 2009 found that in the 15 studies (24 cohort samples with 474,684 participants) short sleep duration (less than five or seven hours of sleep) was associated with an increased risk of developing or dying of coronary heart disease (RR = 1.48) and stroke (RR = 1.15) (Cappuccio 2011). A large prospective cohort study of nurses in the United States found that short sleep duration has a significant impact on coronary heart disease. Compared to the

reference group of nurses that reported an average of eight hours of daily sleep, nurses who slept six hours had a relative risk of 1.30 for developing coronary health disease and nurses who slept less than five hours had a relative risk of 1.82 (Ayas 2003b). The same study also found that nurses who slept less than five hours nightly had an increased risk for diabetes (RR=1.57) (Ayas 2003a).

Obesity
Patel and Hu (2008) conducted a systematic review of manuscripts published between 1966 and 2007 on the relationship between short sleep duration and weight gain, finding there was a clear and strong association between short sleep duration and concurrent and future obesity among children. Among adults, there was a more mixed association with 17 of 23 studies finding an independent association between short sleep duration and weight gain. Though the association wanes with age, three longitudinal studies also found a positive association between short sleep duration and future weight gain in adults (Patel 2008). Cappuccio and colleagues (2008) conducted a meta-analysis of articles analyzing a relationship between short sleep duration and obesity at different ages. The authors found a pooled odds ratio of 1.89 for children (95% Confidence Interval: 1.46 to 2.43; P < 0.0001) and 1.55 for adults (95% Confidence Interval: 1.43 to 1.68; P < 0.0001), suggesting that short sleep duration consistently increases risk of obesity among both children and adults. However, the authors note that drawing any definite conclusion "is difficult due to lack of control for important confounders and inconsistent evidence of temporal sequence in prospective studies." (Cappuccio 2008)

Insufficient sleep duration is also associated with increased risk of metabolic syndrome (Karlsson 1999). DiMilia et al. (2009) conducted a cross sectional survey of 346 shift and day workers in the coal industry and found that long working hours (OR=2.82), age (OR=2.05) and short sleep duration (OR=1.92) were the most important predictors of obesity. A study of middle-aged adults in Pennsylvania found similar results of increased risk for metabolic syndrome associated with short sleep duration (Hall 2008).

7.2.3 Sleep, Stress and Mental Health

Sleep deprivation studies show that short-term reduced sleep duration among healthy volunteers is associated with stress-related health effects such as elevated blood pressure and increased production of cortisol[28] (Ulmer 2009, Colten 2006, Lee-Chiong 2006, Pandi-Perumal 2007). Over time, chronic stress negatively impacts the health of adults and children through its impacts on neuroendocrine, vascular, immune and inflammatory mechanisms. Specifically, chronic stress can accelerate aging and increase risk of heart disease, stroke, diabetes, low birth weight or premature birth, depression, anxiety, stroke, and other conditions (McEwen 1998, Harvard CDC 2007, Bauer 2004, Hertzman 2003).

Research shows that shortened sleep hours are related to increased depression, anger, frustration, tension, and anxiety (Kahn-Green 2007, Sagaspe 2006, Babson 2010). Lack of adequate sleep can result in the magnification of negative reactions to adverse experiences and mitigation of positive reactions to pleasant events (Zohar 2005). Negative reactions to adverse experiences could negatively impact caregiving and the ability of care providers to provide empathetic and positive care for care-recipients.

7.2.4 Cognitive and Motor Performance

Experimental research shows that sleep deprivation significantly impacts cognitive and motor performance. Cognitive and motor performance lapses are of particular concern in a caregiving setting because those performance lapses lead to errors and decreased quality of care (Ulmer 2009, Estabrooks 2009, Surani 2008). Experimental research has consistently shown that individuals who sleep less than five hours a night experience acute sleepiness and fatigue that is manifested in the short term in decreased cognitive and motor performance (Belensky 2003, Dongen 2003).

---

[28] Often called the "stress hormone," cortisol in the saliva is increasingly used as a physiologic measure of stress. Although cortisol can support quicker reactions in adverse moments (e.g. "fight or flight responses"), long-term exposure can harm health.

A review and meta-analysis of sixty studies published between 1971 and 2005 involving 959 physician and 1028 non-physician participants found that sleep deprivation impacts human performance measures including cognitive function, vigilance, fine motor skills and mood. In pooled analysis, sleep deprivation reduced cognitive performance by nearly one standard deviation (-.951). The meta-analysis also showed significant and large effects on clinical performance, memory and vigilance. The authors also identified several aspects of sleep deprivation that have not been studied with respect to performance: chronic partial sleep deprivation, work task duration, pacing and complexity of tasks (Philbert 2005).

Another review and meta-analysis of nineteen studies found that "sleep deprivation strongly impairs human functioning" in the areas of cognitive performance, motor performance and mood. In pooled analysis, sleep deprivation reduced cognitive performance by 1.37 standard deviations. The authors found that mood was most affected by sleep deprivation, followed by cognitive performance and motor performance. Partial sleep deprivation was found to have a surprisingly strong overall effect, which points to the importance of circadian rhythms in day-to-day mood and function (Pilcher 1996).

Figure 6 illustrates the dose-response relationship between sleep restrictions and cumulative cognitive impairment. Belenky et al. (2003) studied the effects of cumulative sleep deprivation on an individual's capacity to detect and respond to a stimulus in the environment (a light) and to sustain attention. Individuals who slept seven and nine hours performed significantly better than those who slept three hours, and the performance gap widened over several days of accumulated sleep deprivation. After seven days, individuals sleeping seven hours a night were averaging one-third as many performance lapses compared to individuals sleeping three hours a night (Belenky 2003).

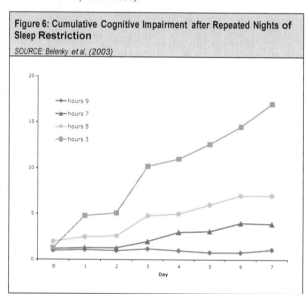

Figure 6: Cumulative Cognitive Impairment after Repeated Nights of Sleep Restriction

SOURCE: Belenky et al. (2003)

7.2.5 Work Errors & Injuries

An indirect effect of impairment in cognitive performance is the increased likelihood of errors and decreased performance which may negatively impact quality of care. Caregivers who are sleepy or fatigued may be more stressed in their relationship with their employer, more likely to have difficulty with problem-solving or detail-oriented tasks, and more prone to household or motor vehicle accidents (McCurry 2007). A one-year randomized intervention study of medical residents compared medical errors among residents who worked a conventional extended 24-hour shift to those who worked an intervention schedule with no extended shifts. Serious medical errors were reduced by 36% among those working the intervention schedule and PAEs (measurement of harm reaching the patient) were reduced by 27% (Ulmer 2009). The American Medical Association evaluated this study, concluding that the performance improvements and reduction in medical errors were largely attributable to the intervention rather than any other confounding factors. Most studies of the effects of shift length on patient care compare eight and twelve-hour shifts, and show a significant difference, with more errors and accidents among nurses who work twelve-hour shifts (Estabrooks 2009). These studies suggest that insufficient sleep may increase the likelihood of a work error that could result in injury to the worker, care-recipient or both.

7.2.6 Traffic Accidents

Drowsy driving is the reported cause of over 100,000 crashes annually in the United States, and according to the Department of Transportation, it is "widely recognized that drowsy driving is underreported as a cause of crashes" (U.S. DOT). One study by the National Highway Traffic Safety Administration placed electronic monitors on a random sample of 100 volunteer drivers over 13 months of driving and found that drowsiness was a contributing factor in 20% of all crashes (Klauer 2006). A systematic review of epidemiological studies that evaluated the role of driver sleepiness found that risk increases substantially when the driver had slept less than five hours or when driving in the early morning hours. Cumulative sleep debt in shift workers also compounded levels of sleepiness. The authors estimate that 15-20% of motor vehicle crashes in high-income countries are attributable to driver sleepiness (Connor 2009).

Recent studies have shown that health care professionals who work long shifts are at significantly increased risk for falling asleep while driving and for motor vehicle crashes. A study of 2737 medical residents found that a documented motor vehicle crash was more than twice as likely to occur after an extended work shift (24 hours) than after a non-extended shift. The odds of a near-motor vehicle crash, as reported by the medical residents, were more than five times as high after working an extended shift (Barger 2005). The same study found that each extended work shift scheduled in a month increased the monthly risk of a motor vehicle crash by 9.1 percent. If residents worked five or more extended shifts in a month, the study also found a significantly increased risk that they would fall asleep while driving (OR=2.39) or while stopped in traffic (OR=3.69) (Barger 2005).

Similarly, a study of 895 hospital nurses found that two-thirds of nurses reported at least one episode of drowsy driving in a month during their return commute. The risk for an episode of drowsy driving doubled when nurses worked shifts over 12 hours. The same study found that 16% of the nurses reported a motor vehicle crash or near-motor vehicle crash, and 60% of those reported incidents occurred following shifts of longer than 12 hours (Scott 2007). These studies show that the risks associated with drowsy driving and motor vehicle accident are not reserved to driving-related professions. Health care and caregiving professionals that work long shifts are at increased risk for falling asleep while driving and for motor vehicle crashes which makes their sleep deprivation a public health concern for all people involved in motor vehicle travel.

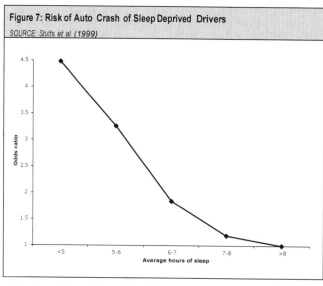

Figure 7: Risk of Auto Crash of Sleep Deprived Drivers
SOURCE: Stutts et al. (1999)

Stutts et al. (1999) and the AAA Foundation for Traffic Safety found a dose-response relationship between average hours of sleep and likelihood of sleep-related crash. The risk for drivers who slept five hours was half the risk of drivers who slept less than five hours, yet was twice the risk for crash for drivers who slept eight hours (Figure 7). The risk of traffic accidents has led to the creation of work limitations for certain occupations including pilots, truck drivers, and railroad conductors (See Appendix B).

7.2   What is the evidence for insufficient sleep among domestic workers?

To date, the number of domestic workers experiencing sleep impairment and the average length of sleep in this population has not been enumerated via survey or other research methods. However, it is reasonable to assume that the work environment contributes to insufficient sleep for a subset of domestic workers. A subset of domestic workers who provide care to children, the elderly, sick or disabled adults often provide care at night during typical sleeping hours. People with dementia or severe chronic disease have nocturnal needs for care (McCurry 1999, McCurry 2007, Carter 2000). Studies conducted over the past fifteen years have found that two-thirds of family caregivers for people with dementia experience sleep disturbances, and 80% of those experience sleep disturbances more than once a week (Wilcox 1999, McCurry 1995).

Other domestic workers are working 24-hour shifts or living in their employer's home. These workers are typically expected to perform work tasks both at night and during the day, depending upon the needs of the employer and care-recipient. This may contribute to an irregular and disrupted sleep schedule, which can also be a contributing factor to the development of sleep disorders such as insomnia that become a further barrier to uninterrupted sleep (Schulz 2004, McCurry 2009).

7.3   Which domestic workers would be impacted by a change in sleep requirements?

The proposed legislative protections for sleep would impact only a subset of California domestic workers — live-in workers or those who work 24 or more hours with one employer. Personal attendants and personal and home care aides are the types of domestic workers most likely to be impacted by this provision since they regularly provide long hours of continuous care. Child care providers, especially live-in nannies, would also be impacted. Housekeepers and maids may be impacted however it is anticipated that the majority of cleaning-related domestic work is performed by domestic workers who live outside their employer's home. According to our estimates, 43% of domestic workers in California are either classified as personal and home care aides or as child care workers (see Table 6). However it is not known what proportion of these workers work 24 or more hours or live in their employers home.

As noted in Section 6, the need for 24-hour care will continue to increase in the coming decades according to the projections of long-term care-recipients who prefer to receive care in their homes rather than enter a long-term care facility. Some care-recipients do not require round-the-clock care but some people with dementia, chronic disease or disability do need to have someone on call 24 hours a day (Smith 2009, U.S. DHHS 2003). Thus the number of home health care and personal care providers in California is projected to double by 2018 (CA EDD 2010), which would significantly increase the number of individuals impacted by the proposed AB 889 legislation.

As currently written, AB 889 allows for domestic workers and their employers to write a bona fide mutually agreed written agreement to forego the law's sleep requirements. This provision would allow for certain exceptions to the law when mutually agreed upon by both the worker and the employer. However, it is assumed that the majority of employers of live-in domestic workers and 24-hour caregivers would be required to comply with this provision.

7.4   How would the legislation change hours or quality of sleep of domestic workers?

AB 889 sleep provisions require employers of domestic workers to provide 1) a minimum of eight consecutive hours of sleep and 2) an adequate, decent, and sanitary sleeping location for domestic workers who work 24 or more consecutive hours. This rule applies both to live-in domestic workers and to personal attendants (Box 4).

Assuming compliance with the law, domestic workers who live in their employers' homes and domestic workers working 24 hours or more would be expected to have improved sleep conditions. Specifically, domestic workers would be expected to be able to rest for at least eight hours without interruption in a location that is suitable and adequate for sleeping.

7.5   How would the legislation impact care-recipients?

The care needs of employers of domestic workers differ. For example, employers of live-in domestic workers who primarily provide housekeeping may already place few nighttime demands on their workers or may more easily be able to meet the sleep requirements. In these cases, the provision is not likely to impact care-recipients.

Where 24 hour care is essential, for example for some disabled individuals, AB 889 sleep provision may result in employers' needing to hire additional employees. However, the total hours of work and thus employer costs should not change as the employer is currently required to pay for all hours worked. Alternatively, the employer may choose to forego care during the eight hour period that the domestic worker is sleeping or have a family member provide the care. It is not possible to judge whether the quality of care would change due to these reasons.

As described above, AB 889 sleep provisions may indirectly improve quality of care for care-recipients by reducing sleep deprivation and resulting impairment of cognitive motor performance. Regular sleep would a) decrease the likelihood of work errors and accidents that may negatively impact the care-recipient and b) result in more well-rested, healthier, and more focused workers.

Currently personal attendants are excluded from overtime laws and meal and rest break requirements. Other provision of AB 889, including overtime provision and paid sick days, could potentially impact the cost of 24 hour care; however, these provisions are not the subject of this HIA.

220

Appendices

7.6 What is the likelihood, certainty, and magnitude of health effects resulting from the legislative changes to sleep requirements?

In summary, based on the available evidence, understanding of the domestic worker population and their socio-economic and work-related vulnerabilities, we predict that the passage of a sleep requirement for domestic workers would protect the health of a sizable and growing subset of domestic workers in California.

Table 12 provides a summary judgment of the likelihood, intensity, and magnitude of the health effect and the uncertainties related to limits of available evidence. A quantitative estimate of the magnitude of health effects related to sleep is not possible due to the lack of data on the following factors:

x   the number of domestic workers working 24 hours or more or working as live-in workers
x   the current distribution of sleep hours for domestic workers impacted by the law.

Table 12: Summary Assessment of Expected Effects of Sleep Protections on Health

Health Outcome	Likelihood	Intensity / Severity	DW	CR	GP	Magnitude	Uncertainties related to limited evidence
			Who Impacted				
Mortality	S S S	High	+			Small	Studies on health effects of sleep not specific to domestic work population
Chronic Disease & Obesity	S S	Mod	+			Small to Moderate	
Stress & Mental Health	S S	Mod	+	?		Small to Moderate	Limited information on current sleep patterns in affected population
Cognitive & Motor Performance	S S S	Mod	+	+		Moderate	
Work Errors & Injuries	S S S	High	+	+		Moderate	
Traffic Accidents	S S S	High	+	+	+	Uncertain	Baseline health status in affected domestic work population
							Data on utilization of protections

Explanations:
x   Likelihood refers to strength of research/evidence showing causal relationship between sleep and the health outcome: S = limited evidence, S S = limited but consistent evidence, S S S = causal relationship established. A causal effect means that the effect is likely to occur, irrespective of the magnitude or severity.
x   Intensity/Severity reflects the nature of the effect its affects on function, life-expectancy and its permanence (High = very severe/intense, Mod = Moderate)
x   Who impacted refers to which populations are impacted by the health outcomes associated with proposed sleep requirements. DW = Domestic Workers, CR = Care Recipient, GP = General Population.
x   Magnitude reflects a qualitative judgment of the size of the anticipated change in the health effect (e.g. the increase in the number of cases of disease, injury, adverse events).

Sample Assessment Section 3:

The following excerpt is taken from the Australian Indigenous Doctors' Association and the Centre for Health Equity Training, Research and Evaluation, University of New South Wales report *Health Impact Assessment of the Northern Territory Emergency Response* (2010).

The excerpt presents the HIA's analysis focusing on housing and health.

housinG

Table 5: housinG: summary of The evidenCe from CommuniTies, sTaKeholders and experT reviewers

	positive impacts				negative impacts			
	sources of evidence				sources of evidence			
	Community visits	Key stake-holders	Expert reviews	Other	Community visits	Key stake-holders	Expert reviews	Other
Significant government investment in housing construction and housing repairs	✓	✓		✓				
Potential employment for community members – housing maintenance and construction	✓	✓						
Lack of recognition that land rights and housing are inextricably linked					✓			
Poor organisation of new housing construction and maintenance					✓	✓		
Continued overcrowding					✓	✓		
Little community engage-ment in decision making and design					✓	✓		
Slow progress in addressing fundamental issues of water and waste disposal					✓	✓		

baCKGround

For Aboriginal people the link between health and attachment to country is inseparable. Land is linked to Indigenous identity, beliefs and rights. Land rights are at the heart of the housing issue for Aboriginal people. Land was taken at the time of colonisation and there has been ongoing struggle by Aboriginal people to achieve government recognition of land rights for Aboriginal Australians.

As a result, there has been no cohesive national or state/territory strategy to provide culturally-acceptable housing of a quality or standard conducive to health and wellbeing as governments have been reluctant to invest in infrastructure and buildings on Aboriginal land over which they (governments) do not have control.

The consequence is the seriously inadequate housing and other public infrastructure in Aboriginal communities. The *Little Children are Sacred* report found that the shortage of housing for Indigenous residents of remote, regional and urban communities of the Northern Territory is severe and desperate. In particular, the inadequate numbers of houses leads to overcrowding; and the houses that are in communities are overcrowded and poorly maintained. There has been little opportunity for families and communities to design housing to suit their needs and limited investment in building local workforces with the capacity to construct and maintain housing (and other public infrastructure).

Ownership and control over land and housing have a positive influence on psychological and physical health. Aboriginal identity is tied to land, cultural practices, systems of authority and social control, intellectual traditions, concepts of spirituality, system of resource ownership and exchange. Loss of control over land, a lack of engagement with non-Aboriginal Australia and resulting powerlessness has had ongoing, serious negative impacts on health.

In addition, there is a strong relationship between the quality of housing and health. Overcrowding, and lack of access to the basic 'health hardware' of safe water, electricity, adequate areas for food preparation and storage, washing facilities, adequate waste disposal have contributed to the poor health of Aboriginal children and communities. Overcrowding and poor quality housing increases the likelihood of infectious disease, family and sexual violence and substance abuse. This has 'knock-on effects' including limits to children's educational attainment, tiredness and inadequate cleanliness that has a devastating impact on employment prospects and reinforces social disruption and marginalisation from mainstream society.

Land ownership was intended to provide a platform to support new housing stock and to improve and maintain existing housing. The measures included in the NTER legislation were:

• acquiring townships through five-year leases;

• land compensation;

• constructing new housing stock and repairs to existing stock;

• urgent repairs to infrastructure and community clean-ups; and

• additional accommodation to be built for 45 Government Business Managers and new police and teachers located in the prescribed communities.

assessmenT

positive impacts

The main positive impact on housing related to the significant investment promised by governments for housing, and higher number of housing repairs occurring.

> 'There's money been promised for houses which is great. I mean there are 4000 dwellings need to be constructed right now. They've earmarked it.'

Non-Aboriginal Senior Bureaucrat

negative impacts

Most of the community responses to the housing measures promised in the Intervention were restatements of the serious, pre-existing housing problems that the Intervention promised to address. Although there was grave concern about the transference of leases to Australian Government control, many people welcomed the thought of there being, finally, a serious effort to provide the housing they need. However, after 12 months the Intervention had, it seemed, disappointed people who had hoped and expected that action would be quicker, particularly in terms of improved maintenance.

Concern was also expressed at the priorities for building houses with most of the new houses being allocated to Business Managers, police and health staff so that there was no impact on the quality of housing and overcrowding among community families. Also there was a perception that if you lived close to existing infrastructure you were given greater priority and also able to negotiate for more flexible arrangements on the ways in which the projects were implemented.

'Housing has got to be one of the most corrupt and incompetent areas of Indigenous affairs. We're looking at houses that you build for $100 000 costing $4 to $5 to $600 000 to build and it's just nonsense and they're not, and a lot of them are falling down within a few years. We must look at the type of housing, the material we're using and look at how we can reduce the cost 'cause that is just a bizarre situation. You cannot tell me just because it's in a remote area, or it's in a rural area that it's going to cost that amount of money to build that type of housing.'

Aboriginal Leader

'The Intervention people would have meeting after meeting and people would say the same thing. We want better housing, we want improved housing. There are houses that have been condemned for 10 or 20 years and the council's suggestion was well you just bulldoze the house. But where do the 20 people go, that live in that house? And the Intervention has come round. They have taken films and interviewed the people and they've been inside these houses but nothing has changed. One year down the track, people are still living the same condemned house.'

Aboriginal Community Member

'They sent 120 garbage bins, wheelie bins out to a remote community. They posted out these holders with chains on them. but when they went to put the bins out, they had 120 garbage bins but only 20 sets of wheels. So they put out 20 garbage bins and the rest just sit there. And there is no garbage service... And the rubbish still gets tipped over by the pigs and dogs.'

Aboriginal Community Member

Overcrowding and poor housing affects everyone in the community including Aboriginal Health Workers.

'There are fifteen in my house including kids. I'm living with my parents. It is a four-bedroom house. All paying rent $400 - 500 per week all together for that house, because it is $50 each. Plus the power cards.'

Aboriginal Community Member

For many people the proposed building program was seen as a missed employment and training opportunity for Aboriginal people in the design, construction, and maintenance of housing and relevant health hardware

'Rather than having people flying in and flying out to build houses while you've got all these white fellas going in, building a house, and then shooting off. You've got the community, you know 50, or 60 or 100 Aboriginals sitting down watching them build a house.'

Non-Aboriginal Doctor

Some people had ambitious long-term vision on ways in which the community could be involved.

'... learn how to fix houses and the plumbing and how it works ... it could have set up maintenance centres where there was proper training, proper apprenticeships and proper pay.'

Aboriginal Health Worker

This speaks to the wider concern expressed by communities and stakeholders that the long-term maintenance of the housing depended on ownership and on the appropriateness of the housing.

'One of the problems with housing histori-cally ... is that there's no consultation with local people about what their needs are.'

Non-Aboriginal Senior Bureaucrat

'The issue for government is that they were going to invest in housing, make a big investment in housing. Investing in housing is all well and good, but if you build houses that are inappropriate, if you allow contrac-tors to dominate the process of building the houses and delivering the infrastructure, without proper Aboriginal eyes overseeing the process then we go through another histori-cal regression... Building houses is needed but it how you build the inside of that house and the family that lives in that house. It is more about making sure that the house on the inside is a shelter indeed, not a shelter that's a temporary solution to a great social problem.'

Aboriginal academic

summary

The commitment by the Australian Government to investment in new housing, and to renovation and improved maintenance on existing housing has the potential to have a very positive impact on the health and wellbeing of Aboriginal children and their families. Reduced overcrowding, improved health hardware, improved water supply and other essential services (e.g. electricity, waste disposal) will all have significant positive effects on health – in the short and longer term. Participation of the local community in the design, building and maintenance of the housing will increase the likelihood of the housing being appropriate, and increased ownership will increase the longevity of quality housing stock.

Delays in providing new or improved housing stock, however, will have a negative impact on the mental health and social functioning of communities. Increased distrust in government, a sense of disillusionment and powerlessness associated with dashed hopes will, in turn, have a negative impact on the psychosocial health and social cohesion of families and communities.

Table 6: housinG: summary of prediCTed heaITh impaCTs

ASPECT oF HEALTH	PoSITIvE HEALTH IMPACTS	NEGATIvE HEALTH IMPACTS
Physical health	- Reduced acute and chronic disease as a result of reduced overcrowding - Reduced acute disease as a result of improved water supply and waste disposal	- Limited improvements to waste disposal
Psychological health	- Potentially, relief from stress associated with overcrowded, inadequate housing	- Lack of trust in government, e.g. Intervention staff housing built first - Lack of Aboriginal control of decision-making, e.g. not involved in decisions on location, allocation, design and construction of new housing - Increased stress associated with long wait for improved housing
Social health and wellbeing	- Building and having access to new housing - Improvements to existing housing - Initial community clean-ups - Increased employment opportunities - Increased education and training opportunities including traineeships and apprenticeships	
Spirituality		- Lack of recognition of Aboriginal views and needs in developing and implementing housing policy and programs - Lack of trust in government which did not recognise the link between housing and Aboriginal connection to country
Cultural integrity		- Loss of control of land title in Intervention communities

reCommendaTions

it is recommended that:

- Aboriginal communities be involved actively in decisions on the design, building, allocation and location of new housing;

- Aboriginal communities be provided with education, training and resources to enable them to undertake systematic maintenance and repair of all existing and future homes;

- priority be given to providing new and renovated housing to community members until 2018;

- benchmarks in National Partnership Agreement on Remote Indigenous Housing be met.

TarGeTs for moniTorinG

at one year

• 20% local Aboriginal employment be included as a procurement requirement in new housing (as per COAG National Partnership Agreement) and housing maintenance contracts

at five years

• 75% of the investment in new or renovated housing until 2018 be for people living permanently in communities

• A recurrently funded rolling maintenance program be established in all prescribed communities

• Each prescribed community will have access to water, sewerage, power and waste disposal

• The average occupancy rate per dwelling in prescribed communities will be no greater than the national average

• 80% of all houses identified as needing repairs and renovation be completed as per the COAG National Partnership Agreement

at ten years

• All dwellings in prescribed communities have operating water, sewerage, power and waste disposal

Index

C. L. Ross et al., *Health Impact Assessment in the United States,*   227
DOI 10.1007/978-1-4614-7303-9, © Springer Science+Business Media New York 2014

Printed by Publishers' Graphics LLC